WORKS OF FREDE

CAMBRIDGE EDITION.

SCHILLER'S

HISTORICAL DRAMAS

MARY STUART.   THE MAID OF ORLEANS.   THE
BRIDE OF MESSINA.

TRANSLATED FROM THE GERMAN.

ILLUSTRATED.

Fredonia Books
Amsterdam, The Netherlands

Historical Dramas
Mary Stuart
The Maid of Orleans
The Bride of Messina

by
Frederick Schiller

Translated from the German

ISBN 0-89875-299-X

Fredonia Books
Amsterdam, The Netherlands
http://www.FredoniaBooks.com

CONTENTS.

MARY STUART.

A TRAGEDY.

DRAMATIS PERSONÆ.

ELIZABETH, *Queen of England.*
MARY STUART, *Queen of Scots, a Prisoner in England.*
RORERT DUDLEY, *Earl of Leicester.*
GEORGE TALBOT, *Earl of Shrewsbury.*
WILLIAM CECIL, *Lord Burleigh, Lord High Treasurer.*
EARL OF KENT.
SIR WILLIAM DAVISON, *Secretary of State.*
SIR AMIAS PAULET, *Keeper of* MARY.
SIR EDWARD MORTIMER, *his Nephew.*
COUNT L'AUBESPINE, *the French Ambassador.*
O'KELLY, *Mortimer's Friend.*

COUNT BELLIEVRE, *Envoy Extraordinary from France.*
SIR DRUE DRURY, *another Keeper of* MARY.
SIR ANDREW MELVIL, *her House Steward.*
BURGOYNE, *her Physician.*
HANNAH KENNEDY, *her Nurse.*
MARGARET CURL, *her Attendant.*
Sheriff of the County.
Officer of the Guard.
French and English Lords.
Soldiers.
Servants of State belonging to ELIZABETH.
Servants and Female Attendants of the Queen of Scots.

ACT I.

SCENE I.

A common apartment in the Castle of Fotheringay.

HANNAH KENNEDY, *contending violently with* PAULET, *who is about to break open a closet;* DRURY *with an iron crow.*

KEN. How now, sir? what fresh outrage have we here?
Back from that cabinet!

PAULET.   Whence came the jewel?
I know 'twas from an upper chamber thrown;
And you would bribe the gardener with your trinkets.
A curse on woman's wiles! In spite of all
My strict precaution and my active search,

5

Still treasures here, still costly gems concealed!
And doubtless there are more where this lay hid.
                    [*Advancing towards the cabinet.*
KEN.   Intruder, back! here lie my lady's secrets.
PAUL.   Exactly what I seek.   [*Drawing forth papers.*
KENNEDY.   Mere trifling papers;
    The amusements only of an idle pen,
    To cheat the dreary tedium of a dungeon.
PAUL.   In idle hours the evil mind is busy.
KEN.   Those writings are in French.
PAULET.   So much the worse!
    That tongue betokens England's enemy.
KEN.   Sketches of letters to the Queen of England.
PAUL.   I'll be their bearer.   Ha! what glitters here?
  [*He touches a secret spring, and draws out jewels from
    a private drawer.*
A royal diadem enriched with stones,
And studded with the fleur-de-lis of France.
                    [*He hands it to his assistant.*
Here, take it, Drury; lay it with the rest.
                            [*Exit* DRURY.
[And ye have found the means to hide from us
Such costly things, and screen them, until now,
From our inquiring eyes?]
KENNEDY.   Oh, insolent
    And tyrant power, to which we must submit.
PAUL.   She can work ill as long as she hath treasures;
    For all things turn to weapons in her hands.
KENNEDY (*supplicating*).
    Oh, sir! be merciful; deprive us not
    Of the last jewel that adorns our life!
    'Tis my poor lady's only joy to view
    This symbol of her former majesty;
    Your hands long since have robbed us of the rest.
PAUL.   'Tis in safe custody; in proper time
    'Twill be restored to you with scrupulous care.
KEN.   Who that beholds these naked walls could say
    That majesty dwelt here?   Where is the throne?
    Where the imperial canopy of state?
    Must she not set her tender foot, still used
    To softest treading, on the rugged ground?

With common pewter, which the lowliest dame
Would scorn, they furnish forth her homely table.
PAUL. Thus did she treat her spouse at Stirling once;
And pledged, the while, her paramour in gold.
KEN. Even the mirror's trifling aid withheld.
PAUL. The contemplation of her own vain image
Incites to hope, and prompts to daring deeds.
KEN. Books are denied her to divert her mind.
PAUL. The Bible still is left to mend her heart.
KEN. Even of her very lute she is deprived!
PAUL. Because she tuned it to her wanton airs.
KEN. Is this a fate for her, the gentle born,
Who in her very cradle was a queen?
Who, reared in Catherine's luxurious court,
Enjoyed the fulness of each earthly pleasure?
Was't not enough to rob her of her power,
Must ye then envy her its paltry tinsel?
A noble heart in time resigns itself
To great calamities with fortitude;
But yet it cuts one to the soul to part
At once with all life's little outward trappings!
PAUL. These are the things that turn the human heart
To vanity, which should collect itself
In penitence; for a lewd, vicious life,
Want and abasement are the only penance.
KEN. If youthful blood has led her into error,
With her own heart and God she must account:—
There is no judge in England over her.
PAUL. She shall have judgment where she hath trans
gressed.
KEN. Her narrow bonds restrain her from transgression
PAUL. And yet she found the means to stretch her arm
Into the world, from out these narrow bonds,
And, with the torch of civil war, inflame
This realm against our queen (whom God preserve
And arm assassin bands. Did she not rouse
From out these walls the malefactor Parry,
And Babington, to the detested crime
Of regicide? And did this iron grate
Prevent her from decoying to her toils
The virtuous heart of Norfolk? Saw we not

The first, best head in all this island fall
A sacrifice for her upon the block?
[The noble house of Howard fell with him.]
And did this sad example terrify
These mad adventurers, whose rival zeal
Plunges for her into this deep abyss?
The bloody scaffold bends beneath the weight
Of her new daily victims; and we ne'er
Shall see an end till she herself, of all
The guiltiest, be offered up upon it.
Oh! curses on the day when England took
This Helen to its hospitable arms.

KEN.   Did England then receive her hospitably?
Oh, hapless queen! who, since that fatal day
When first she set her foot within this realm,
And, as a suppliant — a fugitive —
Came to implore protection from her sister,
Has been condemmed, despite the law of nations,
And royal privilege, to weep away
The fairest years of youth in prison walls.
And now, when she hath suffered everything
Which in imprisonment is hard and bitter,
Is like a felon summoned to the bar,
Foully accused, and though herself a queen,
Constrained to plead for honor and for life.

PAUL.   She came amongst us as a murderess,
Chased by her very subjects from a throne
Which she had oft by vilest deeds disgraced.
Sworn against England's welfare came she hither,
To call the times of bloody Mary back,
Betray our church to Romish tyranny,
And sell our dear-bought liberties to France.
Say, why disdained she to subscribe the treaty
Of Edinborough — to resign her claim
To England's crown — and with one single word,
Traced by her pen, throw wide her prison gates?
No: — she had rather live in vile confinement,
And see herself ill-treated, than renounce
The empty honors of her barren title.
Why acts she thus?   Because she trusts to wiles,
And treacherous arts of base conspiracy;

And, hourly plotting schemes of mischief, hopes
To conquer, from her prison, all this isle.
KEN. You mock us, sir, and edge your cruelty
With words of bitter scorn : — that she should form
Such projects; she, who's here immured alive,
To whom no sound of comfort, not a voice
Of friendship comes from her beloved home;
Who hath so long no human face beheld,
Save her stern gaoler's unrelenting brows;
Till now, of late, in your uncourteous cousin
She sees a second keeper, and beholds
Fresh bolts and bars against her multiplied.
PAUL. No iron-grate is proof against her wiles.
How do I know these bars are not filed through?
How that this floor, these walls, that seem so strong
Without, may not be hollow from within,
And let in felon treachery when I sleep?
Accursed office, that's intrusted to me,
To guard this cunning mother of all ill!
Fear scares me from my sleep ; and in the night
I, like a troubled spirit, roam and try
The strength of every bolt, and put to proof
Each guard's fidelity : — I see, with fear,
The dawning of each morn, which may confirm
My apprehensions : — yet, thank God, there's hope
That all my fears will soon be at an end ;
For rather would I at the gates of hell
Stand sentinel, and guard the devilish host
Of damned souls, than this deceitful queen.
KEN. Here comes the queen.
PAULET.   Christ's image in her hand.
Pride, and all worldly lusts within her heart.

SCENE II.

The same. Enter MARY, *veiled, a crucifix in her hand.*
KENNEDY (*hastening toward her*).
O gracious queen ! they tread us under foot;
No end of tyranny and base oppression;
Each coming day heaps fresh indignities,
New sufferings on thy royal head.

MARY.   Be calm —
    Say, what has happened ?
KENNEDY.   See ! thy cabinet
    Is forced — thy papers — and thy only treasure,
    Which with such pains we had secured, the last
    Poor remnant of thy bridal ornaments
    From France, is in his hands — naught now remains
    Of royal state — thou art indeed bereft !
MARY.   Compose yourself, my Hannah ! and believe
        me,
    'Tis not these baubles that can make a queen —
    Basely indeed they may behave to us,
    But they cannot debase us. I have learned
    To use myself to many a change in England ;
    I can support this too. Sir, you have taken
    By force what I this very day designed
    To have delivered to you. There's a letter
    Amongst these papers for my royal sister
    Of England. Pledge me, sir, your word of honor,
    To give it to her majesty's own hands,
    And not to the deceitful care of Burleigh.
PAUL.   I shall consider what is best to do.
MARY.   Sir, you shall know its import. In this letter
    I beg a favor, a great favor of her, —
    That she herself will give me audience, — she !
    Whom I have never seen. I have been summoned
    Before a court of men, whom I can ne'er
    Acknowledge as my peers — of men to whom
    My heart denies its confidence. The queen
    Is of my family, my rank, my sex ;
    To her alone — a sister, queen, and woman —
    Can I unfold my heart.
PAULET.   Too oft, my lady,
    Have you intrusted both your fate and honor
    To men less worthy your esteem than these.
MARY.   I, in the letter, beg another favor,
    And surely naught but inhumanity
    Can here reject my prayer. These many years
    Have I, in prison, missed the church's comfort,
    The blessings of the sacraments — and she
    Who robs me of my freedom and my crown,

Who seeks my very life, can never wish
To shut the gates of heaven upon my soul.
PAUL. Whene'er you wish, the dean shall wait upon you.
MARY (*interrupting him sharply*).
Talk to me not of deans. I ask the aid
Of one of my own church — a Catholic priest.
PAUL. [That is against the published laws of England.
MARY. The laws of England are no rule for me.
I am not England's subject; I have ne'er
Consented to its laws, and will not bow
Before their cruel and despotic sway.
If 'tis your will, to the unheard-of rigor
Which I have borne, to add this new oppression,
I must submit to what your power ordains;
Yet will I raise my voice in loud complaints.]
I also wish a public notary,
And secretaries, to prepare my will —
My sorrows and my prison's wretchedness
Prey on my life — my days, I fear, are numbered —
I feel that I am near the gates of death.
PAUL. These serious contemplations well become you.
MARY. And know I then that some too ready hand
May not abridge this tedious work of sorrow?
I would indite my will and make disposal
Of what belongs to me.
PAUL. This liberty
May be allowed to you, for England's queen
Will not enrich herself by plundering you.
MARY. I have been parted from my faithful women,
And from my servants; tell me, where are they?
What is their fate? I can indeed dispense
At present with their service, but my heart
Will feel rejoiced to know these faithful ones
Are not exposed to suffering and to want!
PAUL. Your servants have been cared for; [and again
You shall behold whate'er is taken from you:
And all shall be restored in proper season.]
[*Going.*
MARY. And will you leave my presence thus again,
And not relieve my fearful, anxious heart
From the fell torments of uncertainty?

Thanks to the vigilance of your hateful spies,
I am divided from the world; no voice
Can reach me through these prison-walls; my fate
Lies in the hands of those who wish my ruin.
A month of dread suspense is passed already
Since when the forty high commissioners
Surprised me in this castle, and erected,
With most unseemly haste, their dread tribunal;
They forced me, stunned, amazed, and unprepared,
Without an advocate, from memory,
Before their unexampled court, to answer
Their weighty charges, artfully arranged.
They came like ghosts, — like ghosts they disap-
　　peared,
And since that day all mouths are closed to me.
In vain I seek to construe from your looks
Which hath prevailed — my cause's innocence
And my friends' zeal — or my foes' cursed counsel.
Oh, break this silence! let me know the worst;
What have I still to fear, and what to hope.

PAUL.　Close your accounts with heaven.
MARY.　　　　　　　　　From heaven I hope
For mercy, sir; and from my earthly judges
I hope, and still expect, the strictest justice.
PAUL.　Justice, depend upon it, will be done you.
MARY.　Is the suit ended, sir?
PAULET.　　　　　　　I cannot tell.
MARY.　Am I condemned?
PAUL.　　　　　　　I cannot answer, lady.
MARY.　[Sir, a good work fears not the light of day.
PAUL.　The day will shine upon it, doubt it not.]
MARY.　Despatch is here the fashion.　Is it meant
The murderer shall surprise me, like the judges?
PAUL.　Still entertain that thought and he will find you
Better prepared to meet your fate than they did.
MARY (*after a pause*).
Sir, nothing can surprise me which a court
Inspired by Burleigh's hate and Hatton's zeal,
Howe'er unjust, may venture to pronounce:
But I have yet to learn how far the queen
Will dare in execution of the sentence.

PAUL. The sovereigns of England have no fear
But for their conscience and their parliament.
What justice hath decreed her fearless hand
Will execute before the assembled world.

SCENE III.

The same. MORTIMER *enters, and without paying attention to the* QUEEN, *addresses* PAULET.

MORT. Uncle, you're sought for.
  [*He retires in the same manner. The* QUEEN *remarks
    it, and turns towards* PAULET, *who is about to
    follow him.*
MARY.   Sir, one favor more :
If you have aught to say to me — from you
I can bear much — I reverence your gray hairs;
But cannot bear that young man's insolence;
Spare me in future his unmannered rudeness.
PAUL. I prize him most for that which makes you hate
  him :
He is not, truly, one of those poor fools
Who melt before a woman's treacherous tears.
He has seen much — has been to Rheims and Paris,
And brings us back his true old English heart.
Lady, your cunning arts are lost on him.   [*Exit.*

SCENE IV.

MARY, KENNEDY.

KEN. And dare the ruffian venture to your face
Such language ! Oh, 'tis hard — tis past endurance.
MARY (*lost in reflection*).
In the fair moments of our former splendor
We lent to flatterers a too willing ear ; —
It is but just, good Hannah, we should now
Be forced to hear the bitter voice of censure.
KEN. So downcast, so depressed, my dearest lady !
You, who before so gay, so full of hope,
Were used to comfort me in my distress;
More gracious were the task to check your mirth
Than chide your heavy sadness.

MARY.   Well I know him —
  It is the bleeding Darnley's royal shade,
  Rising in anger from his darksome grave :
  And never will he make his peace with me
  Until the measures of my woes be full.
KEN. What thoughts are these —
MARY.   Thou may'st forget it, Hannah;
  But I've a faithful memory — 'tis this day
  Another wretched anniversary
  Of that regretted, that unhappy deed —
  Which I must celebrate with fast and penance.
KEN. Dismiss at length in peace this evil spirit.
  The penitence of many a heavy year,
  Of many a suffering, has atoned the deed ;
  The church, which holds the key of absolution,
  Pardons the crime, and heaven itself's appeased.
MARY. This long-atoned crime arises fresh
  And bleeding from its lightly-covered grave ;
  My husband's restless spirit seeks revenge ;
  No sacred bell can exorcise, no host
  In priestly hands dismiss it to his tomb.
KEN. You did not murder him ; 'twas done by others.
MARY. But it was known to me ; I suffered it,
  And lured him with my smiles to death's embrace.
KEN. Your youth extenuates your guilt. You were
  Of tender years.
MARY.   So tender, yet I drew
  This heavy guilt upon my youthful head.
KEN. You were provoked by direst injuries,
  And by the rude presumption of the man,
  Whom out of darkness, like the hand of heaven,
  Your love drew forth, and raised above all others.
  Whom through your bridal chamber you conducted
  Up to your throne, and with your lovely self,
  And your hereditary crown, distinguished :
  [Your work was his existence, and your grace
  Bedewed him like the gentle rains of heaven.]
  Could he forget that his so splendid lot
  Was the creation of your generous love?
  Yet did he, worthless as he was, forget it.
  With base suspicions, and with brutal manners,

He wearied your affections, and became
An object to you of deserved disgust:
The illusion, which till now had overcast
Your judgment, vanished; angrily you fled
His foul embrace, and gave him up to scorn.
And did he seek again to win your love?
Your favor? Did he e'er implore your pardon?
Or fall in deep repentance at your feet?
No; the base wretch defied you; he, who was
Your bounty's creature, wished to play your king,
[And strove, through fear, to force your inclination.]
Before your eyes he had your favorite singer,
Poor Rizzio, murdered; you did but avenge
With blood the bloody deed ——

MARY.   And bloodily,
I fear, too soon 'twill be avenged on me:
You seek to comfort me, and you condemn me.

KEN.   You were, when you consented to this deed,
No more yourself; belonged not to yourself;
The madness of a frantic love possessed you,
And bound you to a terrible seducer,
The wretched Bothwell.   That despotic man
Ruled you with shameful, overbearing will,
And with his philters and his hellish arts
Inflamed your passions.

MARY.   All the arts he used
Were man's superior strength and woman's weakness.

KEN.   No, no, I say.   The most pernicious spirits
Of hell he must have summoned to his aid,
To cast this mist before your waking senses.
Your ear no more was open to the voice
Of friendly warning, and your eyes were shut
To decency; soft female bashfulness
Deserted you; those cheeks, which were before
The seat of virtuous, blushing modesty,
Glowed with the flames of unrestrained desire.
You cast away the veil of secrecy,
And the flagitious daring of the man
O'ercame your natural coyness: you exposed
Your shame, unblushingly, to public gaze:
You let the murderer, whom the people followed

With curses, through the streets of Edinburgh,
Before you bear the royal sword of Scotland
In triumph. You begirt your parliament
With armed bands ; and by this shameless farce,
There, in the very temple of great justice,
You forced the judges of the land to clear
The murderer of his guilt. You went still further —
O God !

MARY.   Conclude — nay, pause not — say for this
I gave my hand in marriage at the altar.

KEN.   O let an everlasting silence veil
That dreadful deed : the heart revolts at it.
A crime to stain the darkest criminal !
Yet you are no such lost one, that I know.
I nursed your youth myself — your heart is framed
For tender softness : 'tis alive to shame,
And all your fault is thoughtless levity.
Yes, I repeat it, there are evil spirits,
Who sudden fix in man's unguarded breast
Their fatal residence, and there delight
To act their dev'lish deeds ; then hurry back
Unto their native hell, and leave behind
Remorse and horror in the poisoned bosom.
Since this misdeed, which blackens thus your life,
You have done nothing ill ; your conduct has
Been pure ; myself can witness your amendment.
Take courage, then ; with your own heart make peace.
Whatever cause you have for penitence,
You are not guilty here. Nor England's queen,
Nor England's parliament can be your judge.
Here might oppresses you : you may present
Yourself before this self-created court
With all the fortitude of innocence.

MARY.   I hear a step.

KENNEDY.   It is the nephew — In.

SCENE V.

The same. Enter MORTIMER, *approaching cautiously.*

MORTIMER (*to* KENNEDY).

Step to the door, and keep a careful watch,
I have important business with the queen.

MARY (*with dignity*).
 I charge thee, Hannah, go not hence — remain.
MORT. Fear not, my gracious lady — learn to know me.
       [*He gives her a card.*
MARY. [*She examines it, and starts back astonished.*
 Heavens! What is this?
MORTIMER (*to* KENNEDY). Retire, good Kennedy;
 See that my uncle comes not unawares.
MARY (*to* KENNEDY, *who hesitates, and looks at the* QUEEN
 inquiringly).
 Go in; do as he bids you.
    [KENNEDY *retires with signs of wonder.*

SCENE VI.

MARY, MORTIMER.

MARY.   From my uncle
 In France — the worthy Cardinal of Lorrain?
         [*She reads.*
 " Confide in Mortimer, who brings you this;
 You have no truer, firmer friend in England."
    [*Looking at him with astonishment.*
 Can I believe it? Is there no delusion
 To cheat my senses? Do I find a friend
 So near, when I conceived myself abandoned
 By the whole world? And find that friend in you,
 The nephew of my gaoler, whom I thought
 My most inveterate enemy?
MORTIMER (*kneeling*).   Oh, pardon,
 My gracious liege, for the detested mask,
 Which it has cost me pain enough to wear;
 Yet through such means alone have I the power
 To see you, and to bring you help and rescue.
MARY. Arise, sir; you astonish me; I cannot
 So suddenly emerge from the abyss
 Of wretchedness to hope : let me conceive
 This happiness, that I may credit it.
MORT. Our time is brief : each moment I expect
 My uncle, whom a hated man attends;
 Hear, then, before his terrible commission
 Surprises you, how heaven prepares your rescue.

MARY.   You come in token of its wondrous power.
MORT.   Allow me of myself to speak.
MARY.   Say on.
MORT.   I scarce, my liege, had numbered twenty years,
    Trained in the path of strictest discipline
    And nursed in deadliest hate to papacy,
    When led by irresistible desire
    For foreign travel, I resolved to leave
    My country and its puritanic faith
    Far, far behind me : soon with rapid speed
    I flew through France, and bent my eager course
    On to the plains of far-famed Italy.
    'Twas then the time of the great jubilee : —
    And crowds of palmers filled the public roads ;
    Each image was adorned with garlands ; 'twas
    As if all human-kind were wandering forth
    In pilgrimage towards the heavenly kingdom.
    The tide of the believing multitude
    Bore me too onward, with resistless force,
    Into the streets of Rome.   What was my wonder,
    As the magnificence of stately columns
    Rushed on my sight ! the vast triumphal arches,
    The Colosseum's grandeur, with amazement
    Struck my admiring senses ; the sublime
    Creative spirit held my soul a prisoner
    In the fair world of wonders it had framed.
    I ne'er had felt the power of art till now.
    The church that reared me hates the charms of
        sense ;
    It tolerates no image, it adores
    But the unseen, the incorporeal word.
    What were my feelings, then, as I approached
    The threshold of the churches, and within,
    Heard heavenly music floating in the air :
    While from the walls and high-wrought roofs there
        streamed
    Crowds of celestial forms in endless train —
    When the Most High, Most Glorious pervaded
    My captivated sense in real presence !
    And when I saw the great and godlike visions,
    The Salutation, the Nativity,

The Holy Mother, and the Trinity's
Descent, the luminous transfiguration:
And last the holy pontiff, clad in all
The glory of his office, bless the people!
Oh! what is all the pomp of gold and jewels
With which the kings of earth adorn themselves!
He is alone surrounded by the Godhead;
His mansion is in truth an heavenly kingdom,
For not of earthly moulding are these forms!
MARY. O spare me, sir! No further. Spread no more
 Life's verdant carpet out before my eyes,
 Remember I am wretched, and a prisoner.
MORT. I was a prisoner, too, my queen; but swift
 My prison-gates flew open, when at once
 My spirit felt its liberty, and hailed
 The smiling dawn of life. I learned to burst
 Each narrow prejudice of education,
 To crown my brow with never-fading wreaths,
 And mix my joy with the rejoicing crowd.
 Full many noble Scots, who saw my zeal,
 Encouraged me, and with the gallant French
 They kindly led me to your princely uncle,
 The Cardinal of Guise. Oh, what a man!
 How firm, how clear, how manly, and how great!
 Born to control the human mind at will!
 The very model of a royal priest;
 A ruler of the church without an equal!
MARY. You've seen him then, — the much loved, honored
  man,
 Who was the guardian of my tender years!
 Oh, speak of him! Does he remember me?
 Does fortune favor him? And prospers still
 His life? And does he still majestic stand,
 A very rock and pillar of the church?
MORT. The holy man descended from his height,
 And deigned to teach me the important creed
 Of the true church, and dissipate my doubts.
 He showed me how the glimmering light of reason
 Serves but to lead us to eternal error:
 That what the heart is called on to believe
 The eye must see: that he who rules the church

Must needs be visible ; and that the spirit
Of truth inspired the councils of the fathers.
How vanished then the fond imaginings
And weak conceptions of my childish soul
Before his conquering judgment, and the soft
Persuasion of his tongue ! So I returned
Back to the bosom of the holy church,
And at his feet abjured my heresies.
MARY. Then of those happy thousands you are one,
Whom he, with his celestial eloquence,
Like the immortal preacher of the mount,
Has turned and led to everlasting joy !
MORT. The duties of his office called him soon
To France, and I was sent by him to Rheims,
Where, by the Jesuits' anxious labor, priests
Are trained to preach our holy faith in England.
There, 'mongst the Scots, I found the noble Morgan,
And your true Lesley, Ross's learned bishop,
Who pass in France their joyless days of exile.
I joined with heartfelt zeal these worthy men,
And fortified my faith. As I one day
Roamed through the bishop's dwelling, I was struck
With a fair female portrait ; it was full
Of touching wond'rous charms ; with magic might
It moved my inmost soul, and there I stood
Speechless, and overmastered by my feelings.
"Well," cried the bishop, "may you linger thus
In deep emotion near this lovely face !
For the most beautiful of womankind,
Is also matchless in calamity.
She is a prisoner for our holy faith,
And in your native land, alas ! she suffers."
            [MARY *is in great agitation. He pauses.*
MARY. Excellent man ! All is not lost, indeed,
While such a friend remains in my misfortunes !
MORT. Then he began, with moving eloquence,
To paint the sufferings of your martyrdom ;
He showed me then your lofty pedigree,
And your descent from Tudor's royal house.
He proved to me that you alone have right
To reign in England, not this upstart queen,

The base-born fruit of an adult'rous bed,
Whom Henry's self rejected as a bastard.
[He from my eyes removed delusion's mist,
And taught me to lament you as a victim,
To honor you as my true queen, whom I,
Deceived, like thousands of my noble fellows,
Had ever hated as my country's foe.]
I would not trust his evidence alone;
I questioned learned doctors; I consulted
The most authentic books of heraldry;
And every man of knowledge whom I asked
Confirmed to me your claim's validity.
And now I know that your undoubted right
To England's throne has been your only wrong,
This realm is justly yours by heritage,
In which you innocently pine as prisoner.

MARY. Oh, this unhappy right!—'tis this alone
Which is the source of all my sufferings.

MORT. Just at this time the tidings reached my ears
Of your removal from old Talbot's charge,
And your committal to my uncle's care.
It seemed to me that this disposal marked
The wond'rous, outstretched hand of favoring heaven;
It seemed to be a loud decree of fate,
That it had chosen me to rescue you.
My friends concur with me; the cardinal
Bestows on me his counsel and his blessing,
And tutors me in the hard task of feigning.
The plan in haste digested, I commenced
My journey homewards, and ten days ago
On England's shores I landed. Oh, my queen.
                              [*He pauses.*
I saw then, not your picture, but yourself—
Oh, what a treasure do these walls enclose!
No prison this, but the abode of gods,
More splendid far than England's royal court.
Happy, thrice happy he, whose envied lot
Permits to breathe the selfsame air with you!
It is a prudent policy in her
To bury you so deep! All England's youth
Would rise at once in general mutiny,

And not a sword lie quiet in its sheath :
Rebellion would uprear its giant head,
Through all this peaceful isle, if Britons once
Beheld their captive queen.

MARY.   'Twere well with her
If every Briton saw her with your eyes !

MORT. Were each, like me, a witness of your wrongs,
Your meekness, and the noble fortitude
With which you suffer these indignities —
Would you not then emerge from all these trials
Like a true queen ?   Your prison's infamy,
Hath it despoiled your beauty of its charms ?
You are deprived of all that graces life,
Yet round you life and light eternal beam.
Ne'er on this threshold can I set my foot,
That my poor heart with anguish is not torn,
Nor ravished with delight at gazing on you.
Yet fearfully the fatal time draws near,
And danger hourly growing presses on.
I can delay no longer — can no more
Conceal the dreadful news.

MARY.   My sentence then !
It is pronounced ?   Speak freely — I can bear it.

MORT. It is pronounced ! The two-and-forty judges
Have given the verdict, " guilty "; and the Houses
Of Lords and Commons, with the citizens
Of London, eagerly and urgently
Demand the execution of the sentence : —
The queen alone still craftily delays,
That she may be constrained to yield, but not
From feelings of humanity or mercy.

MARY (*collected*).
Sir, I am not surprised, nor terrified.
I have been long prepared for such a message.
Too well I know my judges.   After all
Their cruel treatment I can well conceive
They dare not now restore my liberty.
I know their aim : they mean to keep me here
In everlasting bondage, and to bury,
In the sepulchral darkness of my prison,
My vengeance with me, and my rightful claims.

MORT. Oh, no, my gracious queen; — they stop not there:
Oppression will not be content to do
Its work by halves: — as long as e'en you live,
Distrust and fear will haunt the English queen.
No dungeon can inter you deep enough;
Your death alone can make her throne secure.
MARY. Will she then dare, regardless of the shame,
Lay my crowned head upon the fatal block?
MORT. She will most surely dare it, doubt it not.
MARY. And can she thus roll in the very dust
Her own, and every monarch's majesty?
MORT. She thinks on nothing now but present danger,
Nor looks to that which is so far removed.
MARY. And fears she not the dread revenge of France?
MORT. With France she makes an everlasting peace;
And gives to Anjou's duke her throne and hand.
MARY. Will not the King of Spain rise up in arms?
MORT. She fears not a collected world in arms?
If with her people she remains at peace.
MARY. Were this a spectacle for British eyes?
MORT. This land, my queen, has, in these latter days,
Seen many a royal woman from the throne
Descend and mount the scaffold : — her own mother
And Catherine Howard trod this fatal path;
And was not Lady Grey a crowned head?
MARY (*after a pause*).
No, Mortimer, vain fears have blinded you;
'Tis but the honest care of your true heart,
Which conjures up these empty apprehensions.
It is not, sir, the scaffold that I fear:
There are so many still and secret means
By which her majesty of England may
Set all my claims to rest.   Oh, trust me, ere
An executioner is found for me,
Assassins will be hired to do their work.
'Tis that which makes me tremble, Mortimer:
I never lift the goblet to my lips
Without an inward shuddering, lest the draught
May have been mingled by my sister's love.
MORT. No : — neither open or disguised murder
Shall e'er prevail against you : — fear no more;

All is prepared; — twelve nobles of the land
Are my confederates, and have pledged to-day,
Upon the sacrament, their faith to free you,
With dauntless arm, from this captivity.
Count Aubespine, the French ambassador,
Knows of our plot, and offers his assistance:
'Tis in his palace that we hold our meetings.

MARY.   You make me tremble, sir, but not for joy!
An evil boding penetrates my heart.
Know you, then, what you risk?   Are you not
　　scared
By Babington and Tichburn's bloody heads,
Set up as warnings upon London's bridge?
Nor by the ruin of those many victims
Who have, in such attempts, found certain death,
And only made my chains the heavier?
Fly' hence, deluded, most unhappy youth!
Fly, if there yet be time for you, before
That crafty spy, Lord Burleigh, track your schemes,
And mix his traitors in your secret plots.
Fly hence: — as yet, success hath never smiled
On Mary Stuart's champions.

MORTIMER.   I am not scared
By Babington and Tichburn's bloody heads
Set up as warnings upon London's bridge;
Nor by the ruin of those many victims
Who have, in such attempts, found certain death:
They also found therein immortal honor,
And death, in rescuing you, is dearest bliss.

MARY.   It is in vain: nor force nor guile can save me: —
My enemies are watchful, and the power
Is in their hands.   It is not Paulet only
And his dependent host; all England guards
My prison gates: Elizabeth's free will
Alone can open them.

MORTIMER.   Expect not that.

MARY.   One man alone on earth can open them.

MORT.   Oh, let me know his name!

MARY.   Lord Leicester.

MORTIMER.   He!
　　　　　　　　　　　　[*Starts back in wonder.*

The Earl of Leicester! Your most bloody foe,
The favorite of Elizabeth! through him ——
MARY. If I am to be saved at all, 'twill be
Through him, and him alone. Go to him, sir;
Freely confide in him: and, as a proof
You come from me, present this paper to him.
  [She takes a paper from her bosom; MORTIMER *draws*
    back, and hesitates to take it.
It doth contain my portrait: — take it, sir;
I've borne it long about me; but your uncle's
Close watchfulness has cut me off from all
Communication with him; — you were sent
By my good angel.   *[He takes it.*
MORTIMER.   Oh, my queen! explain
This mystery.
MARY.   Lord Leicester will resolve it.
Confide in him, and he'll confide in you.
Who comes?
KENNEDY (*entering hastily*).
            'Tis Paulet; and he brings with him
A nobleman from court.
MORTIMER.   It is Lord Burleigh.
Collect yourself, my queen, and strive to hear
The news he brings with equanimity.
  [He retires through a side door, and KENNEDY *follows*
    him.

SCENE VII.

Enter LORD BURLEIGH, *and* PAULET.

PAULET (*to* MARY).
You wished to-day assurance of your fate;
My Lord of Burleigh brings it to you now;
Hear it with resignation, as beseems you.
MARY. I hope with dignity, as it becomes
My innocence, and my exalted station.
BUR. I come deputed from the court of justice.
MARY. Lord Burleigh lends that court his willing tongue,
Which was already guided by his spirit.
PAUL. You speak as if no stranger to the sentence.
MARY. Lord Burleigh brings it; therefore do I know it.

PAUL.   [It would become you better, Lady Stuart,
 To listen less to hatred.
MARY.   I but name
 My enemy: I said not that I hate him.]
 But to the matter, sir.
BURLEIGH.   You have acknowledged
 The jurisdiction of the two-and-forty.
MARY.   My lord, excuse me, if I am obliged
 So soon to interrupt you.   I acknowledged,
 Say you, the competence of the commission?
 I never have acknowledged it, my lord ;
 How could I so?   I could not give away
 My own prerogative, the intrusted rights
 Of my own people, the inheritance
 Of my own son, and every monarch's honor
 [The very laws of England say I could not.]
 It is enacted by the English laws
 That every one who stands arraigned of crime
 Shall plead before a jury of his equals :
 Who is my equal in this high commission ?
 Kings only are my peers.
BURLEIGH.   But yet you heard
 The points of accusation, answered them
 Before the court——
MARY.   'Tis true, I was deceived
 By Hatton's crafty counsel : — he advised me,
 For my own honor, and in confidence
 In my good cause, and my most strong defence,
 To listen to the points of accusation,
 And prove their falsehoods.   This, my lord, I did
 From personal respect for the lords' names,
 Not their usurped charge, which I disclaim.
BUR.   Acknowledge you the court, or not, that is
 Only a point of mere formality,
 Which cannot here arrest the course of justice.
 You breathe the air of England ; you enjoy
 The law's protection, and its benefits ;
 You therefore are its subject.
MARY.   Sir, I breathe
 The air within an English prison walls : —
 Is that to live in England ; to enjoy

Protection from its laws ?   I scarcely know
And never have I pledged my faith to keep them.
I am no member of this realm ; I am
An independent, and a foreign queen.
Bur.   And do you think that the mere name of queen
Can serve you as a charter to foment
In other countries, with impunity,
This bloody discord ?   Where would be the state's
Security, if the stern sword of justice
Could not as freely smite the guilty brow
Of the imperial stranger as the beggar's ?
Mary.   I do not wish to be exempt from judgment,
It is the judges only I disclaim.
Bur.   The judges ?   How now, madam ?   Are they then
Base wretches, snatched at hazard from the crowd ?
Vile wranglers that make sale of truth and justice ;
Oppression's willing hirelings, and its tools ?
Are they not all the foremost of this land,
Too independent to be else than honest,
And too exalted not to soar above
The fear of kings, or base servility ?
Are they not those who rule a generous people
In liberty and justice ; men, whose names
I need but mention to dispel each doubt,
Each mean suspicion which is raised against them ?
Stands not the reverend primate at their head,
The pious shepherd of his faithful people,
The learned Talbot, keeper of the seals,
And Howard, who commands our conquering fleets ?
Say, then, could England's sovereign do more
Than, out of all the monarchy, elect
The very noblest, and appoint them judges
In this great suit ?   And were it probable
That party hatred could corrupt one heart ;
Can forty chosen men unite to speak
A sentence just as passion gives command ?
Mary (*after a short pause*).
I am struck dumb by that tongue's eloquence,
Which ever was so ominous to me.
And how shall I, a weak, untutored woman,
Cope with so subtle, learned an orator ?

Yes truly; were these lords as you describe them,
I must be mute; my cause were lost indeed,
Beyond all hope, if they pronounce me guilty.
But, sir, these names, which you are pleased to praise,
These very men, whose weight you think will crush
        me,
I see performing in the history
Of these dominions very different parts:
I see this high nobility of England,
This grave majestic senate of the realm,
Like to an eastern monarch's vilest slaves,
Flatter my uncle Henry's sultan fancies:
I see this noble, reverend House of Lords,
Venal alike with the corrupted Commons,
Make statutes and annul them, ratify
A marriage and dissolve it, as the voice
Of power commands: to-day it disinherits,
And brands the royal daughters of the realm
With the vile name of bastards, and to-morrow
Crowns them as queens, and leads them to the throne.
I see them in four reigns, with pliant conscience,
Four times abjure their faith; renounce the pope
With Henry, yet retain the old belief;
Reform themselves with Edward; hear the mass
Again with Mary; with Elizabeth,
Who governs now, reform themselves again.
BUR.   You say you are not versed in England's laws,
    You seem well read, methinks, in her disasters.
MARY.   And these men are my judges?
            [*As* LORD BURLEIGH *seems to wish to speak.*
                        My lord treasurer,
Towards you I will be just, be you but just
To me.   'Tis said that you consult with zeal
The good of England, and of England's queen;
Are honest, watchful, indefatigable;
I will believe it.   Not your private ends,
Your sovereign and your country's weal alone,
Inspire your counsels and direct your deeds.
Therefore, my noble lord, you should the more
Distrust your heart; should see that you mistake not
The welfare of the government for justice.

I do not doubt, besides yourself, there are
Among my judges many upright men:
But they are Protestants, are eager all
For England's quiet, and they sit in judgment
On me, the Queen of Scotland, and the papist.
It is an ancient saying, that the Scots
And England to each other are unjust;
And hence the rightful custom that a Scot
Against an Englishman, or Englishman
Against a Scot, cannot be heard in judgment.
Necessity prescribed this cautious law;
Deep policy oft lies in ancient customs:
My lord, we must respect them. Nature cast
Into the ocean these two fiery nations
Upon this plank, and she divided it
Unequally, and bade them fight for it.
The narrow bed of Tweed alone divides
These daring spirits; often hath the blood
Of the contending parties dyed its waves.
Threatening, and sword in hand, these thousand
    years,
From both its banks they watch their rival's
    motions,
Most vigilant and true confederates,
With every enemy of the neighbor state.
No foe oppresses England, but the Scot
Becomes his firm ally; no civil war
Inflames the towns of Scotland, but the English
Add fuel to the fire: this raging hate
Will never be extinguished till, at last,
One parliament in concord shall unite them,
One common sceptre rule throughout the isle.
BUR.   And from a Stuart, then, should England hope
    This happiness?
MARY.   Oh! why should I deny it?
Yes, I confess, I cherished the fond hope;
I thought myself the happy instrument
To join in freedom, 'neath the olive's shade,
Two generous realms in lasting happiness!
I little thought I should become the victim
Of their old hate, their long-lived jealousy;

And the sad flames of that unhappy strife,
I hoped at last to smother, and forever :
And, as my ancestor, great Richmond, joined
The rival roses after bloody contest,
To join in peace the Scotch and English crowns.

BUR.   An evil way you took to this good end,
To set the realm on fire, and through the flames
Of civil war to strive to mount the throne.

MARY.   I wished not that : — I wished it not, by Heaven!
When did I strive at that?   Where are your
     proofs?

BUR.   I came not hither to dispute ; your cause
Is no more subject to a war of words.
The great majority of forty voices
Hath found that you have contravened the law
Last year enacted, and have now incurred
Its penalty.   [*Producing the verdict.*

MARY.   Upon this statute, then,
My lord, is built the verdict of my judges?

BURLEIGH (*reading*).
Last year it was enacted, "If a plot
Henceforth should rise in England, in the name,
Or for the benefit of any claimant
To England's crown, that justice should be done
On such pretender, and the guilty party
Be prosecuted unto death."   Now, since
It has been proved ——

MARY.   Lord Burleigh, I can well
Imagine that a law expressly aimed
At me, and framed to compass my destruction
May to my prejudice be used.   Oh! woe
To the unhappy victim, when the tongue
That frames the law shall execute the sentence.
Can you deny it, sir, that this same statute
Was made for my destruction, and naught else?

BUR.   It should have acted as a warning to you :
By your imprudence it became a snare.
You saw the precipice which yawned before you ;
Yet, truly warned, you plunged into the deep.
With Babington, the traitor, and his bands
Of murderous companions, were you leagued.

You knew of all, and from your prison led
Their treasonous plottings with a deep-laid plan.
MARY. When did I that, my lord? Let them produce
The documents.
BURLEIGH. You have already seen them:
They were before the court, presented to you.
MARY. Mere copies written by another hand;
Show me the proof that they were dictated
By me, that they proceeded from my lips,
And in those very terms in which you read them.
BUR. Before his execution, Babington
Confessed they were the same which he received.
MARY. Why was he in his lifetime not produced
Before my face? Why was he then despatched
So quickly that he could not be confronted
With her whom he accused?
BURLEIGH. Besides, my lady,
Your secretaries, Curl and Nau, declare
On oath, they are the very selfsame letters
Which from your lips they faithfully transcribed.
MARY. And on my menials' testimony, then,
I am condemned; upon the word of those
Who have betrayed me, me, their rightful queen!
Who in that very moment, when they came
As witnesses against me, broke their faith!
BUR. You said yourself, you held your countryman
To be an upright, conscientious man.
MARY. I thought him such; but 'tis the hour of danger
Alone, which tries the virtue of a man:
[He ever was an honest man, but weak
In understanding; and his subtle comrade,
Whose faith, observe, I never answered for,
Might easily seduce him to write down
More than he should;] the rack may have compelled
him
To say and to confess more than he knew.
He hoped to save himself by this false witness,
And thought it could not injure me — a queen.
BUR. The oath he swore was free and unconstrained.
MARY. But not before my face! How now, my lord?
The witnesses you name are still alive;

Let them appear against me face to face,
And there repeat what they have testified.
Why am I then denied that privilege,
That right which e'en the murderer enjoys?
I know from Talbot's mouth, my former keeper,
That in this reign a statute has been passed
Which orders that the plaintiff be confronted
With the defendant; is it so, good Paulet?
I e'er have known you as an honest man;
Now prove it to me; tell me, on your conscience,
If such a law exist or not in England?

PAUL. Madam, there does: that is the law in England.
I must declare the truth.

MARY. Well, then, my lord,
If I am treated by the law of England
So hardly, when that law oppresses me,
Say, why avoid this selfsame country's law,
When 'tis for my advantage? Answer me;
Why was not Babington confronted with me?
Why not my servants, who are both alive?

BUR. Be not so hasty, lady; 'tis not only
Your plot with Babington——

MARY. 'Tis that alone
Which arms the law against me; that alone
From which I'm called upon to clear myself.
Stick to the point, my lord; evade it not.

BUR. It has been proved that you have corresponded
With the ambassador of Spain, Mendoza——

MARY. Stick to the point, my lord.

BURLEIGH. That you have formed
Conspiracies to overturn the fixed
Religion of the realm; that you have called
Into this kingdom foreign powers, and roused
All kings in Europe to a war with England.

MARY. And were it so, my lord — though I deny it —
But e'en suppose it were so: I am kept
Imprisoned here against all laws of nations.
I came not into England sword in hand;
I came a suppliant; and at the hands
Of my imperial kinswoman I claimed
The sacred rights of hospitality,

When power seized upon me, and prepared
To rivet fetters where I hoped protection.
Say, is my conscience bound, then, to this realm?
What are the duties that I owe to England?
I should but exercise a sacred right,
Derived from sad necessity, if I
Warred with these bonds, encountered might with
    might,
Roused and incited every state in Europe
For my protection to unite in arms.
Whatever in a rightful war is just
And loyal, 'tis my right to exercise:
Murder alone, the secret, bloody deed,
My conscience and my pride alike forbid.
Murder would stain me, would dishonor me:
Dishonor me, my lord, but not condemn me,
Nor subject me to England's courts of law:
For 'tis not justice, but mere violence,
Which is the question 'tween myself and England.
BURLEIGH (*significantly*).
    Talk not, my lady, of the dreadful right
Of power: 'tis seldom on the prisoner's side.
MARY.   I am the weak, she is the mighty one:
    'Tis well, my lord; let her, then, use her power;
Let her destroy me; let me bleed, that she
May live secure; but let her, then, confess
That she hath exercised her power alone,
And not contaminate the name of justice.
Let her not borrow from the laws the sword
To rid her of her hated enemy;
Let her not clothe in this religious garb
The bloody daring of licentious might;
Let not these juggling tricks deceive the world.
                    [*Returning the sentence.*
Though she may murder me, she cannot judge me:
Let her no longer strive to join the fruits
Of vice with virtue's fair and angel show;
But let her dare to seem the thing she is.   [*Exit.*

Scene VIII.

Burleigh, Paulet.

Bur. She scorns us, she defies us! will defy us,
Even at the scaffold's foot. This haughty heart
Is not to be subdued. Say, did the sentence
Surprise her? Did you see her shed one tear,
Or even change her color? She disdains
To make appeal to our compassion. Well
She knows the wavering mind of England's queen.
Our apprehensions make her bold.
Paulet.   My lord,
Take the pretext away which buoys it up,
And you shall see this proud defiance fail
That very moment. I must say, my lord,
Irregularities have been allowed
In these proceedings; Babington and Ballard
Should have been brought, with her two secretaries,
Before her, face to face.
Burleigh.   No, Paulet, no.
That was not to be risked; her influence
Upon the human heart is too supreme;
Too strong the female empire of her tears.
Her secretary, Curl, if brought before her,
And called upon to speak the weighty word
On which her life depends, would straight shrink
    back
And fearfully revoke his own confession.
Paul. Then England's enemies will fill the world
With evil rumors; and the formal pomp
Of these proceedings to the minds of all
Will only signalize an act of outrage.
Bur. That is the greatest torment of our queen,
[That she can never 'scape the blame. Oh God!]
Had but this lovely mischief died before
She set her faithless foot on English ground.
Paul. Amen, say I!
Burleigh.   Had sickness but consumed her!
Paul. England had been secured from such mis-
    fortune.

BUR. And yet, if she had died in nature's course,
The world would still have called us murderers.
PAUL. 'Tis true, the world will think, despite of us,
Whate'er it list.
BURLEIGH.   Yet could it not be proved?
And it would make less noise.
PAULET.   Why, let it make
What noise it may. It is not clamorous blame,
'Tis righteous censure only which can wound.
BUR. We know that holy justice cannot 'scape
The voice of censure; and the public cry
Is ever on the side of the unhappy:
Envy pursues the laurelled conqueror;
The sword of justice, which adorns the man,
Is hateful in a woman's hand; the world
Will give no credit to a woman's justice
If woman be the victim. Vain that we,
The judges, spoke what conscience dictated;
She has the royal privilege of mercy;
She must exert it: 'twere not to be borne,
Should she let justice take its full career.
PAUL. And therefore ——
BURLEIGH.   Therefore should she live? Oh, no,
She must not live; it must not be. 'Tis this,
Even this, my friend, which so disturbs the queen,
And scares all slumber from her couch; I read
Her soul's distracting contest in her eyes:
She fears to speak her wishes, yet her looks,
Her silent looks, significantly ask,
" Is there not one amongst my many servants
To save me from this sad alternative?
Either to tremble in eternal fear
Upon my throne, or else to sacrifice
A queen of my own kindred on the block?"
PAUL. 'Tis even so; nor can it be avoided ——
BUR. Well might it be avoided, thinks the queen,
If she had only more attentive servants.
PAUL. How more attentive?
BURLEIGH.   Such as could interpret
A silent mandate.
PAULET.   What? A silent mandate!

BUR. Who, when a poisonous adder is delivered
    Into their hands, would keep the treacherous charge
    As if it were a sacred, precious jewel?
PAUL. A precious jewel is the queen's good name
    And spotless reputation: good my lord,
    One cannot guard it with sufficient care.
BUR. When out of Shrewsbury's hands the Queen of Scots
    Was trusted to Sir Amias Paulet's care,
    The meaning was ——
PAULET.   I hope to God, my lord,
    The meaning was to give the weightiest charge
    Into the purest hands; my lord, my lord!
    By heaven I had disdained this bailiff's office
    Had I not thought the service claimed the care
    Of the best man that England's realm can boast.
    Let me not think I am indebted for it
    To anything but my unblemished name.
BUR. Spread the report she wastes; grows sicker still
    And sicker; and expires at last in peace;
    Thus will she perish in the world's remembrance,
    And your good name is pure.
PAULET.   But not my conscience.
BUR. Though you refuse us, sir, your own assistance,
    You will not sure prevent another's hand.
PAUL. No murderer's foot shall e'er approach her
        threshold
    Whilst she's protected by my household gods.
    Her life's a sacred trust; to me the head
    Of Queen Elizabeth is not more sacred.
    Ye are the judges; judge, and break the staff;
    And when 'tis time then let the carpenter
    With axe and saw appear to build the scaffold.
    My castle's portals shall be open to him,
    The sheriff and the executioners:
    Till then she is intrusted to my care;
    And be assured I will fulfil my trust,
    She shall nor do nor suffer what's unjust. [*Exeunt.*

ACT II.

Scene I.

London, a Hall in the Palace of Westminster. The
Earl of Kent *and* Sir William Davison *meeting.*

Dav. Is that my Lord of Kent? So soon returned?
    Is then the tourney, the carousal over?
Kent. How now? Were you not present at the tilt?
Dav. My office kept me here.
Kent.   Believe me, sir,
    You've lost the fairest show which ever state
    Devised, or graceful dignity performed:
    For beauty's virgin fortress was presented
    As by desire invested; the Earl-Marshal,
    The Lord-High Admiral, and ten other knights
    Belonging to the queen defended it,
    And France's cavaliers led the attack.
    A herald marched before the gallant troop,
    And summoned, in a madrigal, the fortress;
    And from the walls the chancellor replied;
    And then the artillery was played, and nosegays
    Breathing delicious fragrance were discharged
    From neat field-pieces; but in vain, the storm
    Was valiantly resisted, and desire
    Was forced, unwillingly, to raise the siege.
Dav. A sign of evil-boding, good my lord,
    For the French suitors.
Kent.   Why, you know that this
    Was but in sport; when the attack's in earnest
    The fortress will, no doubt, capitulate.
Dav. Ha! think you so? I never can believe it.
Kent. The hardest article of all is now
    Adjusted and acceded to by France;
    The Duke of Anjou is content to hold
    His holy worship in a private chapel;
    And openly he promises to honor
    And to protect the realm's established faith.
    Had ye but heard the people's joyful shouts
    Where'er the tidings spread, for it has been
    The country's constant fear the queen might die

Without immediate issue of her body;
And England bear again the Romish chains
If Mary Stuart should ascend the throne.
DAV.   This fear appears superfluous; she goes
Into the bridal chamber; Mary Stuart
Enters the gates of death.
KENT.   The queen approaches.

SCENE II.

Enter ELIZABETH, *led in by* LEICESTER, COUNT AUBESPINE,
  BELLIEVRE, LORDS SHREWSBURY *and* BURLEIGH, *with other
  French and English gentlemen.*

ELIZABETH (*to* AUBESPINE).
    Count, I am sorry for these noblemen
    Whose gallant zeal hath brought them over sea
    To visit these our shores, that they, with us,
    Must miss the splendor of St. Germain's court.
    Such pompous festivals of godlike state
    I cannot furnish as the royal court
    Of France. A sober and contented people,
    Which crowd around me with a thousand blessings
    Whene'er in public I present myself:
    This is the spectacle which I can show,
    And not without some pride, to foreign eyes.
    The splendor of the noble dames who bloom
    In Catherine's beauteous garden would, I know,
    Eclipse myself, and my more modest merits.
AUB.   The court of England has one lady only
    To show the wondering foreigner; but all
    That charms our hearts in the accomplished sex
    Is seen united in her single person.
BEL.   Great majesty of England, suffer us
    To take our leave, and to our royal master,
    The Duke of Anjou, bring the happy news.
    The hot impatience of his heart would not
    Permit him to remain at Paris; he
    At Amiens awaits the joyful tidings;
    And thence to Calais reach his posts to bring
    With winged swiftness to his tranced ear

The sweet consent which, still we humbly hope,
Your royal lips will graciously pronounce.
ELIZ. Press me no further now, Count Bellievre.
It is not now a time, I must repeat,
To kindle here the joyful marriage torch.
The heavens lower black and heavy o'er this land;
And weeds of mourning would become me better
Than the magnificence of bridal robes.
A fatal blow is aimed against my heart;
A blow which threatens to oppress my house.
BEL. We only ask your majesty to promise
Your royal hand when brighter days shall come.
ELIZ. Monarchs are but the slaves of their condition;
They dare not hear the dictates of their hearts;
My wish was ever to remain unmarried,
And I had placed my greatest pride in this,
That men hereafter on my tomb might read,
" Here rests the virgin queen." But my good subjects
Are not content that this should be: they think,
E'en now they often think upon the time
When I shall be no more. 'Tis not enough
That blessings now are showered upon this land;
They ask a sacrifice for future welfare,
And I must offer up my liberty,
My virgin liberty, my greatest good,
To satisfy my people. Thus they'd force
A lord and master on me. 'Tis by this
I see that I am nothing but a woman
In their regard; and yet mtehought that I
Had governed like a man, and like a king.
Well wot I that it is not serving God
To quit the laws of nature; and that those
Who here have ruled before me merit praise,
That they have oped the cloister gates, and given
Thousands of victims of ill-taught devotion
Back to the duties of humanity.
But yet a queen who hath not spent her days
In fruitless, idle contemplation; who,
Without murmur, indefatigably
Performs the hardest of all duties; she
Should be exempted from that natural law

    Which doth ordain one half of human kind
Shall ever be subservient to the other.
AUB.   Great queen, you have upon your throne done honor
    To every virtue ; nothing now remains
    But to the sex, whose greatest boast you are
    To be the leading star, and give the great
    Example of its most consistent duties.
    'Tis true, the man exists not who deserves
    That you to him should sacrifice your freedom ;
    Yet if a hero's soul, descent, and rank,
    And manly beauty can make mortal man
    Deserving of this honor ——
ELIZABETH.   Without doubt,
    My lord ambassador, a marriage union
    With France's royal son would do me honor ;
    Yes, I acknowledge it without disguise,
    If it must be, if I cannot prevent it,
    If I must yield unto my people's prayers,
    And much I fear they will o'erpower me,
    I do not know in Europe any prince
    To whom with less reluctance I would yield
    My greatest treasure, my dear liberty.
    Let this confession satisfy your master.
BEL.   It gives the fairest hope, and yet it gives
    Nothing but hope ; my master wishes more.
ELIZ.   What wishes he ?
        [*She takes a ring from her finger, and thought-
        fully examines it.*
                 In this a queen has not
    One privilege above all other women.
    This common token marks one common duty,
    One common servitude ; the ring denotes
    Marriage, and 'tis of rings a chain is formed.
    Convey this present to his highness ; 'tis
    As yet no chain, it binds me not as yet,
    But out of it may grow a link to bind me.
BELLIEVRE (*kneeling*).
    This present, in his name, upon my knees,
    I do receive, great queen, and press the kiss
    Of homage on the hand of her who is
    Henceforth my princess.

ELIZABETH (*to the* EARL OF LEICESTER, *whom she, during the last speeches, had continually regarded*).

By your leave, my lord.

[*She takes the blue ribbon from his neck,* and invests Bellievre with it.*

Invest his highness with this ornament,
As I invest you with it, and receive you
Into the duties of my gallant order.
And, "*Honi soit qui mal y pense.*" Thus perish
All jealousy between our several realms,
And let the bond of confidence unite
Henceforth, the crowns of Britain and of France.

BEL. Most sovereign queen, this is a day of joy;
Oh that it could be so for all, and no
Afflicted heart within this island mourn.
See! mercy beams upon thy radiant brow;
Let the reflection of its cheering light
Fall on a wretched princess, who concerns
Britain and France alike.

ELIZABETH.   No further, count!
Let us not mix two inconsistent things;
If France be truly anxious for my hand,
It must partake my interests, and renounce
Alliance with my foes.

AUBESPINE.   In thine own eyes
Would she not seem to act unworthily,
If in this joyous treaty she forgot
This hapless queen, the widow of her king;
In whose behalf her honor and her faith
Are bound to plead for grace.

ELIZABETH.   Thus urged, I know
To rate this intercession at its worth;
France has discharged her duties as a friend,
I will fulfil my own as England's queen.

[*She bows to the French ambassadors, who, with the other gentlemen, retire respectfully.*

---

* Till the time of Charles the First, the Knights of the Garter wore the blue ribbon with the George about their necks, as they still do the collars, on great days.—TRANSLATOR.

Scene III.

Enter Burleigh, Leicester, *and* Talbot.   *The* Queen
takes her seat.

Bur.   Illustrious sovereign, thou crown'st to-day
 The fervent wishes of thy people ; now
 We can rejoice in the propitious days
 Which thou bestowest upon us ; and we look
 No more with fear and trembling towards the time
 Which, charged with storms, futurity presented.
 Now, but one only care disturbs this land ;
 It is a sacrifice which every voice
 Demands ; Oh ! grant but this and England's peace
 Will be established now and evermore.
Eliz.   What wish they still, my lord ?   Speak.
Burleigh.   They demand
 The Stuart's head.   If to thy people thou
 Wouldst now secure the precious boon of freedom,
 And the fair light of truth so dearly won,
 Then she must die ; if we are not to live
 In endless terror for thy precious life
 The enemy must fall ; for well thou know'st
 That all thy Britons are not true alike ;
 Romish idolatry has still its friends
 In secret, in this island, who foment
 The hatred of our enemies.   Their hearts
 All turn toward this Stuart ; they are leagued
 With the two plotting brothers of Lorrain,
 The foes inveterate of thy house and name.
 'Gainst thee this raging faction hath declared
 A war of desolation, which they wage
 With the deceitful instruments of hell.
 At Rheims, the cardinal archbishop's see,
 There is the arsenal from which they dart
 These lightnings ; there the school of regicide ;
 Thence, in a thousand shapes disguised, are sent
 Their secret missionaries to this isle ;
 Their bold and daring zealots ; for from thence
 Have we not seen the third assassin come?
 And inexhausted is the direful breed
 Of secret enemies in this abyss.

While in her castle sits at Fotheringay,
The *Até* * of this everlasting war,
Who, with the torch of love, spreads flames around ;
For her who sheds delusive hopes on all,
Youth dedicates itself to certain death ;
To set her free is the pretence — the aim
Is to establish her upon the throne.
For this accursed House of Guise denies
Thy sacred right ; and in their mouths thou art
A robber of the throne, whom chance has crowned.
By them this thoughtless woman was deluded,
Proudly to style herself the Queen of England ;
No peace can be with her, and with her house ;
[Their hatred is too bloody, and their crimes
Too great ;] thou must resolve to strike, or suffer —
Her life is death to thee, her death thy life.

ELIZ.   My lord, you bear a melancholy office ;
I know the purity which guides your zeal,
The solid wisdom which informs your speech ;
And yet I hate this wisdom, when it calls
For blood, I hate it in my inmost soul.
Think of a milder counsel — Good my Lord
Of Shrewsbury, we crave your judgment here.

TAL.   [Desire you but to know, most gracious queen,
What is for your advantage, I can add
Nothing to what my lord-high-treasurer
Has urged ; then, for your welfare, let the sentence
Be now confirmed — this much is proved already :
There is no surer method to avert
The danger from your head and from the state.
Should you in this reject our true advice,

---

* The picture of Até, the goddess of mischief, we are acquainted with
from Homer, ll. v. 91. 130. I. 501. She is a daughter of Jupiter, and eager
to prejudice every one, even the immortal gods. She counteracted Jupiter
himself, on which account he seized her by her beautiful hair, and hurled
her from heaven to the earth, where she now, striding over the heads of men,
excites them to evil in order to involve them in calamity.—HERDER.
Shakspeare has, in Julius Cæsar, made a fine use of this image : —

> "And Cæsar's spirit, ranging for revenge,
> With Até by his side, come hot from hell,
> Shall in these confines, with a monarch's voice,
> Cry havoc, and let slip the dogs of war."

I need not point out to the reader the beautiful propriety of introducing
the evil spirit on this occasion.—TRANSLATOR.

You can dismiss your council. We are placed
Here as your counsellors, but to consult
The welfare of this land, and with our knowledge
And our experience we are bound to serve you !
But in what's good and just, most gracious queen,
You have no need of counsellors, your conscience
Knows it full well, and it is written there.
Nay, it were overstepping our commission
If we attempted to instruct you in it.

ELIZ. Yet speak, my worthy Lord of Shrewsbury,
'Tis not our understanding fails alone,
Our heart too feels it wants some sage advice.]

TAL. Well did you praise the upright zeal which fires
Lord Burleigh's loyal breast; my bosom, too,
Although my tongue be not so eloquent,
Beats with no weaker, no less faithful pulse.
Long may you live, my queen, to be the joy
Of your delighted people, to prolong
Peace and its envied blessings in this realm.
Ne'er hath this isle beheld such happy days
Since it was governed by its native kings.
Oh, let it never buy its happiness
With its good name ; at least, may Talbot's eyes
Be closed in death e'er this shall come to pass.

ELIZ. Forbid it, heaven, that our good name be stained !

TAL. Then must you find some other way than this
To save thy kingdom, for the sentence passed
Of death against the Stuart is unjust.
You cannot upon her pronounce a sentence
Who is not subject to you.

ELIZABETH.   Then, it seems,
My council and my parliament have erred ;
Each bench of justice in the land is wrong,
Which did with one accord admit this right.

TALBOT (after a pause).
The proof of justice lies not in the voice
Of numbers ; England's not the world, nor is
Thy parliament the focus, which collects
The vast opinion of the human race.
This present England is no more the future
Than 'tis the past ; as inclination changes,

Thus ever ebbs and flows the unstable tide
Of public judgment. Say not, then, that thou
Must act as stern necessity compels,
That thou must yield to the importunate
Petitions of thy people; every hour
Thou canst experience that thy will is free.
Make trial, and declare thou hatest blood,
And that thou wilt protect thy sister's life;
Show those who wish to give thee other counsels,
That here thy royal anger is not feigned,
And thou shalt see how stern necessity
Can vanish, and what once was titled justice
Into injustice be converted : thou
Thyself must pass the sentence, thou alone:
Trust not to this unsteady, trembling reed,
But hear the gracious dictates of thy heart.
God hath not planted rigor in the frame
Of woman; and the founders of this realm,
Who to the female hand have not denied
The reins of government, intend by this
To show that mercy, not severity,
Is the best virtue to adorn a crown.

ELIZ.   Lord Shrewsbury is a fervent advocate
For mine and England's enemy; I must
Prefer those counsellors who wish my welfare.

TAL.   Her advocates have an invidious task !
None will, by speaking in her favor, dare
To meet thy anger : suffer, then, an old
And faithful counsellor (whom naught on earth
Can tempt on the grave's brink) to exercise
The pious duty of humanity.
It never shall be said that, in thy council,
Passion and interest could find a tongue,
While mercy's pleading voice alone was mute,
All circumstances have conspired against her;
Thou ne'er hast seen her face, and nothing speaks
Within thy breast for one that's stranger to thee.
I do not take the part of her misdeeds;
They say 'twas she who planned her husband's
    murder :
'Tis true that she espoused his murderer.

A grievous crime, no doubt; but then it happened
In darksome days of trouble and dismay,
In the stern agony of civil war,
When she, a woman, helpless and hemmed in
By a rude crowd of rebel vassals, sought
Protection in a powerful chieftain's arms.
God knows what arts were used to overcome her!
For woman is a weak and fragile thing.

ELIZ. Woman's not weak; there are heroic souls
Among the sex; and, in my presence, sir,
I do forbid to speak of woman's weaknes.

TAL. Misfortune was for thee a rigid school;
Thou wast not stationed on the sunny side
Of life; thou sawest no throne, from far, before thee;
The grave was gaping for thee at thy feet.
At Woodstock, and in London's gloomy tower,
'Twas there the gracious father of this land
Taught thee to know thy duty, by misfortune.
No flatterer sought thee there: there learned thy
	soul,
Far from the noisy world and its distractions,
To commune with itself, to think apart,
And estimate the real goods of life.
No God protected this poor sufferer:
Transplanted in her early youth to France,
The court of levity and thoughtless joys,
There, in the round of constant dissipation,
She never heard the earnest voice of truth;
She was deluded by the glare of vice,
And driven onward by the stream of ruin.
Hers was the vain possession of a face,
And she outshone all others of her sex
As far in beauty, as in noble birth.

ELIZ. Collect yourself, my Lord of Shrewsbury;
Bethink you we are met in solemn council.
Those charms must surely be without compare,
Which can engender, in an elder's blood,
Such fire. My Lord of Leicester, you alone
Are silent; does the subject which has made
Him eloquent, deprive you of your speech?

LEIC. Amazement ties my tongue, my queen, to think

That they should fill thy soul with such alarms,
And that the idle tales, which, in the streets
Of London, terrify the people's ears,
Should reach the enlightened circle of thy council,
And gravely occupy our statesmen's minds.
Astonishment possesses me, I own,
To think this lackland Queen of Scotland, she
Who could not save her own poor throne, the jest
Of her own vassals, and her country's refuse,
[Who in her fairest days of freedom, was
But thy despised puppet,] should become
At once thy terror when a prisoner.
What, in Heaven's name, can make her formidable?
That she lays claim to England? that the Guises
Will not acknowledge thee as queen?   [Did then
Thy people's loyal fealty await
These Guises' approbation?]   Can these Guises,
With their objections, ever shake the right
Which birth hath given thee; which, with   one
      consent,
The votes of parliament have ratified?
And is not she, by Henry's will, passed o'er
In silence?   Is it probable that England,
As yet so blessed in the new light's enjoyment,
Should throw itself into this papist's arms?
From thee, the sovereign it adores, desert
To Darnley's murderess?   What will they then,
These restless men, who even in thy lifetime
Torment thee with a successor ; who cannot
Dispose of thee in marriage soon enough
To rescue church and state from fancied peril?
Stand'st thou not blooming there in youthful prime
While each step leads her towards the expecting
      tomb?
By Heavens, I hope thou wilt full many a year
Walk o'er the Stuart's grave, and ne'er become
Thyself the instrument of her sad end.
BUR. Lord Leicester hath not always held this tone.
LEIC. 'Tis true, I in the court of justice gave
      My verdict for her death ; here, in the council,
      I may consistently speak otherwise :

Here, right is not the question, but advantage.
Is this a time to fear her power, when France,
Her only succor, has abandoned her?
When thou preparest with thy hand to bless
The royal son of France, when the fair hope
Of a new, glorious stem of sovereigns
Begins again to blossom in this land?
Why hasten then her death? She's dead already.
Contempt and scorn are death to her; take heed
Lest ill-timed pity call her into life.
'Tis therefore my advice to leave the sentence,
By which her life is forfeit, in full force.
Let her live on; but let her live beneath
The headsman's axe, and, from the very hour
One arm is lifted for her, let it fall.

ELIZABETH (*rises*).
My lords, I now have heard your several thoughts,
And give my ardent thanks for this your zeal.
With God's assistance, who the hearts of kings
Illumines, I will weigh your arguments,
And choose what best my judgment shall approve.

[*To* BURLEIGH

[Lord Burleigh's honest fears, I know it well,
Are but the offspring of his faithful care;
But yet, Lord Leicester has most truly said,
There is no need of haste; our enemy
Hath lost already her most dangerous sting —
The mighty arm of France: the fear that she
Might quickly be the victim of their zeal
Will curb the blind impatience of her friends.]

SCENE IV.

Enter SIR AMIAS PAULET *and* MORTIMER.

ELIZ.   There's Sir Amias Paulet; noble sir,
    What tidings bring you?
PAUL.   Gracious sovereign,
    My nephew, who but lately is returned
    From foreign travel, kneels before thy feet,
    And offers thee his first and earliest homage,

Grant him thy royal grace, and let him grow
And flourish in the sunshine of thy favor.

MORTIMER *(kneeling on one knee)*.
Long live my royal mistress! Happiness
And glory from a crown to grace her brows!

ELIZ. Arise, sir knight; and welcome here in England;
You've made, I hear, the tour, have been in France
And Rome, and tarried, too, some time at Rheims:
Tell me what plots our enemies are hatching?

MORT. May God confound them all! And may the darts
Which they shall aim against my sovereign,
Recoiling, strike their own perfidious breasts!

ELIZ. Did you see Morgan, and the wily Bishop
Of Ross?

MORT. I saw, my queen, all Scottish exiles
Who forge at Rheims their plots against this realm.
I stole into their confidence in hopes
To learn some hint of their conspiracies.

PAUL. Private despatches they intrusted to him,
In cyphers, for the Queen of Scots, which he,
With loyal hand, hath given up to us.

ELIZ. Say, what are then their latest plans of treason?

MORT. It struck them all as 'twere a thunderbolt,
That France should leave them, and with England close
This firm alliance; now they turn their hopes
Towards Spain ——

ELIZABETH. This, Walsingham hath written us.

MORT. Besides, a bull, which from the Vatican
Pope Sixtus lately levelled at thy throne,
Arrived at Rheims, as I was leaving it;
With the next ship we may expect it here.

LEIC. England no more is frightened by such arms.

BUR. They're always dangerous in bigots' hands.

ELIZABETH *(looking steadfastly at* MORTIMER).
Your enemies have said that you frequented
The schools at Rheims, and have abjured your faith.

MORT. So I pretended, that I must confess;
Such was my anxious wish to serve my queen.

ELIZABETH *(to* PAULET, *who presents papers to her*).
What have you there?

PAULET.   'Tis from the Queen of Scots.
   'Tis a petition, and to thee addressed.
BURLEIGH (*hastily catching at it*).
   Give me the paper.
PAULET (*giving it to the* QUEEN).
                    By your leave, my lord
   High-treasurer; the lady ordered me
   To bring it to her majesty's own hands.
   She says I am her enemy; I am
   The enemy of her offences only,
   And that which is consistent with my duty
   I will, and readily, oblige her in.
  [*The* QUEEN *takes the letter : as she reads it* MORTIMER
     and LEICESTER *speak some words in private.*
BURLEIGH (*to* PAULET).
   What may the purport of the letter be?
   Idle complaints, from which one ought to screen
   The queen's too tender heart.
PAULET.   What it contains
   She did not hide from me; she asks a boon;
   She begs to be admitted to the grace
   Of speaking with the queen.
BURLEIGH.   It cannot be.
TAL.   Why not? Her supplication's not unjust.
BUR.   For her, the base encourager of murder;
   Her, who hath thirsted for our sovereign's blood,
   The privilege to see the royal presence
   Is forfeited : a faithful counsellor
   Can never give this treacherous advice.
TAL.   And if the queen is gracious, sir, are you
   The man to hinder pity's soft emotions?
BUR.   She is condemned to death; her head is laid
   Beneath the axe, and it would ill become
   The queen to see a death-devoted head.
   The sentence cannot have its execution
   If the queen's majesty approaches her,
   For pardon still attends the royal presence,
   As sickness flies the health-dispensing hand.
ELIZABETH (*having read the letter, dries her tears*).
   Oh, what is man! What is the bliss of earth!
   To what extremities is she reduced

Who with such proud and splendid hopes began!
Who, called to sit on the most ancient throne
Of Christendom, misled by vain ambition,
Hoped with a triple crown to deck her brows!
How is her language altered, since the time
When she assumed the arms of England's crown,
And by the flatterers of her court was styled
Sole monarch of the two Britannic isles!
Forgive me, lords, my heart is cleft in twain,
Anguish possesses me, and my soul bleeds
To think that earthly goods are so unstable,
And that the dreadful fate which rules mankind
Should threaten mine own house, and scowl so near
 me.
TAL. Oh, queen! the God of mercy hath informed
Your heart; Oh! hearken to this heavenly guidance.
Most grievously, indeed, hath she atoned
Her grievous crime, and it is time that now,
At last, her heavy penance have an end.
Stretch forth your hand to raise this abject queen,
And, like the luminous vision of an angel,
Descend into her gaol's sepulchral night.
BUR. Be steadfast, mighty queen; let no emotion
Of seeming laudable humanity
Mislead thee; take not from thyself the power
Of acting as necessity commands.
Thou canst not pardon her, thou canst not save her:
Then heap not on thyself the odious blame,
That thou, with cruel and contemptuous triumph,
Didst glut thyself with gazing on thy victim.
LEIC. Let us, my lords, remain within our bounds;
The queen is wise, and doth not need our counsels
To lead her to the most becoming choice.
This meeting of the queens hath naught in common
With the proceedings of the court of justice.
The law of England, not the monarch's will,
Condemns the Queen of Scotland, and 'twere worthy
Of the great soul of Queen Elizabeth,
To follow the soft dictates of her heart,
Though justice swerves not from its rigid path.
ELIZ. Retire, my lords. We shall, perhaps, find means

To reconcile the tender claims of pity
With what necessity imposes on us.
And now retire.
  [*The* LORDS *retire ; she calls* SIR EDWARD MOR-
  TIMER *back.*
     Sir Edward Mortimer!

SCENE V.

ELIZABETH, MORTIMER.

ELIZABETH (*having measured him for some time with her
eyes in silence*).

You've shown a spirit of adventurous courage
And self-possession, far beyond your years.
He who has timely learnt to play so well
The difficult dissembler's needful task
Becomes a perfect man before his time,
And shortens his probationary years.
Fate calls you to a lofty scene of action ;
I prophesy it, and can, happily
For you, fulfil, myself, my own prediction.
MORT. Illustrious mistress, what I am, and all
I can accomplish, is devoted to you.
ELIZ. You've made acquaintance with the foes of
  England.
Their hate against me is implacable ;
Their fell designs are inexhaustible.
As yet, indeed, Almighty Providence
Hath shielded me ; but on my brows the crown
Forever trembles, while she lives who fans
Their bigot-zeal, and animates their hopes.
MORT. She lives no more, as soon as you command it.
ELIZ. Oh, sir! I thought I saw my labors end,
And I am come no further than at first,
I wished to let the laws of England act,
And keep my own hands pure from blood's defilement.
The sentence is pronounced — what gain I by it?
It must be executed, Mortimer,
And I must authorize the execution.

The blame will ever light on me, I must
Avow it, nor can save appearances.
That is the worst ——
MORTIMER.   But can appearances
Disturb your conscience where the cause is just?
ELIZ.   You are unpractised in the world, sir knight;
What we appear, is subject to the judgment
Of all mankind, and what we are, of no man.
No one will be convinced that I am right:
I must take care that my connivance in
Her death be wrapped in everlasting doubt.
In deeds of such uncertain double visage
Safety lies only in obscurity.
Those measures are the worst that stand avowed;
What's not abandoned, is not wholly lost.
MORTIMER (*seeking to learn her meaning*).
Then it perhaps were best ——
ELIZABETH (*quick*).   Ay, surely 'twere
The best; Oh, sir, my better angel speaks
Through you; — go on then, worthy sir, conclude
You are in earnest, you examine deep,
Have quite a different spirit from your uncle.
MORTIMER (*surprised*).
Have you imparted then your wishes to him?
ELIZ.   I am sorry that I have.
MORTIMER.   Excuse his age,
The old man is grown scrupulous; such bold
Adventures ask the enterprising heart
Of youth ——
ELIZABETH.   And may I venture then on you ——
MORT.   My hand I'll lend thee; save then as thou caust
Thy reputation ——
ELIZABETH.   Yes, sir; if you could
But waken me some morning with this news
" Maria Stuart, your bloodthirsty foe,
Breathed yesternight her last " ——
MORTIMER.   Depend on me.
ELIZ.   When shall my head lie calmly down to sleep?
MORT.   The next new moon will terminate thy fears.
ELIZ.   And be the selfsame happy day the dawn
Of your preferment — so God speed you, sir;

And be not hurt, if, chance, my thankfulness
Should wear the mask of darkness.   Silence is
The happy suitor's god.   The closest bonds,
The dearest, are the works of secrecy.   [*Exit.*

SCENE VI.

MORTIMER (*alone*).

Go, false, deceitful queen!   As thou deludest
The world, e'en so I cozen thee; 'tis right,
Thus to betray thee; 'tis a worthy deed.
Look I then like a murderer?   Hast thou read
Upon my brow such base dexterity?
Trust only to my arm, and keep thine own
Concealed — assume the pious outward show
Of mercy 'fore the world, while reckoning
In secret on my murderous aid ; and thus
By gaining time we shall insure her rescue.
Thou wilt exalt me! — show'st me from afar
The costly recompense : but even were
Thyself the prize, and all thy woman's favor,
What art thou, poor one, and what canst thou
        proffer?
I scorn ambition's avaricious strife,
With her alone is all the charm of life,
O'er her, in rounds of endless glory, hover
Spirits with grace, and youth eternal blessed,
Celestial joy is throned upon her breast.
Thou hast but earthly, mortal goods to offer —
That sovereign good, for which all else be slighted,
When heart in heart, delighting and delighted ;
Together flow in sweet forgetfulness ; —
Ne'er didst thou woman's fairest crown possess,
Ne'er hast thou with thy hand a lover's heart
        requited.
I must attend Lord Leicester, and deliver
Her letter to him — 'tis a hateful charge —
I have no confidence in this court puppet —
I can effect her rescue, I alone ;
Be danger, honor, and the prize my own.
        [*As he is going,* PAULET *meets him.*

Scene VII.

Mortimer, Paulet.

Paul. What said the queen to you?

Mortimer. 'Twas nothing, sir;
Nothing of consequence ——

Paulet (*looking at him earnestly*). Hear, Mortimer!
It is a false and slippery ground on which
You tread. The grace of princes is alluring,
Youth loves ambition — let not yours betray you.

Mort. Was it not yourself that brought me to the
court?

Paul. Oh, would to God I had not done as much!
The honor of our house was never reaped
In courts — stand fast, my nephew — purchase not
Too dear, nor stain your conscience with a crime.

Mort. What are these fears? What are you dreaming
of?

Paul. How high soever the queen may pledge herself
To raise you, trust not her alluring words.
[The spirit of the world's a lying spirit,
And vice is a deceitful, treacherous friend.]
She will deny you, if you listen to her;
And, to preserve her own good name, will punish
The bloody deed, which she herself enjoined.

Mort. The bloody deed! ——

Paulet. Away, dissimulation! —
I know the deed the queen proposed to you.
She hopes that your ambitious youth will prove
More docile than my rigid age. But say,
Have you then pledged your promise, have you?

Mortimer. Uncle!

Paul. If you have done so, I abandon you,
And lay my curse upon you ——

Leicester (*entering*). Worthy sir!
I with your nephew wish a word. The queen
Is graciously inclined to him; she wills
That to his custody the Scottish queen
Be with full powers intrusted. She relies
On his fidelity.

Paulet. Relies! — 'tis well ——

LEIC. What say you, sir ?
PAULET.   Her majesty relies
     On him; and I, my noble lord, rely
     Upon myself, and my two open eyes.   [*Exit.*

SCENE VIII.

LEICESTER, MORTIMER.

LEICESTER (*surprised*). What ailed the knight?
MORTIMER.   My lord, I cannot tell
     What angers him : the confidence, perhaps,
     The queen so suddenly confers on me.
LEIC. Are you deserving then of confidence?
MORT. This would I ask of you, my Lord of Leicester.
LEIC. You said you wished to speak with me in private.
MORT. Assure me first that I may safely venture.
LEIC. Who gives me an assurance on your side?
     Let not my want of confidence offend you ;
     I see you, sir, exhibit at this court
     Two different aspects; one of them must be
     A borrowed one; but which of them is real?
MORT. The selfsame doubts I have concerning you.
LEIC. Which, then, shall pave the way to confidence?
MORT. He, who by doing it, is least in danger.
LEIC. Well, that are you ——
MORTIMER.   No, you ; the evidence
     Of such a weighty, powerful peer as you
     Can overwhelm my voice. My accusation
     Is weak against your rank and influence.
LEIC. Sir, you mistake. In everything but this
     I'm powerful here ; but in this tender point
     Which I am called upon to trust you with,
     I am the weakest man of all the court,
     The poorest testimony can undo me.
MORT. If the all-powerful Earl of Leicester deign
     To stoop so low to meet me, and to make
     Such a confession to me, I may venture
     To think a little better of myself,
     And lead the way in magnanimity.
LEIC. Lead you the way of confidence, I'll follow.

MORTIMER (*producing suddenly the letter*).
　Here is a letter from the Queen of Scotland.
LEICESTER (*alarmed, catches hastily at the letter*).
　Speak softly, sir! what see I? Oh, it is
　Her picture!
　[*Kisses and examines it with speechless joy — a pause.*
MORTIMER (*who has watched him closely the whole time*).
　　　　　　　Now, my lord, I can believe you.
LEICESTER (*having hastily run through the letter*).
　You know the purport of this letter, sir.
MORT. Not I.
LEICESTER. 　　Indeed! She surely hath informed you.
MORT. Nothing hath she informed me of. She said
　You would explain this riddle to me — 'tis
　To me a riddle, that the Earl of Leicester,
　The far-famed favorite of Elizabeth,
　The open, bitter enemy of Mary,
　And one of those who spoke her mortal sentence,
　Should be the man from whom the queen expects
　Deliverance from her woes; and yet it must be;
　Your eyes express too plainly what your heart
　Feels for the hapless lady.
LEICESTER. 　　　　　　　Tell me, sir,
　First, how it comes that you should take so warm
　An interest in her fate; and what it was
　Gained you her confidence?
MORTIMER. 　　　　　　　My lord, I can,
　And in few words, explain this mystery.
　I lately have at Rome abjured my creed,
　And stand in correspondence with the Guises.
　A letter from the cardinal archbishop
　Was my credential with the Queen of Scots.
LEIC. I am acquainted, sir, with your conversion;
　'Twas that which waked my confidence towards you.
　[Each remnant of distrust be henceforth banished;]
　Your hand, sir, pardon me these idle doubts,
　I cannot use too much precaution here.
　Knowing how Walsingham and Burleigh hate me,
　And, watching me, in secret spread their snares;
　You might have been their instrument, their creature
　To lure me to their toils.

MORTIMER.   How poor a part
    So great a nobleman is forced to play
    At court! My lord, I pity you.
LEICESTER.   With joy
    I rest upon the faithful breast of friendship,
    Where I can ease me of this long constraint.
    You seem surprised, sir, that my heart is turned
    So suddenly towards the captive queen.
    In truth, I never hated her; the times
    Have forced me to be her enemy.
    She was, as you well know, my destined bride,
    Long since, ere she bestowed her hand on Darnley
    While yet the beams of glory round her smiled,
    Coldly I then refused the proffered boon.
    Now in confinement, at the gates of death,
    I claim her at the hazard of my life.
MORT.   True magnanimity, my lord.
LEICESTER.   The state
    Of circumstances since that time is changed.
    Ambition made me all insensible
    To youth and beauty.   Mary's hand I held
    Too insignificant for me; I hoped
    To be the husband of the Queen of England.
MORT.   It is well known she gave you preference
    Before all others.
LEICESTER.   So, indeed, it seemed.
    Now, after ten lost years of tedious courtship
    And hateful self-constraint — oh, sir, my heart
    Must ease itself of this long agony.
    They call me happy!   Did they only know
    What the chains are, for which they envy me!
    When I had sacrificed ten bitter years
    To the proud idol of her vanity;
    Submitted with a slave's humility
    To every change of her despotic fancies
    The plaything of each little wayward whim.
    At times by seeming tenderness caressed,
    As oft repulsed with proud and cold disdain;
    Alike tormented by her grace and rigor:
    Watched like a prisoner by the Argus eyes
    Of jealousy; examined like a schoolboy,

And railed at like a servant.   Oh, no tongue
Can paint this hell.
MORTIMER.   My lord, I feel for you.
LEIC. To lose, and at the very goal, the prize !
Another comes to rob me of the fruits
Of my so anxious wooing.   I must lose
To her young blooming husband all those rights
Of which I was so long in full possession ;
And I must from the stage descend, where I
So long have played the most distinguished part.
'Tis not her hand alone this envious stranger
Threatens, he'd rob me of her favor too ;
She is a woman, and he formed to please.
MORT.   He is the son of Catherine.   He has learn
In a good school the arts of flattery.
LEIC.   Thus fall my hopes ; I strove to seize a plank
To bear me in this shipwreck of my fortunes,
And my eye turned itself towards the hope
Of former days once more ; then Mary's image
Within me was renewed, and youth and beauty
Once more asserted all their former rights.
No more 'twas cold ambition ; 'twas my heart
Which now compared, and with regret I felt
The value of the jewel I had lost.
With horror I beheld her in the depths.
Of misery, cast down by my transgression ;
Then waked the hope in me that I might still
Deliver and possess her ; I contrived
To send her, through a faithful hand, the news
Of my conversion to her interests ;
And in this letter which you brought me, she
Assures me that she pardons me, and offers
Herself as guerdon if I rescue her.
MORT.   But you attempted nothing for her rescue.
You let her be condemned without a word :
You gave, yourself, your verdict for her death ;
A miracle must happen, and the light
Of truth must move me, *me*, her keeper's nephew,
And heaven must in the Vatican at Rome
Prepare for her an unexpected succour,
Else had she never found the way to you.

LEIC.   Oh, sir, it has tormented me enough!
About this time it was that they removed her
From Talbot's castle, and delivered her
Up to your uncle's stricter custody.
Each way to her was shut.   I was obliged
Before the world to persecute her still;
But do not think that I would patiently
Have seen her led to death.   No, sir; I hoped,
And still I hope, to ward off all extremes,
Till I can find some certain means to save her.

MORT.   These are already found: my Lord of Leicester;
Your generous confidence in me deserves
A like return.   I will deliver her.
That is my object here; my dispositions
Are made already, and your powerful aid
Assures us of success in our attempt.

LEIC.   What say you?   You alarm me!   How?   You
would ——

MORT.   I'll open forcibly her prison-gates;
I have confederates, and all is ready.

LEIC.   You have confederates, accomplices?
Alas! In what rash enterprise would you
Engage me?   And these friends, know they my
secret?

MORT.   Fear not; our plan was laid without your help,
Without your help it would have been accomplished,
Had she not signified her resolution
To owe her liberty to you alone.

LEIC.   And can you, then, with certainty assure me
That in your plot my name has not been mentioned?

MORT.   You may depend upon it.   How, my lord,
So scrupulous when help is offered you?
You wish to rescue Mary, and possess her;
You find confederates; sudden, unexpected,
The readiest means fall, as it were from Heaven,
Yet you show more perplexity than joy.

LEIC.   We must avoid all violence; it is
Too dangerous an enterprise.

MORTIMER.   Delay
Is also dangerous.

LEICESTER.   I tell you, sir,
'Tis not to be attempted ——

MORTIMER. My lord,
    Too hazardous for you, who would possess her;
    But we, who only wish to rescue her,
    We are more bold.
LEICESTER. Young man, you are too hasty
    In such a thorny, dangerous attempt.
MORT. And you too scrupulous in honor's cause.
LEIC. I see the trammels that are spread around us.
MORT. And I feel courage to break through them all.
LEIC. Foolhardiness and madness, is this courage?
MORT. This prudence is not bravery, my lord.
LEIC. You surely wish to end like Babington.
MORT. You not to imitate great Norfolk's virtue.
LEIC. Norfolk ne'er won the bride he wooed so fondly.
MORT. But yet he proved how truly he deserved her.
LEIC. If we are ruined, she must fall with us.
MORT. If we risk nothing, she will ne'er be rescued.
LEIC. You will not weigh the matter, will not hear;
    With blind and hasty rashness you destroy
    The plans which I so happily had framed.
MORT. And what were then the plans which you had
       framed?
    What have you done then to deliver her?
    And how, if I were miscreant enough
    To murder her, as was proposed to me
    This moment by Elizabeth, and which
    She looks upon as certain; only name
    The measures you have taken to protect her?
LEIC. Did the queen give you, then, this bloody order?
MORT. She was deceived in me, as Mary is
    In you.
LEICESTER. And have you promised it? Say, have you?
MORT. That she might not engage another's hand,
    I offered mine.
LEICESTER. Well done, sir; that was right;
    This gives us leisure, for she rests secure
    Upon your bloody service, and the sentence
    Is unfulfilled the while, and we gain time.
MORTIMER (*angrily*).
    No, we are losing time.
LEICESTER. The queen depends

On you, and will the readier make a show
Of mercy; and I may prevail on her
To give an audience to her adversary;
And by this stratagem we tie her hands:
Yes! I will make the attempt, strain every nerve.

MORT. And what is gained by this? When she dis
          covers
That I am cheating her, that Mary lives;
Are we not where we were? She never will
Be free; the mildest doom which can await her
At best is but perpetual confinement.
A daring deed must one day end the matter;
Why will you not with such a deed begin?
The power is in your hands, would you but rouse
The might of your dependents round about
Your many castles, 'twere an host; and still
Has Mary many secret friends. The Howards
And Percies' noble houses, though their chiefs
Be fallen, are rich in heroes; they but wait
For the example of some potent lord.
Away with feigning — act an open part,
And, like a loyal knight, protect your fair;
Fight a good fight for her! You know you are
Lord of the person of the Queen of England,
Whene'er you will: invite her to your castle,
Oft hath she thither followed you — then show
That you're a man; then speak as master; keep
          her
Confined till she release the Queen of Scots.

LEIC. I am astonished — I am terrified!
Where would your giddy madness hurry you?
Are you acquainted with this country? Know you
The deeps and shallows of this court? With what
A potent spell this female sceptre binds
And rules men's spirits round her? 'Tis in vain
You seek the heroic energy which once
Was active in this land! it is subdued,
A woman holds it under lock and key,
And every spring of courage is relaxed.
Follow my counsel — venture nothing rashly.
Some one approaches — go ——

MORTIMER.   And Mary hopes —
  Shall I return to her with empty comfort?
LEIC. Bear her my vows of everlasting love.
MORT. Bear them yourself! I offered my assistance
  As her deliverer, not your messenger.   [*Exit.*

SCENE IX.

ELIZABETH, LEICESTER.

ELIZ. Say, who was here? I heard the sound of voices.
LEICESTER (*turning quickly and perplexed round on
         hearing the* QUEEN).
  It was young Mortimer ——
ELIZABETH.   How now, my lord :
  Why so confused?
LEICESTER (*collecting himself*).
             Your presence is the cause.
  Ne'er did I see thy beauty so resplendent,
  My sight is dazzled by thy heavenly charms.
  Oh!
ELIZABETH. Whence this sigh?
LEICESTER.   Have I no reason, then,
  To sigh? When I behold you in your glory,
  I feel anew, with pain unspeakable,
  The loss which threatens me.
ELIZABETH.   What loss, my lord?
LEIC. Your heart; your own inestimable self :
  Soon will you feel yourself within the arms
  Of your young ardent husband, highly blessed ;
  He will possess your heart without a rival.
  He is of royal blood, that am not I.
  Yet, spite of all the world can say, there lives not
  One on this globe who with such fervent zeal
  Adores you as the man who loses you.
  Anjou hath never seen you, can but love
  Your glory and the splendor of your reign ;
  But I love you, and were you born of all
  The peasant maids the poorest, I the first
  Of kings, I would descend to your condition,
  And lay my crown and sceptre at your feet!
ELIZ. Oh, pity me, my Dudley; do not blame me ;

I cannot ask my heart. Oh, that had chosen
Far otherwise! Ah, how I envy others
Who can exalt the object of their love!
But I am not so blest: 'tis not my fortune
To place upon the brows of him, the dearest
Of men to me, the royal crown of England.
The Queen of Scotland was allowed to make
Her hand the token of her inclination;
She hath had every freedom, and hath drunk,
Even to the very dregs, the cup of joy.
LEIC.   And now she drinks the bitter cup of sorrow.
ELIZ.   She never did respect the world's opinion;
Life was to her a sport; she never courted
The yoke to which I bowed my willing neck.
And yet, methinks, I had as just a claim
As she to please myself and taste the joys
Of life: but I preferred the rigid duties
Which royalty imposed on me; yet she,
She was the favorite of all the men
Because she only strove to be a woman;
And youth and age became alike her suitors.
Thus are the men voluptuaries all!
The willing slaves of levity and pleasure;
Value that least which claims their reverence.
And did not even Talbot, though gray-headed,
Grow young again when speaking of her charms?
LEIC.   Forgive him, for he was her keeper once,
And she has fooled him with her cunning wiles.
ELIZ.   And is it really true that she's so fair?
So often have I been obliged to hear
The praises of this wonder — it were well
If I could learn on what I might depend:
Pictures are flattering, and description lies;
I will trust nothing but my own conviction.
Why gaze you at me thus?
LEICESTER.   I placed in thought
You and Maria Stuart side by side.
Yes! I confess I oft have felt a wish,
If it could be but secretly contrived,
To see you placed beside the Scottish queen,
Then would you feel, and not till then, the full

Enjoyment of your triumph: she deserves
To be thus humbled; she deserves to see,
With her own eyes, and envy's glance is keen,
Herself surpassed, to feel herself o'ermatched,
As much by thee in form and princely grace
As in each virtue that adorns the sex.

ELIZ. In years she has the advantage ——

LEICESTER. Has she so?
I never should have thought it. But her griefs,
Her sufferings, indeed! 'tis possible
Have brought down age upon her ere her time.
Yes, and 'twould mortify her more to see thee
As bride — she hath already turned her back
On each fair hope of life, and she would see thee
Advancing towards the open arms of joy.
See thee as bride of France's royal son,
She who hath always plumed herself so high
On her connection with the house of France,
And still depends upon its mighty aid.

ELIZABETH (*with a careless air*).
I'm teazed to grant this interview.

LEICESTER. She asks it
As a favor; grant it as a punishment.
For though you should conduct her to the block,
Yet would it less torment her than to see
Herself extinguished by your beauty's splendor.
Thus can you murder her as she hath wished
To murder you. When she beholds your beauty,
Guarded by modesty, and beaming bright,
In the clear glory of unspotted fame
(Which she with thoughtless levity discarded),
Exalted by the splendor of the crown,
And blooming now with tender bridal graces —
Then is the hour of her destruction come.
Yes — when I now behold you — you were never,
No, never were you so prepared to seal
The triumph of your beauty. As but now
You entered the apartment, I was dazzled
As by a glorious vision from on high.
Could you but now, now as you are, appear
Before her, you could find no better moment.

ELIZ. Now? no, not now; no, Leicester; this must be
    Maturely weighed — I must with Burleigh —
LEICESTER.   Burleigh!
    To him you are but sovereign, and as such
    Alone he seeks your welfare; but your rights,
    Derived from womanhood, this tender point
    Must be decided by your own tribunal,
    Not by the statesman; yet e'en policy
    Demands that you should see her, and allure
    By such a generous deed the public voice.
    You can hereafter act as it may please you,
    To rid you of the hateful enemy.
ELIZ. But would it then become me to behold
    My kinswoman in infamy and want?
    They say she is not royally attended;
    Would not the sight of her distress reproach me?
LEIC. You need not cross her threshold; hear my
           counsel:
    A fortunate conjuncture favors it.
    The hunt you mean to honor with your presence
    Is in the neighborhood of Fotheringay;
    Permission may be given to Lady Stuart
    To take the air; you meet her in the park,
    As if by accident; it must not seem
    To have been planned, and should you not incline,
    You need not speak to her.
ELIZABETH.   If I am foolish,
    Be yours the fault, not mine. I would not care
    To-day to cross your wishes; for to-day
    I've grieved you more than all my other subjects.
                               [*Tenderly.*
    Let it then be your fancy. Leicester, hence
    You see the free obsequiousness of love.
    Which suffers that which it cannot approve.
    [LEICESTER *prostrates himself before her, and the
       curtain falls.*

ACT III.

SCENE I.

In a park. In the foreground trees; in the background a distant prospect.

MARY advances, running from behind the trees. HANNAH KENNEDY follows slowly.

KEN. You hasten on as if endowed with wings;
I cannot follow you so swiftly; wait.

MARY. Freedom returns! Oh let me enjoy it.
Let me be childish; be thou childish with me.
Freedom invites me! Oh, let me employ it
Skimming with winged step light o'er the lea;
Have I escaped from this mansion of mourning?
Holds me no more the sad dungeon of care?
Let me, with joy and with eagerness burning,
Drink in the free, the celestial air.

KEN. Oh, my dear lady! but a very little
Is your sad gaol extended; you behold not
The wall that shuts us in; these plaited tufts
Of trees hide from your sight the hated object.

MARY. Thanks to these friendly trees, that hide from me
My prison walls, and flatter my illusion!
Happy I now may deem myself, and free;
Why wake me from my dream's so sweet confusion?
The extended vault of heaven around me lies,
Free and unfettered range my wandering eyes
O'er space's vast, immeasurable sea!
From where yon misty mountains rise on high
I can my empire's boundaries explore;
And those light clouds which, steering southwards, fly,
Seek the mild clime of France's genial shore.

    Fast fleeting clouds! ye meteors that fly;
    Could I but with you sail through the sky!
    Tenderly greet the dear land of my youth!
    Here I am captive! oppressed by my foes,
    No other than you may carry my woes.
    Free through the ether your pathway is seen,
    Ye own not the power of this tyrant queen.

KEN.   Alas! dear lady!   You're beside yourself,
  This long-lost, long-sought freedom makes you rave.
MARY.   Yonder's a fisher returning to his home;
  Poor though it be, would he lend me his wherry,
  Quick to congenial shores would I ferry.
  Spare is his trade, and labor's his doom;
  Rich would I freight his vessel with treasure;
  Such a draught should be his as he never had seen;
  Wealth should he find in his nets without measure,
  Would he but rescue a poor captive queen.
KEN.   Fond, fruitless wishes!   See you not from far
  How we are followed by observing spies?
  A dismal, barbarous prohibition scares
  Each sympathetic being from our path.
MARY.   No, gentle Hannah!   Trust me, not in vain
  My prison gates are opened.   This small grace
  Is harbinger of greater happiness.
  No!   I mistake not; 'tis the active hand
  Of love to which I owe this kind indulgence.
  I recognize in this the mighty arm
  Of Leicester.   They will by degrees expand
  My prison; will accustom me, through small,
  To greater liberty, until at last
  I shall behold the face of him whose hand
  Will dash my fetters off, and that forever.
KEN.   Oh, my dear queen!   I cannot reconcile
  These contradictions.   'Twas but yesterday
  That they announced your death, and all at once,
  To-day, you have such liberty.   Their chains
  Are also loosed, as I have oft been told,
  Whom everlasting liberty awaits.
                    [*Hunting horns at a distance.*
MARY.   Hear'st thou the bugle, so blithely resounding?
  Hear'st thou its echoes through wood and through
      plain?
  Oh, might I now, on my nimble steed bounding,
  Join with the jocund, the frolicsome train.
                    [*Hunting horns again heard.*
  Again!   Oh, this sad and this pleasing remembrance!
  These are the sounds which, so sprightly and clear,
  Oft, when with music the hounds and the horn

So cheerfully welcomed the break of the morn,
On the heaths of the Highlands delighted my ear.

SCENE II.

Enter PAULET.

PAUL. Well, have I acted right at last, my lady?
  Do I for once, at least, deserve your thanks?
MARY. How! Do I owe this favor, sir, to you?
PAUL. Why not to me? I visited the court,
  And gave the queen your letter.
MARY.   Did you give it?
  In very truth did you deliver it?
  And is this freedom which I now enjoy
  The happy consequence?
PAULET (*significantly*).   Nor that alone;
  Prepare yourself to see a greater still.
MARY. A greater still! What do you mean by that?
PAUL. You heard the bugle-horns?
MARY (*starting back with foreboding apprehension*).
                     You frighten me.
PAUL. The queen is hunting in the neighborhood ——
MARY.   What!
PAUL. In a few moments she'll appear before you.
KENNEDY (*hastening towards* MARY, *and about to fall*).
  How fare you, dearest lady? You grow pale.
PAUL. How? Is't not well? Was it not then your
        prayer?
  'Tis granted now, before it was expected;
  You who had ever such a ready speech,
  Now summon all your powers of eloquence,
  The important time to use them now is come.
MARY. Oh, why was I not told of this before?
  Now I am not prepared for it — not now ——
  What, as the greatest favor, I besought,
  Seems to me now most fearful; Hannah, come,
  Lead me into the house, till I collect
  My spirits.
PAULET.   Stay; you must await her here.
  Yes! I believe you may be well alarmed
  To stand before your judge.

Scene III.

Enter the Earl of Shrewsbury.

MARY. 'Tis not for that
O God! Far other thoughts possess me now.
Oh, worthy Shrewsbury! You come as though
You were an angel sent to me from heaven.
I cannot, will not see her. Save me, save me
From the detested sight!

SHREWSBURY. Your majesty,
Command yourself, and summon all your courage,
'Tis the decisive moment of your fate.

MARY. For years I've waited, and prepared myself.
For this I've studied, weighed, and written down
Each word within the tablet of my memory
That was to touch and move her to compassion.
Forgotten suddenly, effaced is all,
And nothing lives within me at this moment
But the fierce, burning feeling of my wrongs.
My heart is turned to direst hate against her ;
All gentle thoughts, all sweet forgiving words,
Are gone, and round me stand with grisly mien,
The fiends of hell, and shake their snaky locks!

SHREW. Command your wild, rebellious blood ; — con-
strain
The bitterness which fills your heart. No good
Ensues when hatred is opposed to hate.
How much soe'er the inward struggle cost
You must submit to stern necessity,
The power is in her hand, be therefore humble.

MARY. To her? I never can.

SHREWSBURY. But pray, submit.
Speak with respect, with calmness! Strive to move
Her magnanimity ; insist not now
Upon your rights, not now — 'tis not the season.

MARY. Ah! woe is me! I've prayed for my destruction,
And, as a curse to me, my prayer is heard.
We never should have seen each other — never !
Oh, this can never, never come to good.
Rather in love could fire and water meet,
The timid lamb embrace the roaring tiger !

I have been hurt too grievously; she hath
Too grievously oppressed me; — no atonement
Can make us friends!
SHREWSBURY.   First see her, face to face:
Did I not see how she was moved at reading
Your letter? How her eyes were drowned in tears?
No — she is not unfeeling; only place
More confidence in her. It was for this
That I came on before her, to entreat you
To be collected — to admonish you ——
MARY (*seizing his hand*).
Oh, Talbot! you have ever been my friend,
Had I but stayed beneath your kindly care!
They have, indeed, misused me, Shrewsbury.
SHREW. Let all be now forgot, and only think
How to receive her with submissiveness.
MARY. Is Burleigh with her, too, my evil genius?
SHREW. No one attends her but the Earl of Leicester.
MARY. Lord Leicester?
SHREWSBURY.   Fear not him; it is not he
Who wishes your destruction; — 'twas his work
That here the queen hath granted you this meeting.
MARY. Ah! well I knew it.
SHREWSBURY.   What?
PAULET.   The queen approaches.
   [*They all draw aside;* MARY *alone remains, leaning
   on* KENNEDY.

SCENE IV.

The same, ELIZABETH, EARL OF LEICESTER, *and Retinue.*

ELIZABETH (*to* LEICESTER),
   What seat is that, my lord?
LEICESTER.   'Tis Fotheringay.
ELIZABETH (*to* SHREWSBURY).
   My lord, send back our retinue to London;
   The people crowd too eager in the roads,
   We'll seek a refuge in this quiet park.
   [TALBOT *sends the train away. She looks steadfastly
   at* MARY, *as she speaks further with* PAULET.
   My honest people love me overmuch.

These signs of joy are quite idolatrous.
Thus should a God be honored, not a mortal.
MARY (*who the whole time had leaned, almost fainting,
on* KENNEDY, *rises now, and her eyes meet the steady,
piercing look of* ELIZABETH; *she shudders and throws
herself again upon* KENNEDY'S *bosom*).
O God! from out these features speaks no heart.
ELIZ.   What lady's that?
                    [*A general, embarrassed silence.*
LEICESTER.   You are at Fotheringay,
        My liege!
ELIZABETH (*as if surprised, casting an angry look at*
LEICESTER.)
                Who hath done this, my Lord of Leicester?
LEIC.   'Tis past, my queen;—and now that heaven hath led
        Your footsteps hither, be magnanimous;
        And let sweet pity be triumphant now.
SHREW.   Oh, royal mistress! yield to our entreaties;
        Oh, cast your eyes on this unhappy one
        Who stands dissolved in anguish.
        [MARY *collects herself, and begins to advance towards*
        ELIZABETH, *stops shuddering at half way:*—*her
        action expresses the most violent internal struggle.*
ELIZABETH.   How, my lords!
        Which of you then announced to me a prisoner
        Bowed down by woe? I see a haughty one
        By no means humbled by calamity.
MARY.   Well, be it so:—to this will I submit.
        Farewell high thought, and pride of noble mind!
        I will forget my dignity, and all
        My sufferings; I will fall before her feet
        Who hath reduced me to this wretchedness.
                        [*She turns towards the* QUEEN.
        The voice of heaven decides for you, my sister.
        Your happy brows are now with triumph crowned,
        I bless the Power Divine which thus hath raised you.
                                [*She kneels.*
        But in your turn be merciful, my sister;
        Let me not lie before you thus disgraced;
        Stretch forth your hand, your royal hand, to raise
        Your sister from the depths of her distress.

ELIZABETH (*stepping back*).
You are where it becomes you, Lady Stuart;
And thankfully I prize my God's protection,
Who hath not suffered me to kneel a suppliant
Thus at your feet, as you now kneel at mine.
MARY (*with increasing energy of feeling*).
Think on all earthly things, vicissitudes.
Oh! there are gods who punish haughty pride:
Respect them, honor them, the dreadful ones
Who thus before thy feet have humbled me!
Before these strangers' eyes dishonor not
Yourself in me: profane not, nor disgrace
The royal blood of Tudor. In my veins
It flows as pure a stream as in your own.
Oh, for God's pity, stand not so estranged
And inaccessible, like some tall cliff,
Which the poor shipwrecked mariner in vain
Struggles to sieze, and labors to embrace.
My all, my life, my fortune now depends
Upon the influence of my words and tears;
That I may touch your heart, oh, set mine free.
If you regard me with those icy looks
My shuddering heart contracts itself, the stream
Of tears is dried, and frigid horror chains
The words of supplication in my bosom!
ELIZABETH (*cold and severe*).
What would you say to me, my Lady Stuart?
You wished to speak with me; and I, forgetting
The queen, and all the wrongs I have sustained,
Fulfil the pious duty of the sister,
And grant the boon you wished for of my presence.
Yet I, in yielding to the generous feelings
Of magnanimity, expose myself
To rightful censure, that I stoop so low.
For well you know you would have had me murdered.
MARY. Oh! how shall I begin? Oh, how shall I
So artfully arrange my cautious words
That they may touch, yet not offend your heart?
Strengthen my words, O Heaven! and take from
them
Whate'er might wound. Alas! I cannot speak

In my own cause without impeaching you,
And that most heavily, I wish not so;
You have not as you ought behaved to me:
I am a queen, like you yet you have held me
Confined in prison. As a suppliant
I came to you, yet you in me insulted
The pious use of hospitality;
Slighting in me the holy law of nations,
Immured me in a dungeon — tore from me
My friends and servants; to unseemly want
I was exposed, and hurried to the bar
Of a disgraceful, insolent tribunal.
No more of this; — in everlasting silence
Be buried all the cruelties I suffered!
See — I will throw the blame of all on fate,
'Twere not your fault, no more than it was mine.
An evil spirit rose from the abyss,
To kindle in our hearts the flame of hate,
By which our tender youth had been divided.
It grew with us, and bad, designing men
Fanned with their ready breath the fatal fire :
Frantics, enthusiasts, with sword and dagger
Armed the uncalled-for hand! This is the curse
Of kings, that they, divided, tear the world
In pieces with their hatred, and let loose
The raging furies of all hellish strife!
No foreign tongue is now between us, sister,
     [*Approaching her confidently, and with a flattering
          tone.*
Now stand we face to face; now, sister, speak :
Name but my crime, I'll fully satisfy you, —
Alas! had you vouchsafed to hear me then,
When I so earnest sought to meet your eye,
It never would have come to this, nor would,
Here in this mournful place, have happened now
This so distressful, this so mournful meeting.
ELIZ.   My better stars preserved me.   I was warned,
And laid not to my breast the poisonous adder!
Accuse not fate! your own deceitful heart
It was, the wild ambition of your house:
As yet no enmities had passed between us,

When your imperious uncle, the proud priest,
Whose shameless hand grasps at all crowns, attacked
  me
With unprovoked hostility, and taught
You, but too docile, to assume my arms,
To vest yourself with my imperial title,
And meet me in the lists in mortal strife:
What arms employed he not to storm my throne?
The curses of the priests, the people's sword,
The dreadful weapons of religious frenzy; —
Even here in my own kingdom's peaceful haunts
He fanned the flames of civil insurrection; —
But God is with me, and the haughty priest
Has not maintained the field. The blow was aimed
Full at my head, but yours it is which falls!

MARY. I'm in the hand of heaven. You never will
Exert so cruelly the power it gives you.

ELIZ. Who shall prevent me? Say, did not your
  uncle
Set all the kings of Europe the example,
How to conclude a peace with those they hate.
Be mine the school of Saint Bartholomew;
What's kindred then to me, or nation's laws?
The church can break the bands of every duty;
It consecrates the regicide, the traitor;
I only practise what your priests have taught!
Say then, what surety can be offered me,
Should I magnanimously loose your bonds?
Say, with what lock can I secure your faith,
Which by Saint Peter's keys cannot be opened?
Force is my only surety; no alliance
Can be concluded with a race of vipers.

MARY. Oh! this is but your wretched, dark suspicion!
For you have constantly regarded me
But as a stranger, and an enemy.
Had you declared me heir to your dominions,
As is my right, then gratitude and love
In me had fixed, for you, a faithful friend
And kinswoman.

ELIZABETH. Your friendship is abroad,
Your house is papacy, the monk your brother.

Name you my successor !   The treacherous snare !
That in my life you might seduce my people ;
And, like a sly Armida, in your net
Entangle all our noble English youth ;
That all might turn to the new rising sun,
And I ——

MARY.   O sister, rule your realm in peace ;
I give up every claim to these domains —
Alas ! the pinions of my soul are lamed ;
Greatness entices me no more : your point
Is gained ; I am but Mary's shadow now —
My noble spirit is at last broke down
By long captivity : — you've done your worst
On me ; you have destroyed me in my bloom !
Now, end your work, my sister ; — speak at length
The word, which to pronounce has brought you
      hither ;
For I will ne'er believe that you are come,
To mock unfeelingly your hapless victim.
Pronounce this word ; — say, " Mary, you are free :
You have already felt my power, — learn now
To honor too my generosity."
Say this, and I will take my life, will take
My freedom, as a present from your hands.
One word makes all undone ; — I wait for it ; —
Oh, let it not be needlessly delayed.
Woe to you if you end not with this word !
For should you not, like some divinity,
Dispensing noble blessings, quit me now,
Then, sister, not for all this island's wealth,
For all the realms encircled by the deep,
Would I exchange my present lot for yours.

ELIZ.   And you confess at last that you are conquered :
Are all your schemes run out ?   No more assassins
Now on the road ?   Will no adventurer
Attempt again for you the sad achievement ?
Yes, madam, it is over : — you'll seduce
No mortal more.   The world has other cares ; —
None is ambitious of the dangerous honor
Of being your fourth husband — you destroy
Your wooers like your husbands.

MARY (*starting angrily*). Sister, sister ! —
Grant me forbearance, all ye powers of heaven !
ELIZABETH (*regards her long with a look of proud contempt*).
Those then, my Lord of Leicester, are the charms
Which no man with impunity can view,
Near which no woman dare to stand ?
In sooth, this honor has been cheaply gained ;
She who to all is common, may with ease
Become the common object of applause.
MARY. This is too much !
ELIZABETH (*laughing insultingly*).
You show us now, indeed,
Your real face ; till now 'twas but the mask.
MARY (*burning with rage, yet dignified and noble*).
My sins were human, and the faults of youth :
Superior force misled me. I have never
Denied or sought to hide it : I despised
All false appearance, as became a queen.
The worst of me is known, and I can say,
That I am better than the fame I bear.
Woe to you ! when, in time to come, the world
Shall draw the robe of honor from your deeds,
With which thy arch-hypocrisy has veiled
The raging flames of lawless, secret lust.
Virtue was not your portion from your mother ;
Well know we what it was which brought the head
Of Anna Boleyn to the fatal block.
SHREWSBURY (*stepping between both* QUEENS).
Oh ! Heaven ! Alas, and must it come to this !
Is this the moderation, the submission,
My lady ? ——
MARY. Moderation ! I've supported
What human nature can support : farewell,
Lamb-hearted resignation, passive patience,
Fly to thy native heaven ; burst at length
Thy bonds, come forward from thy dreary cave,
In all thy fury, long suppressed rancor !
And thou, who to the angered basilisk
Impart'st the murderous glance, oh, arm my tongue
With poisoned darts !

SHREWSBURY.   She is beside herself!
    Exasperated, mad! My liege, forgive her.
    [ELIZABETH, *speechless with anger, casts enraged looks
        at* MARY.
LEICESTER (*in the most violent agitation; he seeks to lead*
    ELIZABETH *away*).
    Attend not to her rage! Away, away,
    From this disastrous place!
MARY (*raising her voice*).   A bastard soils,
    Profanes the English throne! The generous Britons
    Are cheated by a juggler, [whose whole figure
    Is false and painted, heart as well as face!]
    If right prevailed, you now would in the dust
    Before me lie, for I'm your rightful monarch!
    [ELIZABETH *hastily quits the stage; the lords follow
        her in the greatest consternation.*

Scene V.

Mary, Kennedy.

KEN.   What have you done? She has gone hence in
        wrath
    All hope is over now!
MARY (*still quite beside herself*).
                        Gone hence in wrath!
    She carries death within her heart! I know it.
                    [*Falling on* KENNEDY'S *bosom.*
    Now I am happy, Hannah! and at last,
    After whole years of sorrow and abasement,
    One moment of victorious revenge!
    A weight falls off my heart, a weight of mountains;
    I plunged the steel in my oppressor's breast!
KEN.   Unhappy lady! Frenzy overcomes you.
    Yes, you have wounded your inveterate foe;
    'Tis she who wields the lightning, she is queen,
    You have insulted her before her minion.
MARY.   I have abased her before Leicester's eyes;
    He saw it, he was witness of my triumph.
    How did I hurl her from her haughty height,
    He saw it, and his presence strengthened me.

Scene VI.

Enter Mortimer.

Ken. Oh, sir! What an occurrence!

Mortimer. I heard all —

[*Gives the nurse a sign to repair to her post, and draws nearer; his whole appearance expresses the utmost violence of passion.*

Thine is the palm; — thou trod'st her to the dust! —
Thou wast the queen, she was the malefactor; —
I am transported with thy noble courage; —
Yes! I adore thee; like a Deity,
My sense is dazzled by thy heavenly beams.

Mary (*with vivacity and expectation*).
You spoke with Leicester, gave my letter to him.
My present, too? — oh, speak, sir.

Mortimer (*beholding her with glowing looks*).
How thy noble,
Thy royal indignation shone, and cast
A glory round thy beauty; yes, by heavens,
Thou art the fairest woman upon earth!

Mary. Sir, satisfy, I beg you, my impatience;
What says his lordship? Say, sir, may I hope?

Mort. Who? — he? — he is a wretch, a very coward,
Hope naught from him; despise him, and forget
him!

Mary. What say you?

Mortimer. He deliver, and possess you!
Why let him dare it: — he! — he must with me
In mortal contest first deserve the prize!

Mary. You gave him not my letter? Then, indeed
My hopes are lost!

Mortimer. The coward loves his life.
Whoe'er would rescue you, and call you his,
Must boldly dare affront e'en death itself!

Mary. Will he do nothing for me?

Mortimer. Speak not of him.
What can he do? What need have we of him?
I will release you; I alone.

Mary. Alas!
What power have you?

MORTIMER.   Deceive yourself no more;
  Think not your case is now as formerly;
  The moment that the queen thus quitted you,
  And that your interview had ta'en this turn,
  All hope was lost, each way of mercy shut.
  Now deeds must speak, now boldness must decide
  To compass all must all be hazarded;
  You must be free before the morning break.
MARY.   What say you, sir — to-night? — impossible!
MORT.   Hear what has been resolved: — I led my friends
  Into a private chapel, where a priest
  Heard our confession, and, for every sin
  We had committed, gave us absolution;
  He gave us absolution too, beforehand,
  For every crime we might commit in future;
  He gave us too the final sacrament,
  And we are ready for the final journey.
MARY.   Oh, what an awful, dreadful preparation!
MORT.   We scale, this very night, the castle's walls;
  The keys are in my power; the guards we murder!
  Then from thy chamber bear thee forcibly.
  Each living soul must die beneath our hands,
  That none remain who might disclose the deed.
MARY.   And Drury, Paulet, my two keepers, they
  Would sooner spill their dearest drop of blood.
MORT.   They fall the very first beneath my steel.
MARY.   What, sir! Your uncle? How! Your second
            father!
MORT.   Must perish by my hand — I murder him!
MARY.   Oh, bloody outrage!
MORTIMER.   We have been absolved
  Beforehand; I may perpetrate the worst;
  I can, I will do so!
MARY.   Oh, dreadful, dreadful!
MORT.   And should I be obliged to kill the queen,
  I've sworn upon the host, it must be done!
MARY.   No, Mortimer; ere so much blood for me ——
MORT.   What is the life of all compared to thee,
  And to my love? The bond which holds the world
  Together may be loosed, a second deluge
  Come rolling on, and swallow all creation!

Henceforth I value nothing; ere I quit
My hold on thee, may earth and time be ended!

MARY *(retiring)*.
Heavens! Sir, what language, and what looks! They scare,
They frighten me!

MORTIMER *(with unsteady looks, expressive of quiet madness)*. Life's but a moment — death
Is but a moment too. Why! let them drag me
To Tyburn, let them tear me limb from limb,
With red-hot pincers —
[*Violently approaching her with extended arms.*
If I clasp but thee
Within my arms, thou fervently beloved!

MARY. Madman, avaunt!

MORTIMER. To rest upon this bosom,
To press upon this passion-breathing mouth ——

MARY. Leave me, for God's sake, sir; let me go in ——

MORT. He is a madman who neglects to clasp
His bliss in folds that never may be loosed,
When Heaven has kindly given it to his arms.
I will deliver you, and though it cost
A thousand lives, I do it; but I swear,
As God's in Heaven I will possess you too!

MARY. Oh! will no God, no angel shelter me?
Dread destiny! thou throwest me, in thy wrath,
From one tremendous terror to the other!
Was I then born to waken naught but frenzy?
Do hate and love conspire alike to fright me!

MORT. Yes, glowing as their hatred is my love;
They would behead thee, they would wound this neck,
So dazzling white, with the disgraceful axe!
Oh! offer to the living god of joy
What thou must sacrifice to bloody hate!
Inspire thy happy lover with those charms
Which are no more thine own. Those golden locks
Are forfeit to the dismal powers of death,
Oh! use them to entwine thy slave forever!

MARY. Alas! alas! what language must I hear!
My woe, my sufferings should be sacred to you,

Although my royal brows are so no more.

MORT.   The crown is fallen from thy brows, thou hast
No more of earthly majesty.   Make trial,
Raise thy imperial voice, see if a friend,
If a deliverer will rise to save you.
Thy moving form alone remains, the high,
The godlike influence of thy heavenly beauty;
This bids me venture all, this arms my hand
With might, and drives me tow'rd the headsman's axe.

MARY.   Oh! who will save me from his raging madness?

MORT.   Service that's bold demands a bold reward.
Why shed their blood the daring?   Is not life
Life's highest good?   And he a madman who
Casts life away?   First will I take my rest,
Upon the breast that glows with love's own fire!
                    [*He presses her violently to his bosom,*

MARY.   Oh, must I call for help against the man
Who would deliver me!

MORTIMER.   Thou'rt not unfeeling,
The world ne'er censured thee for frigid rigor;
The fervent prayer of love can touch thy heart.
Thou mad'st the minstrel Rizzio blest, and gavest
Thyself a willing prey to Bothwell's arms.

MARY.   Presumptuous man!

MORTIMER.   He was indeed thy tyrant,
Thou trembled'st at his rudeness, whilst thou loved'st
     him;
Well, then — if only terror can obtain thee —
By the infernal gods!

MARY.   Away — you're mad!

MORT.   I'll teach thee then before me, too, to tremble.

KENNEDY (*entering suddenly*).
They're coming — they approach — the park is filled
With men in arms.

MORTIMER (*starting and catching at his sword*).
                    I will defend you — I ——

MARY.   O Hannah! save me, save me from his hands.
Where shall I find, poor sufferer, an asylum?
Oh! to what saint shall I address my prayers?
Here force assails me, and within is murder!
          [*She flies towards the house,* KENNEDY *follows her.*

Scene VII.

Mortimer, Paulet, *and* Drury *rush in in the greatest
consternation.   Attendants hasten over the stage.*

Paul.   Shut all the portals — draw the bridges up.
Mort.   What is the matter, uncle?
Paulet.   Where is the murderess?
Down with her, down into the darkest dungeon!
Mort.   What is the matter?   What has passed?
Paulet.   The queen!
Accursed hand!   Infernal machination!
Mort.   The queen!   What queen?
Paul.   What queen!
The Queen of England;
She has been murdered on the road to London.
                        [*Hastens into the house.*

Scene VIII.

Mortimer, *soon after* O'Kelly.

Mortimer (*after a pause*).
Am I then mad?   Came not one running by
But now, and cried aloud, the queen is murdered!
No, no!   I did but dream.   A feverish fancy
Paints that upon my mind as true and real,
Which but existed in my frantic thoughts
Who's there?   It is O'Kelly.   So dismayed!
O'Kelly (*rushing in*).
Flee, Mortimer, oh!   flee — for all is lost!
Mort.   What then is lost?
O'Kelly.   Stand not on question.   Think
On speedy flight.
Mortimer.   What has occurred?
O'Kelly.   Sauvage,
That madman, struck the blow.
Mortimer.   It is then true!
O'Kelly.   True, true — oh!   save yourself.
Mortimer (*exultingly*).   The queen is murdered —
And Mary shall ascend the English throne!
O'Kel.   Is murdered!   Who said that?
Mortimer.   Yourself.

O'KELLY.   She lives,
    And I, and you, and all of us are lost.
MORT.   She lives!
O'KELLY.   The blow was badly aimed, her cloak
    Received it.   Shrewsbury disarmed the murderer.
MORT.   She lives!
O'KELLY.   She lives to whelm us all in ruin;
    Come, they surround the park already; come.
MORT.   Who did this frantic deed?
O'KELLY.   It was the monk
    From Toulon, whom you saw immersed in thought,
    As in the chapel the pope's bull was read,
    Which poured anathemas upon the queen.
    He wished to take the nearest, shortest way,
    To free, with one bold stroke, the church of God,
    And gain the crown of martyrdom : he trusted
    His purpose only to the priest, and struck
    The fatal blow upon the road to London.
MORTIMER (*after a long silence*).
    Alas! a fierce, destructive fate pursues thee,
    Unhappy one!   Yes — now thy death is fixed ;
    Thy very angel has prepared thy fall !
O'KEL.   Say, whither will you take your flight?   I go
    To hide me in the forests of the north.
MORT.   Fly thither, and may God attend your flight ;
    I will remain, and still attempt to save
    My love ; if not, my bed shall be upon her grave.
                [*Exeunt at different sides.*

ACT IV.

SCENE I. — *Antechamber.*

COUNT AUBESPINE, *the* EARLS *of* KENT *and* LEICESTER.

AUB.   How fares her majesty?   My lords, you see me
    Still stunned, and quite beside myself for terror !
    How happened it ?   How was it possible
    That in the midst of this most loyal people ——
LEIC.   The deed was not attempted by the people.
    The assassin was a subject of your king,
    A Frenchman.

AUBESPINE.   Sure a lunatic.
LEIC.   A papist,
   Count Aubespine!

SCENE II.

Enter BURLEIGH, *in conversation with* DAVISON.

BURLEIGH.   Sir; let the death-warrant
   Be instantly made out, and pass the seal;
   Then let it be presented to the queen;
   Her majesty must sign it. Hasten, sir,
   We have no time to lose.
DAVISON.   It shall be done.   [*Exit.*
AUB. My lord high-treasurer, my faithful heart
   Shares in the just rejoicings of the realm.
   Praised be almighty Heaven, who hath averted
   Assassination from our much-loved queen!
BUR. Praised be His name, who thus hath turned to
     scorn
   The malice of our foes!
AUBESPINE.   May heaven confound
   The perpetrator of this cursed deed!
BUR. Its perpetrator and its base contriver!
AUB. Please you, my lord, to bring me to the queen,
   That I may lay the warm congratulations
   Of my imperial master at her feet.
BUR. There is no need of this.
AUBESPINE (*officiously*).   My Lord of Burleigh,
   I know my duty.
BURLEIGH.   Sir, your duty is
   To quit, and that without delay, this kingdom.
AUBESPINE (*stepping back with surprise*).
   What! How is this?
BURLEIGH.   The sacred character
   Of an ambassador to-day protects you,
   But not to-morrow.
AUBESPINE.   What's my crime?
BURLEIGH.   Should I
   Once name it, there were then no pardon for it.
AUB. I hope, my lord, my charge's privilege ——
BUR. Screens not a traitor.

LEICESTER *and* KENT.   Traitor! How?
AUBESPINE.   My lord
    Consider well ——
BURLEIGH.   Your passport was discovered
    In the assassin's pocket.
KENT.   Righteous heaven!
AUB.   Sir, many passports are subscribed by me;
    I cannot know the secret thoughts of men.
BUR.   He in your house confessed, and was absolved.
AUB.   My house is open ——
BURLEIGH.   To our enemies.
AUB.   I claim a strict inquiry.
BURLEIGH.   Tremble at it.
AUB.   My monarch in my person is insulted,
    He will annul the marriage contract.
BURLEIGH.   That
    My royal mistress has annulled already;
    England will not unite herself with France.
    My Lord of Kent, I give to you the charge
    To see Count Aubespine embarked in safety.
    The furious populace has stormed his palace,
    Where a whole arsenal of arms was found;
    Should he be found, they'll tear him limb from limb,
    Conceal him till the fury is abated —
    Your answer for his life.
AUBESPINE.   I go — I leave
    This kingdom where they sport with public treaties
    And trample on the laws of nations. Yet
    My monarch, be assured, will vent his rage
    In direst vengeance!
BURLEIGH.   Let him seek it here.
                        [*Exeunt* KENT *and* AUBESPINE

SCENE III.

LEICESTER, BURLEIGH.

LEIC.   And thus you loose yourself the knot of union
    Which you officiously, uncalled for, bound!
    You have deserved but little of your country,
    My lord; this trouble was superfluous.

BUR. My aim was good, though fate declared against it;
 Happy is he who has so fair a conscience!
LEIC. Well know we the mysterious mien of Burleigh
 When he is on the hunt for deeds of treason.
 Now you are in your element, my lord;
 A monstrous outrage has been just committed,
 And darkness veils as yet its perpetrators:
 Now will a court of inquisition rise;
 Each word, each look be weighed; men's very
  thoughts
 Be summoned to the bar. You are, my lord,
 The mighty man, the Atlas of the state,
 All England's weight lies upon your shoulders.
BUR. In you, my lord, I recognize my master;
 For such a victory as your eloquence
 Has gained I cannot boast.
LEICESTER.   What means your lordship?
BUR. You were the man who knew, behind my back,
 To lure the queen to Fotheringay Castle.
LEIC. Behind your back! When did I fear to act
 Before your face?
BURLEIGH.   You led her majesty?
 Oh, no — you led her not — it was the queen
 Who was so gracious as to lead you thither.
LEIC. What mean you, my lord, by that?
BURLEIGH.   The noble part
 You forced the queen to play! The glorious
  triumph
 Which you prepared for her! Too gracious princess!
 So shamelessly, so wantonly to mock
 Thy unsuspecting goodness, to betray thee
 So pitiless to thy exulting foe!
 This, then, is the magnanimity, the grace
 Which suddenly possessed you in the council!
 The Stuart is for this so despicable,
 So weak an enemy, that it would scarce
 Be worth the pains to stain us with her blood.
 A specious plan! and sharply pointed too;
 'Tis only pity this sharp point is broken.
LEIC. Unworthy wretch! this instant follow me,
 And answer at the throne this insolence.

BUR.   You'll find me there, my lord ; and look you well
    That there your eloquence desert you not.   [*Exit.*

SCENE IV.

LEICESTER *alone ; then* MORTIMER.

LEIC.   I am detected !   All my plot's disclosed !
    How has my evil genius tracked my steps !
    Alas ! if he has proofs, if she should learn
    That I have held a secret correspondence
    With her worst enemy ; how criminal
    Shall I appear to her !   How false will then
    My counsel seem, and all the fatal pains
    I took to lure the queen to Fotheringay !
    I've shamefully betrayed, I have exposed her
    To her detested enemy's revilings !
    Oh ! never, never can she pardon that.
    All will appear as if premeditated.
    The bitter turn of this sad interview,
    The triumph and the tauntings of her rival ;
    Yes, e'en the murderous hand which had prepared
    A bloody, monstrous, unexpected fate ;
    All, all will be ascribed to my suggestions !
    I see no rescue ! nowhere — ha !   Who comes ?
    [MORTIMER *enters in the most violent uneasiness, and
        looks with apprehension round him.*
MORT.   Lord Leicester !   Is it you !   Are we alone ?
LEIC.   Ill-fated wretch, away !   What seek you here ?
MORT.   They are upon our track — upon yours, too ;
    Be vigilant !
LEICESTER.   Away, away !
MORTIMER.   They know
    That private conferences have been held
    At Aubespine's ———
LEICESTER.   What's that to me ?
MORTIMER.   They know, too,
    That the assassin ———
LEICESTER.   That is your affair —
    Audacious wretch ! to dare to mix my name
    In your detested outrage : go ; defend
    Your bloody deeds yourself !

MORTIMER.   But only hear me.
LEICESTER (*violently enraged*).
Down, down to hell! Why cling you at my heels
Like an infernal spirit! I disclaim you;
I know you not; I make no common cause
With murderers!
MORTIMER.   You will not hear me, then!
I came to warn you; you too are detected.
LEIC. How! What?
MORTIMER.   Lord Burleigh went to Fotheringay
Just as the luckless deed had been attempted;
Searched with strict scrutiny the queen's apartments,
And found there ——
LEICESTER.   What?
MORTIMER.   A letter which the queen
Had just addressed to you ——
LEICESTER.   Unhappy woman!
MORT. In which she calls on you to keep your word,
Renews the promise of her hand, and mentions
The picture which she sent you.
LEICESTER.   Death and hell!
MORT. Lord Burleigh has the letter.
LEICESTER.   I am lost!
    [*During the following speech of* MORTIMER, LEICESTER
    goes up and down as in despair.
MORT. Improve the moment; be beforehand with him,
And save yourself — save her! An oath can clear
Your fame; contrive excuses to avert
The worst. I am disarmed, can do no more;
My comrades are dispersed — to pieces fallen
Our whole confederacy. For Scotland I
To rally such new friends as there I may.
'Tis now your turn, my lord; try what your weight,
What bold assurance can effect.
LEICESTER (*stops suddenly as if resolved*). I will.
                    [*Goes to the door, opens it, and calls.*
Who waits without? Guards! seize this wretched
    traitor!
                    [*To the officer, who comes in with soldiers.*
And guard him closely! A most dreadful plot
Is brought to light — I'll to her majesty.

MORTIMER (*stands for a time petrified with wonder; col-
lects himself soon, and follows* LEICESTER *with his looks
expressive of the most sovereign contempt*).
 Infamous wretch! But I deserve it all.
 Who told me then to trust this practised villain?
 Now o'er my head he strides, and on my fall
 He builds the bridge of safety! be it so;
 Go, save thyself — my lips are sealed forever;
 I will not join even thee in my destruction;
 I would not own thee, no, not even in death;
 Life is the faithless villain's only good!
[*To the officer of the guard, who steps forward to seize
 him.*
 What wilt thou, slave of tyranny, with me?
 I laugh to scorn thy threatenings; I am free.
          [*Drawing a dagger.*
OFFIC. He's armed; rush in and wrest his weapon from
 him. [*They rush upon him, he defends himself.*
MORTIMER (*raising his voice*).
 And in this latest moment shall my heart
 Expand itself in freedom, and my tongue
 Shall break this long constraint. Curse and destruc-
  tion
 Light on you all who have betrayed your faith,
 Your God, and your true sovereign! Who, alike
 To earthly Mary false as to the heavenly,
 Have sold your duties to this bastard queen!
OFFIC. Hear you these blasphemies? Rush forward —
 seize him.
MORT. Beloved queen! I could not set thee free;
 Yet take a lesson from me how to die.
 Mary, thou holy one, O! pray for me!
 And take me to thy heavenly home on high.
[*Stabs himself, and falls into the arms of the guard.*

SCENE V.

The apartment of the Queen.

ELIZABETH, *with a letter in her hand,* BURLEIGH.

ELIZ. To lure me thither! trifle with me thus!
 The traitor! Thus to lead me, as in triumph,

Into the presence of his paramour!
Oh, Burleigh! ne'er was woman so deceived.
BUR.   I cannot yet conceive what potent means,
What magic he exerted, to surprise
My queen's accustomed prudence.
ELIZABETH.   Oh, I die
For shame! How must he laugh to scorn my weak-
I thought to humble her, and was myself   [ness!
The object of her bitter scorn.
BURLEIGH.   By this
You see how faithfully I counselled you.
ELIZ.   Oh, I am sorely punished, that I turned
My ear from your wise counsels; yet I thought
I might confide in him. Who could suspect
Beneath the vows of faithfullest devotion
A deadly snare? In whom can I confide
When he deceives me? He, whom I have made
The greatest of the great, and ever set
The nearest to my heart, and in this court
Allowed to play the master and the king.
BUR.   Yet in that very moment he betrayed you,
Betrayed you to this wily Queen of Scots.
ELIZ.   Oh, she shall pay me for it with her life!
Is the death-warrant ready?
BURLEIGH.   'Tis prepared
As you commanded.
ELIZABETH.   She shall surely die —
He shall behold her fall, and fall himself!
I've driven him from my heart. No longer love,
Revenge alone is there : and high as once
He stood, so low and shameful be his fall!
A monument of my severity,
As once the proud example of my weakness.
Conduct him to the Tower; let a commission
Of peers be named to try him. He shall feel
In its full weight the rigor of the law.
BUR.   But he will seek thy presence; he will clear——
ELIZ.   How can he clear himself? Does not the letter
Convict him. Oh, his crimes are manifest!
BUR.   But thou art mild and gracious! His appearance,
His powerful presence ——

ELIZABETH.   I will never see him;
  No never, never more. Are orders given
  Not to admit him should he come?
BURLEIGH.   'Tis done.
PAGE (*entering*).
  The Earl of Leicester!
ELIZABETH.   The presumptuous man!
  I will not see him. Tell him that I will not.
PAGE. I am afraid to bring my lord this message,
  Nor would he credit it.
ELIZABETH.   And I have raised him
  So high that my own servants tremble more
  At him than me!
BURLEIGH (*to the* PAGE). The queen forbids his presence.
                             [*The* PAGE *retires slowly.*
ELIZABETH (*after a pause*).
  Yet, if it still were possible? If he
  Could clear himself? Might it not be a snare
  Laid by the cunning one, to sever me
  From my best friends — the ever-treacherous harlot!
  She might have writ the letter, but to raise
  Poisonous suspicion in my heart, to ruin
  The man she hates.
BURLEIGH.   Yet, gracious queen, consider.

SCENE VI.

LEICESTER (*bursts open the door with violence, and enters
          with an imperious air*).

LEIC. Fain would I see the shameless man who dares
  Forbid me the apartments of my queen!
ELIZABETH (*avoiding his sight*).
  Audacious slave!
LEICESTER.   To turn me from the door!
  If for a Burleigh she be visible,
  She must be so to me!
BURLEIGH.   My lord, you are
  Too bold, without permission to intrude.
LEIC. My lord, you are too arrogant, to take
  The lead in these apartments. What! Permission!

I know of none who stands so high at court
As to permit my doings, or refuse them.
        [*Humbly approaching* ELIZABETH.
'Tis from my sovereign's lips alone that I ——
ELIZABETH (*without looking at him*).
Out of my sight, deceitful, worthless traitor!
LEIC. 'Tis not my gracious queen I hear, but Burleigh,
My enemy, in these ungentle words.
To my imperial mistress I appeal;
Thou hast lent him thine ear; I ask the like.
ELIZ. Speak, shameless wretch! Increase your crime —
    deny it.
LEIC. Dismiss this troublesome intruder first.
Withdraw, my lord; it is not of your office
To play the third man here: between the queen
And me there is no need of witnesses.
Retire ——
ELIZABETH (*to* BURLEIGH).
    Remain, my lord; 'tis my command.
LEIC. What has a third to do 'twixt thee and me?
I have to clear myself before my queen,
My worshipped queen; I will maintain the rights
Which thou hast given me; these rights are sacred,
And I insist upon it, that my lord
Retire.
ELIZABETH. This haughty tone befits you well.
LEIC. It well befits me; am not I the man,
The happy man, to whom thy gracious favor
Has given the highest station? this exalts me
Above this Burleigh, and above them all.
Thy heart imparted me this rank, and what
Thy favor gave, by heavens I will maintain
At my life's hazard. Let him go, it needs
Two moments only to exculpate me.
ELIZ. Think not, with cunning words, to hide the truth.
LEIC. That fear from him, so voluble of speech:
But what I say is to the heart addressed;
And I will justify what I have dared
To do, confiding in thy generous favor,
Before thy heart alone. I recognize
No other jurisdiction.

ELIZABETH.   Base deceiver!
    'Tis this, e'en this, which above all condemns you.
    My lord, produce the letter.   [*To* BURLEIGH.
BURLEIGH.   Here it is.
LEICESTER (*running over the letter without losing his
                presence of mind*).
    'Tis Mary Stuart's hand ——
ELIZABETH.   Read and be dumb!
LEICESTER (*having read it quietly*).
    Appearance is against me, yet I hope
    I shall not by appearances be judged.
ELIZ.   Can you deny your secret correspondence
    With Mary?— that she sent and you received
    Her picture, that you gave her hopes of rescue?
LEIC.   It were an easy matter, if I felt
    That I were guilty of a crime, to challenge
    The testimony of my enemy:
    Yet bold is my good conscience.   I confess
    That she hath said the truth.
ELIZABETH.   Well then, thou wretch!
BUR.   His own words sentence him ——
ELIZABETH.   Out of my sight!
    Away!   Conduct the traitor to the Tower!
LEIC.   I am no traitor; it was wrong, I own,
    To make a secret of this step to thee;
    Yet pure was my intention, it was done
    To search into her plots and to confound them.
ELIZ.   Vain subterfuge!
BUR.   And do you think, my lord ——
LEIC.   I've played a dangerous game, I know it well,
    And none but Leicester dare be bold enough
    To risk it at this court.   The world must know
    How I detest this Stuart, and the rank
    Which here I hold; my monarch's confidence,
    With which she honors me, must sure suffice
    To overturn all doubt of my intentions.
    Well may the man thy favor above all
    Distinguishes pursue a daring course
    To do his duty!
BURLEIGH.   If the course was good,
    Wherefore conceal it?

LEICESTER. You are used, my lord,
  To prate before you act; the very chime
  Of your own deeds. This is your manner, lord;
  But mine is first to act, and then to speak.
BUR. Yes, now you speak because you must.
LEICESTER (*measuring him proudly and disdainfully
  with his eyes*).
                              And you
  Boast of a wonderful, a mighty action,
  That you have saved the queen, have snatched
      away
  The mask from treachery; all is known to you;
  You think, forsooth, that nothing can escape
  Your penetrating eyes. Poor, idle boaster!
  In spite of all your cunning, Mary Stuart
  Was free to-day, had I not hindered it.
BUR. How? You?
LEICESTER.   Yes, I, my lord; the queen confided
  In Mortimer; she opened to the youth
  Her inmost soul! Yes, she went further still;
  She gave him, too, a secret, bloody charge,
  Which Paulet had before refused with horror.
  Say, is it so, or not?
  [*The* QUEEN *and* BURLEIGH *look at one another with
      astonishment.*
BURLEIGH.   Whence know ye this?
LEIC. Nay, is it not a fact? Now answer me.
  And where, my lord, where were your thousand
      eyes,
  Not to discover Mortimer was false?
  That he, the Guise's tool, and Mary's creature,
  A raging papist, daring fanatic,
  Was come to free the Stuart, and to murder
  The Queen of England!
ELIZABETH (*with the utmost astonishment*).
                              How! This Mortimer!
LEIC. 'Twas he through whom our correspondence passed.
  This plot it was which introduced me to him.
  This very day she was to have been torn
  From her confinement; he, this very moment,
  Disclosed his plan to me: I took him prisoner,

And gave him to the guard, when in despair
To see his work o'erturned, himself unmasked,
He slew himself!

ELIZABETH.   Oh, I indeed have been
Deceived beyond example, Mortimer!

BUR. This happened then but now? Since last we
  parted?

LEIC. For my own sake, I must lament the deed;
That he was thus cut off. His testimony,
Were he alive, had fully cleared my fame,
And freed me from suspicion; 'twas for this
That I surrendered him to open justice.
I thought to choose the most impartial course
To verify and fix my innocence
Before the world.

BURLEIGH.   He killed himself, you say!
Is't so? Or did you kill him?

LEICESTER.   Vile suspicion!
Hear but the guard who seized him.

      [He goes to the door, and calls.
      Ho! who waits?
      [Enter the officer of the guard.
Sir, tell the queen how Mortimer expired.

OFFIC. I was on duty in the palace porch,
When suddenly my lord threw wide the door,
And ordered me to take the knight in charge,
Denouncing him a traitor: upon this
He grew enraged, and with most bitter curses
Against our sovereign and our holy faith,
He drew a dagger, and before the guards
Could hinder his intention, plunged the steel
Into his heart, and fell a lifeless corpse.

LEIC. 'Tis well; you may withdraw. Her majesty
Has heard enough.

      [The officer withdraws.
ELIZABETH.   Oh, what a deep abyss
Of monstrous deeds?

LEICESTER.   Who was it, then, my queen,
Who saved you? Was it Burleigh? Did he
  know
The dangers which surrounded you? Did he

Avert them from your head? Your faithful Leicester
Was your good angel.
BURLEIGH.   This same Mortimer
Died most conveniently for you, my lord.
ELIZ. What I should say I know not. I believe you,
And I believe you not. I think you guilty,
And yet I think you not. A curse on her
Who caused me all this anguish.
LEICESTER. She must die;
I now myself consent unto her death.
I formerly advised you to suspend
The sentence, till some arm should rise anew
On her behalf; the case has happened now,
And I demand her instant execution.
BUR. You give this counsel? You?
LEICESTER.   Howe'er it wound
My feelings to be forced to this extreme,
Yet now I see most clearly, now I feel
That the queen's welfare asks this bloody victim.
'Tis my proposal, therefore, that the writ
Be drawn at once to fix the execution.
BURLEIGH (to the QUEEN).
Since, then, his lordship shows such earnest zeal,
Such loyalty, 'twere well were he appointed
To see the execution of the sentence.
LEIC. Who? I?
BURLEIGH. Yes, you; you surely ne'er could find
A better means to shake off the suspicion
Which rests upon you still, than to command
Her, whom 'tis said you love, to be beheaded.
ELIZABETH (looking steadfastly at LEICESTER).
My lord advises well. So be it, then.
LEIC. It were but fit that my exalted rank
Should free me from so mournful a commission,
Which would indeed, in every sense, become
A Burleigh better than the Earl of Leicester.
The man who stands so near the royal person
Should have no knowledge of such fatal scenes:
But yet to prove my zeal, to satisfy
My queen, I waive my charge's privilege,
And take upon myself this hateful duty.

Eliz. Lord Burleigh shall partake this duty with you.
                                    [*To* Burleigh.
    So be the warrant instantly prepared.
        [Burleigh *withdraws; a tumult heard without.*

Scene VII.

The Queen, *the* Earl of Kent.

Eliz. How now, my Lord of Kent? What uproar's this
    I hear without?
Kent.   My queen, it is thy people,
    Who, round the palace ranged, impatiently
    Demand to see their sovereign.
Elizabeth.   What's their wish?
Kent. A panic terror has already spread
    Through London, that thy life has been attempted;
    That murderers commissioned from the pope
    Beset thee; that the Catholics have sworn
    To rescue from her prison Mary Stuart,
    And to proclaim her queen. Thy loyal people
    Believe it, and are mad; her head alone
    Can quiet them; this day must be her last.
Eliz. How! Will they force me, then?
Kent.   They are resolved——

Scene VIII.

Enter Burleigh *and* Davison, *with a paper.*

Eliz. Well, Davison?
Dav. (*approaches earnestly*). Your orders are obeyed,
    My queen——
Elizabeth.   What orders, sir?
    [*As she is about to take the paper, she shudders, and
    starts back.*

                                    Oh, God!
Burleigh.   Obey
    Thy people's voice; it is the voice of God.
Elizabeth (*irresolute, as if in contest with herself*)
    Oh, my good lord, who will assure me now
    That what I hear is my whole people's voice,

The voice of all the world! Ah! much I fear,
That, if I now should listen to the wish
Of the wild multitude, a different voice
Might soon be heard; — and that the very men,
Who now by force oblige me to this step,
May, when 'tis taken, heavily condemn me!

SCENE IX.

Enter the EARL OF SHREWSBURY (*who enters with great emotion*).

SHREW. Hold fast, my queen, they wish to hurry thee;
      [*Seeing* DAVISON *with the paper.*
Be firm — or is it then decided? — is it
Indeed decided? I behold a paper
Of ominous appearance in his hand;
Let it not at this moment meet thy eyes,
My queen!——
ELIZ.   Good Shrewsbury! I am constrained——
SHREW. Who can constrain thee? Thou art Queen of
   England,
Here must thy majesty assert its rights:
Command those savage voices to be silent,
Who take upon themselves to put constraint
Upon thy royal will, to rule thy judgment.
Fear only, blind conjecture, moves thy people;
Thou art thyself beside thyself; thy wrath
Is grievously provoked: thou art but mortal,
And canst not thus ascend the judgment seat.
BUR. Judgment has long been past. It is not now
The time to speak but execute the sentence.
KENT (*who upon* SHREWSBURY'S *entry had retired, comes
back*). The tumult gains apace; there are no means
To moderate the people.
ELIZABETH (*to* SHREWSBURY). See, my lord,
How they press on.
SHREWSBURY.   I only ask a respite;
A single word traced by thy hand decides
The peace, the happiness of all thy life!
Thou hast for years considered, let not then
A moment ruled by passion hurry thee —

But a short respite — recollect thyself !
Wait for a moment of tranquillity.
BURLEIGH (*violently*).
    Wait for it — pause — delay — till flames of fire
Consume the realm ; until the fifth attempt
Of murder be successful !   God, indeed,
Hath thrice delivered thee ; thy late escape
Was marvellous, and to expect again
A miracle would be to tempt thy God !
SHREW.   That God, whose potent hand hath thrice pre
          served thee,
Who lent my aged feeble arm the strength
To overcome the madman : — he deserves
Thy confidence.   I will not raise the voice
Of justice now, for now is not the time ;
Thou canst not hear it in this storm of passion.
Yet listen but to this !   Thou tremblest now
Before this living Mary — tremble rather
Before the murdered, the beheaded Mary.
She will arise, and quit her grave, will range
A fiend of discord, an avenging ghost,
Around thy realm, and turn thy people's hearts
From their allegiance.   For as yet the Britons
Hate her, because they fear her ; but most surely
Will they avenge her when she is no more.
They will no more behold the enemy
Of their belief, they will but see in her
The much-lamented issue of their kings
A sacrifice to jealousy and hate.
Then quickly shalt thou see the sudden change
When thou hast done the bloody deed ; then go
Through London, seek thy people, which till now
Around thee swarmed delighted ; thou shalt see
Another England, and another people ;
For then no more the godlike dignity
Of justice, which subdued thy subjects' hearts,
Will beam around thee.   Fear, the dread ally
Of tyranny, will shuddering march before thee,
And make a wilderness in every street —
The last, extremest crime thou hast committed.
What head is safe, if the anointed fall ?

Eliz. Ah ! Shrewsbury, you saved my life, you turned
 The murderous steel aside ; why let you not
 The dagger take its course ? then all these broils
 Would have been ended ; then, released from doubt,
 And free from blame, I should be now at rest
 In my still, peaceful grave. In very sooth
 I'm weary of my life, and of my crown.
 If Heaven decree that one of us two queens
 Must perish, to secure the other's life —
 And sure it must be so — why should not I
 Be she who yields ? My people must decide ;
 I give them back the sovereignty they gave.
 God is my witness that I have not lived
 For my own sake, but for my people's welfare.
 If they expect from this false, fawning Stuart,
 The younger sovereign, more happy days,
 I will descend with pleasure from the throne,
 Again repair to Woodstock's quiet bowers,
 Where once I spent my unambitious youth ;
 Where far removed from all the vanities
 Of earthly power, I found within myself
 True majesty. I am not made to rule —
 A ruler should be made of sterner stuff :
 My heart is soft and tender. I have governed
 These many years this kingdom happily,
 But then I only needed to make happy :
 Now, comes my first important regal duty,
 And now I feel how weak a thing I am.
Bur. Now by mine honor, when I hear my queen,
 My royal liege, speak such unroyal words,
 I should betray my office, should betray
 My country, were I longer to be silent.
 You say you love your people 'bove yourself,
 Now prove it. Choose not peace for your own heart,
 And leave your kingdom to the storms of discord.
 Think on the church. Shall, with this papist queen
 The ancient superstition be renewed ?
 The monk resume his sway, the Roman legate
 In pomp march hither ; lock our churches up,
 Dethrone our monarchs ? I demand of you
 The souls of all your subjects — as you now

Shall act, they all are saved, or all are lost!
Here is no time for mercy;—to promote
Your people's welfare is your highest duty.
If Shrewsbury has saved your life, then I
Will save both you and England — that is more!

ELIZ. I would be left alone. No consolation,
No counsel can be drawn from human aid
In this conjecture : — I will lay my doubts
Before the Judge of all : — I am resolved
To act as He shall teach. Withdraw, my lords.

       [*To* DAVISON, *who lays the paper on the table.*
You, sir, remain in waiting — close at hand.

  [*The lords withdraw ;* SHREWSBURY *alone stands for a*
    few moments before the QUEEN, *regards her signi-*
    ficantly, then withdraws slowly, and with an ex-
    pression of the deepest anguish.

SCENE X.

ELIZABETH *alone.*

Oh! servitude of popularity!
Disgraceful slavery! How weary am I
Of flattering this idol, which my soul
Despises in its inmost depth! Oh! when
Shall I once more be free upon this throne?
I must respect the people's voice, and strive
To win the favor of the multitude,
And please the fancies of a mob, whom naught
But jugglers' tricks delight. O call not him
A king who needs must please the world: 'tis he
Alone, who in his actions does not heed
The fickle approbation of mankind.
Have I then practised justice, all my life
Shunned each despotic deed ; have I done this
Only to bind my hands against this first,
This necessary act of violence?
My own example now condemns myself!
Had I but been a tyrant, like my sister,
My predecessor, I could fearless then
Have shed this royal blood : — but am I now
Just by my own free choice? No — I was forced

By stern necessity to use this virtue;
Necessity, which binds e'en monarch's wills.
Surrounded by my foes, my people's love
Alone supports me on my envied throne.
All Europe's powers confederate to destroy me;
The pope's inveterate decree declares me
Accursed and excommunicated.   France
Betrays me with a kiss, and Spain prepares
At sea a fierce exterminating war;
Thus stand I, in contention with the world,
A poor defenceless woman : I must seek
To veil the spot in my imperial birth,
By which my father cast disgrace upon me:
In vain with princely virtues would I hide it;
The envious hatred of my enemies
Uncovers it, and places Mary Stuart,
A threatening fiend, before me evermore!
[*Walking up and down, with quick and agitated
     steps.*
Oh, no! this fear must end.   Her head must fall!
I will have peace.   She is the very fury
Of my existence; a tormenting demon,
Which destiny has fastened on my soul.
Wherever I had planted me a comfort,
A flattering hope, my way was ever crossed
By this infernal viper! She has torn
My favorite, and my destined bridegroom from me.
The hated name of every ill I feel
Is Mary Stuart — were but she no more
On earth I should be free as mountain air.
                                   [*Standing still.*
With what disdain did she look down on me,
As if her eye should blast me like the lightning!
Poor feeble wretch !   I bear far other arms,
Their touch is mortal, and thou art no more.
[*Advancing to the table hastily, and taking the pen.*
I am a bastard, am I ?   Hapless wretch,
I am but so the while thou liv'st and breath'st.
Thy death will make my birth legitimate.
The moment I destroy thee is the doubt
Destroyed which hangs o'er my imperial right.

As soon as England has no other choice,
My mother's honor and my birthright triumphs!
[*She signs with resolution; lets her pen then fall, and
    steps back with an expression of terror. After a
    pause she rings.*

Scene XI.

Elizabeth, Davison.

Eliz. Where are their lordships?
Davison.   They are gone to quell
The tumult of the people. The alarm
Was instantly appeased when they beheld
The Earl of Shrewsbury. That's he! exclaimed
A hundred voices — that's the man — he saved
The queen; hear him — the bravest man in England!
And now began the gallant Talbot, blamed
In gentle words the people's violence,
And used such strong, persuasive eloquence,
That all were pacified, and silently
They slunk away.
Elizabeth.   The fickle multitude!
Which turns with every wind. Unhappy he
Who leans upon this reed! 'Tis well, Sir William;
You may retire again ——
                     [*As he is going towards the door.*
                     And, sir, this paper,
Receive it back; I place it in your hands.
Davison (*casts a look upon the paper, and starts back.*)
My gracious queen — thy name! 'tis then decided.
Eliz. I had but to subscribe it — I have done so —
A paper sure cannot decide — a name
Kills not.
Davison.   Thy name, my queen, beneath this paper
Is most decisive — kills — 'tis like the lightning,
Which blasteth as it flies! This fatal scroll
Commands the sheriff and commissioners
To take departure straight for Fotheringay,
And to the Queen of Scots announce her death,
Which must at dawn be put in execution.
There is no respite, no discretion here.

As soon as I have parted with this writ
Her race is run.
ELIZABETH. Yes, sir, the Lord has placed
This weighty business in your feeble hands;
Seek him in prayer to light you with his wisdom;
I go — and leave you, sir, to do your duty. [*Going.*
DAV. No; leave me not, my queen, till I have heard
Your will. The only wisdom that I need
Is, word for word, to follow your commands.
Say, have you placed this warrant in my hands
To see that it be speedily enforced?
ELIZ. That you must do as your own prudence dic-
tates.
DAVISON (*interrupting her quickly, and alarmed*).
Not mine — oh, God forbid! Obedience is
My only prudence here. No point must now
Be left to be decided by your servant.
A small mistake would here be regicide,
A monstrous crime, from which my soul recoils
Permit me, in this weighty act, to be
Your passive instrument, without a will: —
Tell me in plain, undoubted terms your pleasure,
What with the bloody mandate I should do.
ELIZ. Its name declares its meaning.
DAVISON. Do you, then,
My liege, command its instant execution?
ELIZ. I said not that; I tremble but to think it.
DAV. Shall I retain it, then, 'till further orders?
ELIZ. At your own risk; you answer the event.
DAV. I! gracious heavens! Oh, speak, my queen, your
pleasure!
ELIZ. My pleasure is that this unhappy business
Be no more mentioned to me; that at last
I may be freed from it, and that forever.
DAV. It costs you but a word — determine then
What shall I do with this mysterious scroll?
ELIZ. I have declared it, plague me, sir, no longer.
DAV. You have declared it, say you? Oh, my queen,
You have said nothing. Please, my gracious mis-
tress,
But to remember ——

ELIZABETH (*stamps on the ground*).
                     Insupportable!
DAV.   Oh, be indulgent to me!   I have entered
     Unwittingly, not many months ago,
     Upon this office; I know not the language
     Of courts and kings.   I ever have been reared
     In simple, open wise, a plain blunt man.
     Be patient with me; nor deny your servant
     A light to lead him clearly to his duty.
    [*He approaches her in a supplicating posture, she turns
      her back on him; he stands in despair; then
      speaks with a tone of resolution.*
     Take, take again this paper — take it back!
     Within my hands it is a glowing fire.
     Select not me, my queen; select not me
     To serve you in this terrible conjecture.
ELIZ.   Go, sir; — fulfil the duty of your office.   [*Exit.*

SCENE XII.

DAVISON, *then* BURLEIGH.

DAV.   She goes!   She leaves me doubting and perplexed
     With this dread paper!   How to act I know not;
     Should I retain it, should I forward it?
                 [*To* BURLEIGH, *who enters.*
     Oh! I am glad that you are come, my lord,
     'Tis you who have preferred me to this charge;
     Now free me from it, for I undertook it,
     Unknowing how responsible it made me.
     Let me then seek again the obscurity
     In which you found me; this is not my place,
BUR.   How now?   Take courage, sir!   Where is the
     warrant?
     The queen was with you.
DAVISON.   She has quitted me
     In bitter anger.   Oh, advise me, help me,
     Save me from this fell agony of doubt!
     My lord, here is the warrant: it is signed!
BUR.   Indeed!   Oh, give it, give it me!
DAVISON.   I may not.
BUR.   How!

DAV. She has not yet explained her final will.

BUR. Explained! She has subscribed it; — give it to me.

DAV. I am to execute it, and I am not.
 Great heavens! I know not what I am to do!

BURLEIGH (*urging more violently*).
 It must be now, this moment, executed.
 The warrant, sir. You're lost if you delay.

DAV. So am I also if I act too rashly.

BUR. What strange infatuation. Give it me.
 [*Snatches the paper from him, and exit with it.*

DAV. What would you? Hold? You will be my
 destruction.

ACT V.

SCENE I.

The Scene the same as in the First Act.

HANNAH KENNEDY *in deep mourning, her eyes still red from weeping, in great but quiet anguish, is employed in sealing letters and parcels. Her sorrow often interrupts her occupation, and she is seen at such intervals to pray in silence.* PAULET *and* DRURY, *also in mourning, enter, followed by many servants, who bear golden and silver vessels, mirrors, paintings, and other valubles, and fill the back part of the stage with them.* PAULET *delivers to the* NURSE *a box of jewels and a paper, and seems to inform her by signs that it contains the inventory of the effects the* QUEEN *had brought with her. At the sight of these riches, the anguish of the* NURSE *is renewed; she sinks into a deep, glowing melancholy, during which* DRURY, PAULET, *and the servants silently retire.*

MELVIL *enters.*

KENNEDY (*screams aloud as soon as she observes him*).
 Melvil! Is it you? Behold I you again?

MEL. Yes, faithful Kennedy, we meet once more.

KEN. After this long, long, painful separation!

MEL. A most unhappy, bitter meeting this!

KEN. You come ——

MELVIL.   To take an everlasting leave
     Of my dear queen — to bid a last farewell!
KEN.   And now at length, now on the fatal morn
     Which brings her death, they grant our royal lady
     The presence of her friends. Oh, worthy sir,
     I will not question you, how you have fared,
     Nor tell you all the sufferings we've endured,
     Since you were torn away from us: alas!
     There will be time enough for that hereafter.
     O, Melvil, Melvil, why was it our fate
     To see the dawn of this unhappy day?
MEL.   Let us not melt each other with our grief.
     Throughout my whole remaining life, as long
     As ever it may be, I'll sit and weep;
     A smile shall never more light up these cheeks,
     Ne'er will I lay this sable garb aside,
     But lead henceforth a life of endless mourning.
     Yet on this last sad day I will be firm;
     Pledge me your word to moderate your grief;
     And when the rest of comfort all bereft,
     Abandoned to despair, wail round her, we
     Will lead her with heroic resolution,
     And be her staff upon the road to death!
KEN.   Melvil! You are deceived if you suppose
     The queen has need of our support to meet
     Her death with firmness. She it is, my friend,
     Who will exhibit the undaunted heart.
     Oh! trust me, Mary Stuart will expire
     As best becomes a heroine and queen!
MEL.   Received she firmly, then, the sad decree
     Of death? — 'tis said that she was not prepared.
KEN.   She was not; yet they were far other terrors
     Which made our lady shudder: 'twas not death,
     But her deliverer, which made her tremble.
     Freedom was promised us; this very night
     Had Mortimer engaged to bear us hence:
     And thus the queen, perplexed 'twixt hope and fear
     And doubting still if she should trust her honor
     And royal person to the adventurous youth,
     Sat waiting for the morning. On a sudden
     We hear a boisterous tumult in the castle;

Our ears are startled by repeated blows
Of many hammers, and we think we hear
The approach of our deliverers : hope salutes us,
And suddenly and unresisted wakes
The sweet desire of life. And now at once
The portals are thrown open — it is Paulet,
Who comes to tell us — that — the carpenters
Erect beneath our feet the murderous scaffold !
  [*She turns aside, overpowered by excessive anguish.*
MEL. O God in Heaven ! Oh, tell me then how bore
    The queen this terrible vicissitude ?
KENNEDY (*after a pause, in which she has somewhat
  collected herself*).
    Not by degrees can we relinquish life ;
    Quick, sudden, in the twinkling of an eye,
    The separation must be made, the change
    From temporal to eternal life ; and God
    Imparted to our mistress at this moment
    His grace, to cast away each earthly hope,
    And firm and full of faith to mount the skies.
    No sign of pallid fear dishonored her ;
    No word of mourning, 'till she heard the tidings
    Of Leicester's shameful treachery, the sad fate
    Of the deserving youth, who sacrificed
    Himself for her ; the deep, the bitter anguish
    Of that old knight, who lost, through her, his last,
    His only hope ; till then she shed no tear —
    'Twas then her tears began to flow, 'twas not
    Her own, but others' woe which wrung them from
        her.
MEL. Where is she now ? Can you not lead me to her ?
KEN. She spent the last remainder of the night
    In prayer, and from her dearest friends she took
    Her last farewell in writing : then she wrote
    Her will * with her own hand. She now enjoys
    A moment of repose, the latest slumber
    Refreshes her weak spirits.
MELVIL.   Who attends her ?
KEN. None but her women and physician Burgoyn :
    You seem to look around you with surprise ;
        * The document is now in the British Museum.

Your eyes appear to ask me what should mean
This show of splendor in the house of death.
Oh, sir, while yet we lived we suffered want;
But at our death plenty returns to us.

SCENE II.

Enter MARGARET CURL.

KEN. How, madam, fares the queen? Is she awake?
CURL (*drying her tears*).
      She is already dressed — she asks for you.
KEN. I go : —
            [*To* MELVIL, *who seems to wish to accompany her*
                  But follow not until the queen
      Has been prepared to see you.   [*Exit*
CURL.   Melvil, sure,
      The ancient steward?
MELVIL.   Yes, the same.
CURL.   Oh, sir,
      This is a house which needs no steward now!
      Melvil, you come from London; can you give
      No tidings of my husband?
MELVIL.   It is said
      He will be set at liberty as soon ——
CURL. As soon as our dear queen shall be no more.
      Oh, the unworthy, the disgraceful traitor!
      He is our lady's murderer — 'tis said
      It was his testimony which condemned her.
MEL. 'Tis true.
CURL.   Oh, curse upon him! be his soul
      Condemned forever! he has borne false witness.
MEL. Think, madam, what you say.
CURL.   I will maintain it
      With every sacred oath before the court,
      I will repeat it in his very face;
      The world shall hear of nothing else. I say
      That she dies innocent!
MELVIL.   God grant it true!

Scene III.

Enter HANNAH KENNEDY.

KENNEDY (*to* CURL).
    Go, madam, and require a cup of wine —
    'Tis for our lady.
MELVIL.   Is the queen then sick?
KEN.   She thinks that she is strong; she is deceived
    By her heroic courage; she believes
    She has no need of nourishment; yet still
    A hard and painful task's allotted her.
    Her enemies shall not enjoy the triumph;
    They shall not say that fear hath blanched her cheeks
    When her fatigues have conquered human weakness.
MEL.   May I approach her?
KENNEDY.   She will come herself.

Scene IV.

Enter BURGOYN; *two women of the chamber follow
him, weeping, and in deep mourning.*

BURG.   Oh, Melvil!
MELVIL.   Oh, Burgoyn!   [*They embrace silently.*
FIRST WOMAN (*to the* NURSE).   She chose to be
    Alone : she wishes, at this awful moment,
    For the last time, to commune with her God.

Scene V.

Enter MARGARET CURL, *bearing a golden cup of wine;
she places it hastily upon the table, and leans, pale and
trembling, against a chair.*

MEL.   How, madam!   What has frightened you?
KENNEDY.   Oh God!
BURG.   Speak, madam!
CURL.   What, alas! have I beheld!
MEL.   Come to yourself, and say what you have seen!
CURL.   As I went down the staircase which conducts
    To the great hall below, a door stood open;
    I looked into the chamber, and I saw —
    Oh heaven!

MELVIL.   What saw you?

CURL.   All the walls were hung
With black; a spacious scaffold, too, o'erspread
With sable cloth, was raised above the floor,
And in the middle of the scaffold stood
A dreadful sable block! upon it lay
A naked, polished axe: — the hall was full
Of cruel people, crowding round the scaffold
Who, with a horrid thirst for human blood,
Seemed waiting for the victim!

THE WOMEN.   Gracious heaven,
Protect our queen!

MELVIL.   Be calm; the queen approaches.

SCENE VI.

Enter MARY *in white and sumptuously arrayed, as for a
festival: she wears hanging from her neck, on a row
of small beads, an Agnus Dei; a rosary hangs from
her girdle; she bears a crucifix in her hand, and a
diadem of precious stones binds her hair; her large
black veil is thrown back.   On her entrance all present
fall back on both sides with the most violent expressions
of anguish.   MELVIL falls involuntarily upon his
knees.*

MARY (*with quiet majesty, looking round the whole circle*).
Why these complaints? Why weep ye? Ye should
    rather
Rejoice with me, that now at length the end
Of my long woe approaches; that my shackles
Fall off, my prison opens, and my soul
Delighted mounts on seraph's wings, and seeks
The land of everlasting liberty.
When I was offered up to the oppression
Of my proud enemy, was forced to suffer
Ignoble taunts, and insults most unfitting
A free and sovereign queen, then was the time
To weep for me; but as an earnest friend,
Beneficent and healing death approaches.
All the indignities which I have suffered

On earth are covered by his sable wings.
The most degraded criminal's ennobled
By his last sufferings, by his final exit;
I feel again the crown upon my brows.
And dignity possess my swelling soul!

                    [Advancing a few steps.

How! Melvil here! My worthy sir, not so;
Arise; you rather come in time to see
The triumph of your mistress than her death.
One comfort, which I never had expected,
Is granted me, that after death my name
Will not be quite abandoned to my foes;
One friend at least, one partner of my faith,
Will be my witness in the hour of death.
Say, honest Melvil, how you fared the while
In this inhospitable, hostile land?
For since the time they tore you from my side
My fears for you have oft depressed my soul.

MEL. No other evil galled me but my grief
For thee, and that I wanted power to serve thee.

MARY. How fares my chamberlain, old Didier?
But sure the faithful servant long has slept
The sleep of death, for he was full of years.

MEL. God hath not granted him as yet this grace;
He lives to see the grave o'erwhelm thy youth.

MARY. Oh! could I but have felt before my death,
The happiness of pressing one descendant
Of the dear blood of Stuart to my bosom.
But I must suffer in a foreign land,
None but my servants to bewail my fate!
Sir; to your loyal bosom I commit
My latest wishes. Bear then, sir, my blessing
To the most Christian king, my royal brother,
And the whole royal family of France.
I bless the cardinal, my honored uncle,
And also Henry Guise, my noble cousin.
I bless the holy father, the vicegerent
Of Christ on earth, who will, I trust, bless me.
I bless the King of Spain, who nobly offered
Himself as my deliverer, my avenger.
They are remembered in my will: I hope

That they will not despise, how poor soe'er
They be, the presents of a heart which loves them.
                        [*Turning to her servants.*
I have bequeathed you to my royal brother
Of France; he will protect you, he will give you
Another country, and a better home;
And if my last desire have any weight,
Stay not in England; let no haughty Briton
Glut his proud heart with your calamities,
Nor see those in the dust who once were mine.
Swear by this image of our suffering Lord
To leave this fatal land when I'm no more.

MELVIL (*touching the crucifix*).
    I swear obedience in the name of all.

MARY.   What I, though poor and plundered, still
            possess,
Of which I am allowed to make disposal,
Shall be amongst you shared; for I have hope
In this at least my will may be fulfilled.
And what I wear upon my way to death
Is yours — nor envy me on this occasion
The pomp of earth upon the road to heaven.
                        [*To the ladies of her chamber.*
To you, my Alice, Gertrude, Rosamund,
I leave my pearls, my garments: you are young,
And ornament may still delight your hearts.
You, Margaret, possess the nearest claims,
To you I should be generous: for I leave you
The most unhappy woman of them all.
That I have not avenged your husband's fault
On you I hope my legacy will prove.
The worth of gold, my Hannah, charms not thee;
Nor the magnificence of precious stones:
My memory, I know, will be to thee
The dearest jewel; take this handkerchief,
I worked it for thee, in the hours of sorrow,
With my own hands, and my hot, scalding tears
Are woven in the texture: — you will bind
My eyes with this, when it is time: this last
Sad service I would wish but from my Hannah.

KEN.   O Melvil! I cannot support it.

MARY. Come,
Come all and now receive my last farewell.
[*She stretches forth her hands ; the* WOMEN *violently
weeping, fall successively at her feet, and kiss her
outstretched hand.*
Margaret, farewell — my Alice, fare thee well ;
Thanks, Burgoyn, for thy honest, faithful service —
Thy lips are hot, my Gertrude : — I have been
Much hated, yet have been as much beloved.
May a deserving husband bless my Gertrude,
For this warm, glowing heart is formed for love.
Bertha, thy choice is better, thou hadst rather
Become the chaste and pious bride of heaven ;
Oh ! haste thee to fulfil thy vows ; the goods
Of earth are all deceitful ; thou may'st learn
This lesson from thy queen. No more ; farewell,
Farewell, farewell, my friends, farewell for ever.
[*She turns suddenly from them ; all but* MELVIL *retire
at different sides.*

SCENE VII.

MARY, MELVIL.

MARY (*after the others are all gone*).
I have arranged all temporal concerns,
And hope to leave the world in debt to none ;
Melvil, one thought alone there is which binds
My troubled soul, nor suffers it to fly
Delighted and at liberty to heaven.
MEL. Disclose it to me ; ease your bosom, trust
Your doubts, your sorrows, to your faithful friend.
MARY. I see eternity's abyss before me ; —
Soon must I stand before the highest Judge,
And have not yet appeased the Holy One.
A priest of my religion is denied me,
And I disdain to take the sacrament,
The holy, heavenly nourishment, from priests
Of a false faith ; I die in the belief
Of my own church, for that alone can save.
MEL. Compose your heart ; the fervent, pious wish
Is prized in heaven as high as the performance.

The might of tyrants can but bind the hands,
The heart's devotion rises free to God,
The word is dead — 'tis faith which brings to life.
MARY.   The heart is not sufficient of itself;
Our faith must have some earthly pledge to ground
Its claim to the high bliss of heaven.   For this
Our God became incarnate, and enclosed
Mysteriously his unseen heavenly grace
Within an outward figure of a body.
The church it is, the holy one, the high one,
Which rears for us the ladder up to heaven : —
'Tis called the Catholic Apostolic church, —
For 'tis but general faith can strengthen faith;
Where thousands worship and adore the heat
Breaks out in flame, and, borne on eagle wings,
The soul mounts upwards to the heaven of heavens
Ah ! happy they, who for the glad communion
Of pious prayer meet in the house of God !
The altar is adorned, the tapers blaze,
The bell invites, the incense soars on high ;
The bishop stands enrobed, he takes the cup,
And blessing it declares the solemn mystery,
The transformation of the elements ;
And the believing people fall delighted
To worship and adore the present Godhead.
Alas ! I only am debarred from this;
The heavenly benediction pierces not
My prison walls : its comfort is denied me.
MEL.   Yes ! it can pierce them — put thy trust in Him
Who is almighty — in the hand of faith,
The withered staff can send forth verdant branches
And he who from the rock called living water,
He can prepare an altar in this prison,
Can change ——
            [*Seizing the cup, which stands upon the table.*
                    The earthly contents of this cup
Into a substance of celestial grace.
MARY.   Melvil ! Oh, yes, I understand you, Melvil !
Here is no priest, no church, no sacrament;
But the Redeemer says, " When two or three
Are in my name assembled, I am with them,"

What consecrates the priest? Say, what ordains him
To be the Lord's interpreter? a heart
Devoid of guile, and a reproachless conduct.
Well, then, though unordained, be you my priest;
To you will I confide my last confession,
And take my absolution from your lips.

MEL. If then thy heart be with such zeal inflamed,
I tell thee that for thine especial comfort,
The Lord may work a miracle. Thou say'st
Here is no priest, no church, no sacrament —
Thou err'st — here is a priest — here is a God;
A God descends to thee in real presence.

[*At these words he uncovers his head, and shows a host
in a golden vessel.*

I am a priest — to hear thy last confession,
And to announce to thee the peace of God
Upon thy way to death. I have received
Upon my head the seven consecrations.
I bring thee, from his Holiness, this host,
Which, for thy use, himself has deigned to bless.

MARY. Is then a heavenly happiness prepared
To cheer me on the very verge of death?
As an immortal one on golden clouds
Descends, as once the angel from on high,
Delivered the apostle from his fetters: —
He scorns all bars, he scorns the soldier's sword,
He steps undaunted through the bolted portals,
And fills the dungeon with his native glory;
Thus here the messenger of heaven appears
When every earthly champion had deceived me.
And you, my servant once, are now the servant
Of the Most High, and his immortal Word!
As before me your knees were wont to bend,
Before you humbled, now I kiss the dust.

[*She sinks before him on her knees.*

MELVIL (*making over her the sign of the cross*).
Hear, Mary, Queen of Scotland: — in the name
Of God the Father, Son, and Holy Ghost,
Hast thou examined carefully thy heart,
Swearest thou, art thou prepared in thy confession
To speak the truth before the God of truth?

MARY. Befoi e my God and thee, my heart lies open.
MEL. What calls thee to the presence of the Highest?
MARY. I humbly do acknowledge to have erred
 Most grievously, I tremble to approach,
 Sullied with sin, the God of purity.
MEL. Declare the sin which weighs so heavily
 Upon thy conscience since thy last confession.
MARY. My heart was filled with thoughts of envious
  hate,
 And vengeance took possession of my bosom.
 I hope forgiveness of my sins from God,
 Yet could I not forgive my enemy.
MEL. Repentest thou of the sin? Art thou, in sooth,
 Resolved to leave this world at peace with all?
MARY. As surely as I wish the joys of heaven.
MEL. What other sin hath armed thy heart against thee?
MARY. Ah! not alone through hate; through lawless
  love
 Have I still more abused the sovereign good.
 My heart was vainly turned towards the man
 Who left me in misfortune, who deceived me.
MEL. Repentest thou of the sin? And hast thou turned
 Thy heart, from this idolatry, to God?
MARY. It was the hardest trial I have passed;
 This last of earthly bonds is torn asunder.
MEL. What other sin disturbs thy guilty conscience?
MARY. A bloody crime, indeed of ancient date,
 And long ago confessed; yet with new terrors
 It now attacks me, black and grisly steps
 Across my path, and shuts the gates of heaven:
 By my connivance fell the king, my husband —
 I gave my hand and heart to a seducer —
 By rigid penance I have made atonement;
 Yet in my soul the worm is gnawing still.
MEL. Has then thy heart no other accusation,
 Which hath not been confessed and washed away?
MARY. All you have heard with which my heart is
  charged.
MEL. Think on the presence of Omniscience;
 Think on the punishments with which the church
 Threatens imperfect and reserved confessions!

This is the sin to everlasting death,
For this is sinning 'gainst his Holy Spirit.
MARY. So may eternal grace with victory
Crown my last contest, as I wittingly
Have nothing hid ——
MELVIL.   How ? Wilt thou then conceal
The crime from God for which thou art condemned ?
Thou tell'st me nothing of the share thou hadst
In Babington and Parry's bloody treason :
Thou diest for this a temporal death ; for this
Wilt thou, too, die the everlasting death ?
MARY. I am prepared to meet eternity ;
Within the narrow limits of an hour
I shall appear before my Judge's throne
But, I repeat it, my confession's ended.
MEL. Consider well — the heart is a deceiver.
Thou hast, perhaps, with sly equivocation,
The word avoided, which would make thee guilty
Although thy will was party to the crime.
Remember, that no juggler's tricks can blind
The eye of fire which darts through every breast.
MARY. 'Tis true that I have called upon all princes
To free me from unworthy chains ; yet 'tis
As true that, neither by intent or deed,
Have I attempted my oppressor's life.
MEL. Your secretaries then have witnessed falsely.
MARY. It is as I have said ; — what they have wit-
nessed
The Lord will judge.
MELVIL.   Thou mountest, then, satisfied
Of thy own innocence, the fatal scaffold ?
MARY. God suffers me in mercy to atone,
By undeserved death, my youth's transgressions.
MELVIL (*making over her the sign of the cross*).
Go, then, and expiate them all by death ;
Sink a devoted victim on the altar,
Thus shall thy blood atone the blood thou'st spilt.
From female frailty were derived thy faults,
Free from the weakness of mortality,
The spotless spirit seeks the blest abodes.
Now, then, by the authority which God

Hath unto me committed, I absolve thee
From all thy sins; be as thy faith thy welfare!
                    [*He gives her the host.*
Receive the body which for thee was offered —
[*He takes the cup which stands upon the table, conse-
    crates it with silent prayer, then presents it to her;
    she hesitates to take it, and makes signs to him to
    withdraw it.*
Receive the blood which for thy sins was shed
Receive it; 'tis allowed thee by the pope
To exercise in death the highest office
Of kings, the holy office of the priesthood.
                    [*She takes the cup.*
And as thou now, in this his earthly body
Hast held with God mysterious communion,
So may'st thou henceforth, in his realm of joy,
Where sin no more exists, nor tears of woe,
A fair, transfigured spirit, join thyself
Forever with the Godhead, and forever.
[*He sets down the cup; hearing a noise, he covers his
    head, and goes to the door;* MARY *remains in silent
    devotion on her knees.*
MELVIL (*returning*).   A painful conflict is in store for thee.
    Feel'st thou within thee strength enough to smother
    Each impulse of malignity and hate?
MARY.   I fear not a relapse.   I have to God
    Devoted both my hatred and my love.
MEL.   Well, then, prepare thee to receive my Lords
    Of Leicester and of Burleigh.   They are here.

SCENE VIII.

Enter BURLEIGH, LEICESTER, *and* PAULET.

[LEICESTER *remains in the background, without raising
    his eyes;* BURLEIGH, *who remarks his confusion,
    steps between him and the* QUEEN.
BUR.   I come, my Lady Stuart, to receive
    Your last commands and wishes.
MARY.   Thanks, my lord.
BUR.   It is the pleasure of my royal mistress
    That nothing reasonable be denied you.

MARY. My will, my lord, declares my last desires;
    I've placed it in the hand of Sir Amias,
    And humbly beg that it may be fulfilled.
PAUL. You may rely on this.
MARY.   I beg that all
    My servants unmolested may return
    To France, or Scotland, as their wishes lead.
BUR. It shall be as you wish.
MARY.   And since my body
    Is not to rest in consecrated ground,
    I pray you suffer this my faithful servant
    To bear my heart to France, to my relations —
    Alas! 'twas ever there.
BURLEIGH.   It shall be done.
    What wishes else?
MARY.   Unto her majesty
    Of England bear a sister's salutation;
    Tell her that from the bottom of my heart
    I pardon her my death; most humbly, too,
    I crave her to forgive me for the passion
    With which I spoke to her. May God preserve her
    And bless her with a long and prosperous reign.
BUR. Say, do you still adhere to your resolve,
    And still refuse assistance from the dean?
MARY. My lord, I've made my peace with God.
                  [*To* PAULET. Good sir,
    I have unwittingly caused you much sorrow,
    Bereft you of your age's only stay.
    Oh, let me hope you do not hate my name.
PAULET (*giving her his hand*).
    The Lord be with you! Go your way in peace.

SCENE IX.

HANNAH KENNEDY, *and the other women of the* QUEEN
crowd into the room with marks of horror. The SHER-
IFF *follows them, a white staff in his hand; behind are
seen, through the open doors, men under arms.*

MARY. What ails thee, Hannah? Yes, my hour is come.
    The sheriff comes to lead me to my fate,
    And part we must. Farewell!

KENNEDY *and* CURL.   We will not leave thee,
    We will not part from thee.
MARY (*to* MELVIL).   You, worthy sir,
    And my dear, faithful Hannah, shall attend me
    In my last moments. I am sure, my lord
    Will not refuse my heart this consolation.
BUR. For this I have no warrant.
MARY.   How, my lord ;
    Can you deny me, then, this small petition ?
    Respect my sex ; who shall attend me else,
    And yield me the last service ? Sure, it never
    Can be my sister's pleasure that in me
    My sex should be insulted ; that these men
    With their rude hands should touch my royal person.
BUR. 'Tis ordered that no woman shall ascend
    The scaffold steps with you.   Their tears and
        moans ——
MARY. She shall not weep, my lord ; she shall not moan ;
    I answer for my Hannah's resolution ;
    Be merciful ; divide me not so soon
    From my true foster-mother, from my friend.
    She bore me on her arms into this life ;
    Let her then gently lead me to my death.
PAULET (*to* BURLEIGH).
    Yield to her wishes.
BURLEIGH.   Be it so.
MARY.   I now
    Have nothing in this world to wish for more.
                    [*She takes the crucifix, and kisses it.*
    My God ! My Comforter ! My blest Redeemer !
    As once thy arms were stretched upon the cross,
    Let them be now extended to receive me !
    [*She turns round to go ; at the same moment her eyes
        fall upon* LEICESTER, *who, on her going, starts in-
        voluntarily, and turns his eyes towards her ; at this
        sight* MARY *trembles, her knees fail her, she is about
        to fall, when* LEICESTER *catches at her, and receives
        her in his arms ; she regards him for some time
        earnestly, and in silence ; he cannot support her
        looks ; at length she speaks.*
    You keep your word, my Lord of Leicester : for

You promised me your arm to lead me forth
From prison, and you lend it to me now.
At length the wished-for day is come, and what
Was oft the object of my fondest dreams
Is now accomplished : and the Earl of Leicester,
The long-expected, the long-wished-for friend,
Appears at length in Fotheringay Castle.
I see him standing in my prison; all
Is ready for the journey; all the gates
Stand open, and at length I cross the threshold,
Conducted by his hand ; and now I leave
These dismal walls behind me, and forever.
All is fulfilled, and you have saved your honor.
[*He stands as if annihilated ; she continues, with a*
gentle voice.
Yes, Leicester; not for liberty alone
I wished to be indebted to your hands.
You should have made me bless that liberty.
Led by your hand, and happy in your love,
I hoped once more to taste the joys of life.
Yes; now that I'm prepared from all the world
To part, and to become a happy spirit,
Whom earthly inclinations tempt no more!
Now, Leicester, I may venture to confess
Without a blush the frailty I have conquered ;
Farewell, my lord ; and, if you can, be happy!
To woo two queens has been your daring aim ;
You have disdained a tender, loving heart,
Betrayed it in the hope to win a proud one:
Kneel at the feet of Queen Elizabeth!
May your reward not prove your punishment.
Farewell ; I now have nothing more on earth.
[*She goes, preceded by the* SHERIFF ; *at her side* MELVIL
and her nurse ; BURLEIGH *and* PAULET *follow ; the*
others, wailing, follow her with their eyes till she dis-
appears ; they then retire through the other two doors.

SCENE X.

LEICESTER (*remaining alone*).
Do I live still ?   Can I still bear to live?
Will not this roof fall down and bury me?

Yawns no abyss to swallow in its gulf
The veriest wretch on earth?   What have I lost?
Oh, what a pearl have I not cast away!
What bliss celestial madly dashed aside!
She's gone, a spirit purged from earthly stain,
And the despair of hell remains for me!
Where is the purpose now with which I came
To stifle my heart's voice in callous scorn?
To see her head descend upon the block
With unaverted and indifferent eyes?
How   doth   her   presence   wake   my   slumbering
     shame?
Must she in death surround me with love's toils?
Lost, wretched man!   No more it suits thee now
To melt away in womanly compassion:
Love's golden bliss lies not upon thy path,
Then arm thy breast in panoply of steel,
And henceforth be thy brows of adamant!
Wouldst thou not lose the guerdon of thy guilt,
Thou must uphold, complete it daringly!
Pity be dumb; mine eyes be petrified!
I'll see — I will be witness of her fall.

[*He advances with resolute steps towards the door
     through which* MARY *passed; but stops suddenly
     half way.*

No! No!   The terrors of all hell possess me.
I cannot look upon the dreadful deed;
I cannot see her die!   Hark!   What was that?
They are already there.   Beneath my feet
The bloody business is preparing.   Hark!
I hear their voices.   Hence!   Away, away
From this abode of misery and death!

[*He attempts to escape by another door; finds it locked,
     and returns.*

How!   Does some demon chain me to this spot?
To hear what I would shudder to behold?
That voice — it is the dean's, exhorting her;
She interrupts him.   Hark — she prays aloud;
Her voice is firm — now all is still, quite still!
And sobs and women's moans are all I hear.

Now, they undress her; they remove the stool;
She kneels upon the cushion; lays her head ——
[*Having spoken these last words, and paused awhile, he
is seen with a convulsive motion suddenly to shrink
and faint away; a confused hum of voices is heard
at the same moment from below, and continues for
some time.*

SCENE XI.

The Second Chamber in the Fourth Act.

ELIZABETH (*entering from a side door; her gait and action
expressive of the most violent uneasiness.*

No message yet arrived! What! no one here!
Will evening never come! Stands the sun still
In its ethereal course? I can no more
Remain upon the rack of expectation!
Is it accomplished? Is it not? I shudder
At both events, and do not dare to ask.
My Lord of Leicester comes not, — Burleigh too,
Whom I appointed to fulfil the sentence.
If they have quitted London then 'tis done,
The bolt has left its rest — it cuts the air —
It strikes; has struck already: were my realm
At stake I could not now arrest its course.
Who's there?

SCENE XII.

Enter a PAGE.

ELIZABETH. Returned alone? Where are the lords?
PAGE. My Lord High-Treasurer and the Earl of Leicester?
ELIZ. Where are they?
PAGE. They are not in London.
ELIZ. No!
Where are they then?
PAGE. That no one could inform me;
Before the dawn, mysteriously, in haste
They quitted London.
ELIZABETH (*exultingly*). I am Queen of England!
[*Walking up and down in the greatest agitation.*
Go — call me — no, remain, boy! She is dead;
Now have I room upon the earth at last.

Why do I shake? Whence comes this aguish dread?
My fears are covered by the grave; who dares
To say I did it? I have tears enough
In store to weep her fall. Are you still here?

                                    [*To the* PAGE.
Command my secretary, Davison,
To come to me this instant. Let the Earl
Of Shrewsbury be summoned. Here he comes.

                                   [*Exit* PAGE.

SCENE XIII.

Enter SHREWSBURY.

ELIZ. Welcome, my noble lord. What tidings; say
    It cannot be a trifle which hath led
    Your footsteps hither at so late an hour.
SHREW. My liege, the doubts that hung upon my heart,
    And dutiful concern for your fair fame,
    Directed me this morning to the Tower,
    Where Mary's secretaries, Nau and Curl,
    Are now confined as prisoners, for I wished
    Once more to put their evidence to proof.
    On my arrival the lieutenant seemed
    Embarrassed and perplexed; refused to show me
    His prisoners; but my threats obtained admittance.
    God! what a sight was there! With frantic looks,
    With hair dishevelled, on his pallet lay
    The Scot like one tormented by a fury.
    The miserable man no sooner saw me
    Than at my feet he fell, and there, with screams,
    Clasping my knees, and writhing like a worm,
    Implored, conjured me to acquaint him with
    His sovereign's destiny, for vague reports
    Had somehow reached the dungeons of the Tower
    That she had been condemned to suffer death.
    When I confirmed these tidings, adding, too,
    That on his evidence she had been doomed, —
    He started wildly up, — caught by the throat
    His fellow-prisoner; with the giant strength
    Of madness tore him to the ground and tried
    To strangle him. No sooner had we saved
    The wretch from his fierce grapple than at once

He turned his rage against himself and beat
His breast with savage fists; then cursed himself
And his companions to the depths of hell!
His evidence was false; the fatal letters
To Babington, which he had sworn were true,
He now denounced as forgeries; for he
Had set down words the queen had never spoken;
The traitor Nau had led him to this treason.
Then ran he to the casement, threw it wide
With frantic force, and cried into the street
So loud that all the people gathered round:
I am the man, Queen Mary's secretary,
The traitor who accused his mistress falsely;
I bore false witness and am cursed forever!

ELIZ.   You said yourself that he had lost his wits;
A madman's words prove nothing.

SHREWSBURY.   Yet this madness
Serves in itself to swell the proof.   My liege,
Let me conjure thee; be not over-hasty;
Prithee, give order for a new inquiry!

ELIZ.   I will, my lord, because it is your wish,
Not that I can believe my noble peers
Have in this case pronounced a hasty judgment.
To set your mind at rest the inquiry shall
Be straight renewed.   Well that 'tis not too late!
Upon the honor of our royal name
No, not the shadow of a doubt shall rest.

SCENE XIV.

Enter DAVISON.

ELIZ.   The sentence, sir, which I but late intrusted
Unto your keeping; where is it?

DAVISON (*in the utmost astonishment*).   The sentence!

ELIZABETH (*more urgent*).
Which yesterday I gave into your charge.

DAV.   Into my charge, my liege!

ELIZABETH.   The people urged
And baited me to sign it.   I perforce
Was driven to yield obedience to their will.
I did so; did so on extreme constraint,

And in your hands deposited the paper.
To gain time was my purpose ; you remember
What then I told you. Now, the paper, sir!
SHREW. Restore it, sir, affairs have changed since then,
The inquiry must be set on foot anew.
DAV. Anew! Eternal mercy!
ELIZABETH.   Why this pause,
This hesitation ? Where, sir, is the paper?
DAV. I am undone! Undone! My fate is sealed!
ELIZABETH (*interrupting him violently*).
Let me not fancy, sir ——
DAVISON.   Oh, I am lost!
I have it not.
ELIZABETH.   How ? What ?
SHREWSBURY.   Oh, God in heaven!
DAV. It is in Burleigh's hands — since yesterday.
ELIZ. Wretch! Is it thus you have obeyed my orders?
Did I not lay my strict injunction on you
To keep it carefully ?
DAVISON.   No such injunction
Was laid on me, my liege.
ELIZABETH.   Give me the lie ?
Opprobrious wretch! When did I order you
To give the paper into Burleigh's hands?
DAV. Never expressly in so many words.
ELIZ. And, paltering villain! dare you then presume
To construe, as you list, my words — and lay
Your bloody meaning on them ? Wo betide you,
If evil come of this officious deed !
Your life shall answer the event to me.
Earl Shrewsbury, you see how my good name
Has been abused !
SHREWSBURY.   I see! Oh, God in heaven!
ELIZ. What say you ?
SHREWSBURY.   If the knight has dared to act
In this, upon his own authority,
Without the knowledge of your majesty,
He must be cited to the Court of Peers
To answer there for subjecting thy name
To the abhorrence of all after time.

SCENE XV.

Enter BURLEIGH.

BURLEIGH (*bowing his knee before the* QUEEN).
Long life and glory to my royal mistress,
And may all enemies of her dominions
End like this Stuart.
[SHREWSBURY *hides his face.* DAVIDSON *wrings his
hands in despair.*
ELIZABETH.   Speak, my lord; did you
From me receive the warrant?
BURLEIGH.   No, my queen;
From Davison.
ELIZABETH.   And did he in my name
Deliver it?
BURLEIGH.   No, that I cannot say.
ELIZ.   And dared you then to execute the writ
Thus hastily, nor wait to know my pleasure?
Just was the sentence — we are free from blame
Before the world; yet it behooved thee not
To intercept our natural clemency.
For this, my lord, I banish you my presence;
And as this forward will was yours alone
Bear you alone the curse of the misdeed!   [*To* DAV.
For you, sir; who have traitorously o'erstepped
The bounds of your commission, and betrayed
A sacred pledge intrusted to your care,
A more severe tribunal is prepared:
Let him be straight conducted to the Tower,
And capital arraignments filed against him.
My honest Talbot, you alone have proved,
'Mongst all my counsellors, an upright man:
You shall henceforward be my guide — my friend.
SHREW.   Oh! banish not the truest of your friends;
Nor cast those into prison, who for you
Have acted; who for you are silent now.
But suffer me, great queen, to give the seal,
Which, these twelve years, I've borne unworthily,
Back to your royal hands, and take my leave.
ELIZABETH (*surprised*).
No, Shrewsbury; you surely would not now
Desert me? No; not now.

SHREWSBURY.   Pardon, I am
    Too old, and this right hand is growing too stiff
    To set the seal upon your later deeds.
ELIZ. Will he forsake me, who has saved my life?
SHREW. 'Tis little I have done : I could not save
    Your nobler part. Live — govern happily!
    Your rival's dead ! Henceforth you've nothing more
    To fear — henceforth to nothing pay regard. [*Exit.*
ELIZABETH (*to the* EARL *of* KENT, *who enters*).
    Send for the Earl of Leicester.
KENT.   He desires
    To be excused — he is embarked for France.
                         The Curtain drops.

THE MAID OF ORLEANS.

DRAMATIS PERSONÆ.

CHARLES THE SEVENTH, *King of France.*
QUEEN ISABEL, *his Mother.*
AGNES SOREL.
PHILIP THE GOOD, *Duke of Burgundy.*
EARL DUNOIS, *Bastard of Orleans.*
LA HIRE, DUCHATEL, *French Officers.*
ARCHBISHOP OF RHEIMS.
CHATILLON, *A Burgundian Knight.*
RAOUL, *a Lotharingian Knight.*
TALBOT, *the English General,*
LIONEL, FASTOLFE, *English Officers.*
MONTGOMERY, *a Welshman.*
COUNCILLORS OF ORLEANS.

AN ENGLISH HERALD.
THIBAUT D'ARC, *a wealthy Countryman.*
MARGOT, LOUISON, JOHANNA, *his Daughters.*
ETIENNE, CLAUDE MARIE, RAIMOND, *their Suitors.*
BERTRAND, *another Countryman.*
APPARITION OF A BLACK KNIGHT.
CHARCOAL-BURNER AND HIS WIFE.
Soldiers and People, Officers of the Crown, Bishops, Monks, Marshals, Magistrates, Courtiers, and other mute persons in the Coronation Procession.

PROLOGUE.

A rural District. To the right, a Chapel with an Image of the Virgin; to the left, an ancient Oak.

SCENE I.

THIBAUT D'ARC. *His Three Daughters. Three young Shepherds, their Suitors.*

THIB. Ay, my good neighbors! we at least to-day
Are Frenchmen still, free citizens and lords
Of the old soil which our forefathers tilled.
Who knows whom we to-morrow must obey?
For England her triumphal banner waves
From every wall: the blooming fields of France
Are trampled down beneath her chargers' hoofs;
Paris hath yielded to her conquering arms,
And with the ancient crown of Dagobert

131

Adorns the scion of a foreign race.
Our king's descendant, disinherited,
Must steal in secret through his own domain;
While his first peer and nearest relative
Contends against him in the hostile ranks;
Ay, his unnatural mother leads them on.
Around us towns and peaceful hamlets burn.
Near and more near the devastating fire
Rolls toward these vales, which yet repose in peace.
Therefore, good neighbors, I have now resolved,
While God still grants us safety, to provide
For my three daughters; for 'midst war's alarms
Women require protection, and true love
Hath power to render lighter every load.
                        [*To the first Shepherd.*
Come, Etienne!   You seek my Margot's hand.
Fields lying side by side and loving hearts
Promise a happy union!   [*To the second.*
                    Claude!   You're silent,
And my Louison looks upon the ground?
How, shall I separate two loving hearts
Because you have no wealth to offer me?
Who now has wealth?   Our barns and homes afford
Spoil to the foe, and fuel to the fires.
In times like these a husband's faithful breast
Affords the only shelter from the storm.
Louis.   My father!
Claude Marie.   My Louison!
Louison (*embracing* Johanna).   My dear sister!
Thib.   I give to each a yard, a stall and herd,
      And also thirty acres; and as God
      Gave me his blessing, so I give you mine!
Margot (*embracing* Johanna).
      Gladden our father — follow our example!
      Let this day see three unions ratified!
Thib.   Now go; make all things ready; for the morn
      Shall see the wedding.   Let our village friends
      Be all assembled for the festival.
                  [*The two couple retire arm in arm*

Scene II.

Thibaut, Raimond, Johanna.

Thib. Thy sisters, Joan, will soon be happy brides;
I see them gladly; they rejoice my age;
But thou, my youngest, giv'st me grief and pain.
Raim. What is the matter? Why upbraid thy child?
Thib. Here is this noble youth, the flower and pride
Of all our village; he hath fixed on thee
His fond affections, and for three long years
Has wooed thee with respectful tenderness;
But thou dost thrust him back with cold reserve.
Nor is there one 'mong all our shepherd youths
Who e'er can win a gracious smile from thee.
I see thee blooming in thy youthful prime;
Thy spring it is, the joyous time of hope;
Thy person, like a tender flower, hath now
Disclosed its beauty, but I vainly wait
For love's sweet blossom genially to blow,
And ripen joyously to golden fruit!
Oh, that must ever grieve me, and betrays
Some sad deficiency in nature's work!
The heart I like not which, severe and cold,
Expands not in the genial years of youth.
Raim. Forbear, good father! Cease to urge her thus!
A noble, tender fruit of heavenly growth
Is my Johanna's love, and time alone
Bringeth the costly to maturity!
Still she delights to range among the hills,
And fears descending from the wild, free heath,
To tarry 'neath the lowly roofs of men,
Where dwell the narrow cares of humble life.
From the deep vale, with silent wonder, oft
I mark her, when, upon a lofty hill
Surrounded by her flock, erect she stands,
With noble port, and bends her earnest gaze
Down on the small domains of earth. To me
She looketh then, as if from other times
She came, foreboding things of import high.
Thib. 'Tis that precisely which displeases me!
She shuns her sisters' gay companionship;

    Seeks out the desert mountains, leaves her couch
Before the crowing of the morning cock,
And in the dreadful hour, when men are wont
Confidingly to seek their fellow-men,
She, like the solitary bird, creeps forth,
And in the fearful spirit-realm of night,
To yon crossway repairs, and there alone
Holds secret commune with the mountain wind.
Wherefore this place precisely doth she choose?
Why hither always doth she drive her flock?
For hours together I have seen her sit
In dreamy musing 'neath the Druid tree,
Which every happy creature shuns with awe.
For 'tis not holy there; an evil spirit
Hath since the fearful pagan days of old
Beneath its branches fixed his dread abode.
The oldest of our villagers relate
Strange tales of horror of the Druid tree;
Mysterious voices of unearthly sound
From its unhallowed shade oft meet the ear.
Myself, when in the gloomy twilight hour
My path once chanced to lead me near this tree,
Beheld a spectral figure sitting there,
Which slowly from its long and ample robe
Stretched forth its withered hand, and beckoned me.
But on I went with speed, nor looked behind,
And to the care of God consigned my soul.

RAIMOND (*pointing to the image of the Virgin*).
    Yon holy image of the Virgin blest,
Whose presence heavenly peace diffuseth round,
Not Satan's work, leadeth thy daughter here.

THIB. No! not in vain hath it in fearful dreams
And apparitions strange revealed itself.
For three successive nights I have beheld
Johanna sitting on the throne at Rheims,
A sparkling diadem of seven stars
Upon her brow, the sceptre in her hand,
From which three lilies sprung, and I, her sire,
With her two sisters, and the noble peers,
The earls, archbishops, and the king himself,
Bowed down before her. In my humble home

How could this splendor enter my poor brain?
Oh, 'tis the prelude to some fearful fall!
This warning dream, in pictured show, reveals
The vain and sinful longing of her heart.
She looks with shame upon her lowly birth.
Because with richer beauty God hath graced
Her form, and dowered her with wondrous gifts
Above the other maidens of this vale,
She in her heart indulges sinful pride,
And pride it is through which the angels fell,
By which the fiend of hell seduces man.

RAIM.   Who cherishes a purer, humbler mind
Than doth thy pious daughter?   Does she not
With cheerful spirit work her sisters' will?
She is more highly gifted far than they,
Yet, like a servant maiden, it is she
Who silently performs the humblest tasks.
Beneath her guiding hands prosperity
Attendeth still thy harvest and thy flocks;
And around all she does there ceaseless flows
A blessing, rare and unaccountable.

THIB.   Ah truly!   Unaccountable indeed!
Sad horror at this blessing seizes me!
But now no more; henceforth I will be silent.
Shall I accuse my own beloved child?
I can do naught but warn and pray for her.
Yet warn I must.   Oh, shun the Druid tree!
Stay not alone, and in the midnight hour
Break not the ground for roots, no drinks prepare,
No characters inscribe upon the sand!
'Tis easy to unlock the realm of spirits;
Listening each sound, beneath a film of earth
They lay in wait, ready to rush aloft.
Stay not alone, for in the wilderness
The prince of darkness tempted e'en the Lord.

SCENE III.

THIBAUT, RAIMOND, JOHANNA.

BERTRAND *enters, a helmet in his hand.*

RAIM.   Hush! here is Bertrand coming back from town;
What bears he in his hand?

BERTRAND.   You look at me
  With wondering gaze; no doubt you are surprised
  To see this martial helm!
THIBAUT.   We are indeed!
  Come, tell us how you come by it?   Why bring
  This fearful omen to our peaceful vale?
   [JOHANNA, *who has remained indifferent during the*
    two previous scenes, becomes attentive, and steps
    nearer.
BERT.   I scarce can tell you how I came by it.
  I had procured some tools at Vaucouleurs;
  A crowd was gathered in the market-place,
  For fugitives were just arrived in haste
  From Orleans, bringing most disastrous news.
  In tumult all the town together flocked,
  And as I forced a passage through the crowds,
  A brown Bohemian woman, with this helm,
  Approached me, eyed me narrowly, and said:
  "Fellow, you seek a helm; I know it well.
  Take this one!   For a trifle it is yours."
  "Go with it to the soldiers," I replied,
  "I am a husbandman, and want no helm."
  She would not cease, however, and went on:
  "None knoweth if he may not want a helm.
  A roof of metal for the head just now
  Is of more value than a house of stone."
  Thus she pursued me closely through the streets,
  Still offering the helm, which I refused.
  I marked it well, and saw that it was bright,
  And fair and worthy of a knightly head;
  And when in doubt I weighed it in my hand,
  The strangeness of the incident revolving,
  The woman disappeared, for suddenly
  The rushing crowd had carried her away.
  And I was left the helmet in my hand.
JOHANNA (*attempting eagerly to seize it*).
  Give me the helmet!
BERTRAND.   Why, what boots it you?
  It is not suited to a maiden's head.
JOHANNA (*seizing it from him*).
  Mine is the helmet — it belongs to me!

THIB.   What whim is this?

RAIMOND.   Nay, let her have her way!
This warlike ornament becomes her well,
For in her bosom beats a manly heart.
Remember how she once subdued the wolf,
The savage monster which destroyed our herds,
And filled the neighb'ring shepherds with dismay.
She all alone — the lion-hearted maid —
Fought with the wolf, and from him snatched the
     lamb
Which he was bearing in his bloody jaws.
How brave soe'er the head this helm adorned,
It cannot grace a worthier one than hers!

THIBAUT (to BERTRAND).
Relate what new disasters have occurred.
What tidings brought the fugitives?

BERTRAND.   May God
Have pity on our land, and save the king!
In two great battles we have lost the day;
Our foes are stationed in the heart of France,
Far as the river Loire our lands are theirs —
Now their whole force they have combined, and lay
Close siege to Orleans.

THIBAUT.   God protect the king!

BERT.   Artillery is brought from every side,
And as the dusky squadrons of the bees
Swarm round the hive upon a summer day,
As clouds of locusts from the sultry air
Descend and shroud the country round for miles,
So doth the cloud of war, o'er Orleans' fields,
Pour forth its many-nationed multitudes,
Whose varied speech, in wild confusion blent,
With strange and hollow murmurs fill the air.
For Burgundy, the mighty potentate,
Conducts his motley host; the Hennegarians,
The men of Liege and of Luxemburg,
The people of Namur, and those who dwell
In fair Brabant; the wealthy men of Ghent,
Who boast their velvets, and their costly silks;
The Zealanders, whose cleanly towns appear
Emerging from the ocean; Hollanders

Who milk the lowing herds; men from Utrecht,
And even from West Friesland's distant realm,
Who look towards the ice-pole — all combine,
Beneath the banner of the powerful duke,
Together to accomplish Orleans' fall.

THIB.   Oh, the unblest, the lamentable strife,
Which turns the arms of France against itself!

BERT.   E'en she, the mother-queen, proud Isabel —
Bavaria's haughty princess — may be seen,
Arrayed in armor, riding through the camp;
With poisonous words of irony she fires
The hostile troops to fury 'gainst her son,
Whom she hath clasped to her maternal breast.

THIB.   A curse upon her, and may God prepare
For her a death like haughty Jezebel's!

BERT.   The fearful Salisbury conducts the siege,
The town-destroyer; with him Lionel,
The brother of the lion; Talbot, too,
Who, with his murd'rous weapon, moweth down
The people in the battle: they have sworn,
With ruthless insolence to doom to shame
The hapless maidens, and to sacrifice
All who the sword have wielded, with the sword.
Four lofty watch-towers, to o'ertop the town,
They have upreared; Earl Salisbury from on high
Casteth abroad his cruel, murd'rous glance,
And marks the rapid wanderers in the streets.
Thousands of cannon-balls, of pond'rous weight,
Are hurled into the city.   Churches lie
In ruined heaps, and Nôtre Dame's royal tower
Begins at length to bow its lofty head.
They also have formed powder-vaults below,
And thus, above a subterranean hell,
The timid city every hour expects,
'Midst crashing thunder, to break forth in flames.

[JOHANNA *listens with close attention, and places the
    helmet on her head..*

THIB.   But where were then our heroes?   Where the
        swords
Of Saintrailles, and La Hire, and brave Dunois,
Of France the bulwark, that the haughty foe

With such impetuous force thus onward rushed?
Where is the king? Can he supinely see
His kingdom's peril and his cities' fall?

BERT. The king at Chinon holds his court; he lacks
Soldiers to keep the field. Of what avail
The leader's courage, and the hero's arm,
When pallid fear doth paralyze the host?
A sudden panic, as if sent from God,
Unnerves the courage of the bravest men.
In vain the summons of the king resounds
As when the howling of the wolf is heard,
The sheep in terror gather side by side,
So Frenchmen, careless of their ancient fame,
Seek only now the shelter of the towns.
One knight alone, I have been told, has brought
A feeble company, and joins the king
With sixteen banners.

JOHANNA (quickly). What's the hero's name?

BERT. 'Tis Baudricour. But much I fear the knight
Will not be able to elude the foe,
Who track him closely with too numerous hosts.

JOHAN. Where halts the knight? Pray tell me, if you
know.

BERT. About a one day's march from Vaucouleurs.

THIBAUT (to JOHANNA).
Why, what is that to thee? Thou dost inquire
Concerning matters which become thee not.

BERT. The foe being now so strong, and from the king
No safety to be hoped, at Vaucouleurs
They have with unanimity resolved
To yield them to the Duke of Burgundy.
Thus we avoid the foreign yoke, and still
Continue by our ancient royal line;
Ay, to the ancient crown we may fall back
Should France and Burgundy be reconciled.

JOHANNA (as if inspired).
Speak not of treaty! Speak not of surrender!
The savior comes, he arms him for the fight.
The fortunes of the foe before the walls
Of Orleans shall be wrecked! His hour is come,
He now is ready for the reaper's hand,

And with her sickle will the maid appear,
And mow to earth the harvest of his pride.
She from the heavens will tear his glory down,
Which he had hung aloft among the stars;
Despair not! Fly not! for ere yonder corn
Assumes its golden hue, or ere the moon
Displays her perfect orb, no English horse
Shall drink the rolling waters of the Loire.

BERT.   Alas! no miracle will happen now!

JOHAN.   Yes, there shall yet be one — a snow-white
          dove
Shall fly, and with the eagle's boldness, tear
The birds of prey which rend her fatherland.
She shall o'erthrow this haughty Burgundy,
Betrayer of the kingdom; Talbot, too,
The hundred-handed, heaven-defying scourge;
This Salisbury, who violates our fanes,
And all these island robbers shall she drive
Before her like a flock of timid lambs.
The Lord will be with her, the God of battle;
A weak and trembling creature he will choose,
And through a tender maid proclaim his power,
For he is the Almighty!

THIBAULT.   What strange power
Hath seized the maiden?

RAIMOND.   Doubtless 'tis the helmet
Which doth inspire her with such martial thoughts.
Look at your daughter. Mark her flashing eye,
Her glowing cheek, which kindles as with fire.

JOHAN.   This realm shall fall! This ancient land of
          fame,
The fairest that, in his majestic course,
The eternal sun surveys — this paradise,
Which, as the apple of his eye, God loves —
Endure the fetters of a foreign yoke?
— Here were the heathen scattered, and the cross
And holy image first were planted here;
Here rest St. Louis' ashes, and from hence
The troops went forth who set Jerusalem free.

BERTRAND (*in astonishment*).
Hark how she speaks! Why, whence can she obtain

This glorious revelation ? Father Arc!
A wond'rous daughter God hath given you!
JOHAN. We shall no longer serve a native prince!
The king, who never dies, shall pass away —
The guardian of the sacred plough, who fills
The earth with plenty, who protects our herds,
Who frees the bondmen from captivity,
Who gathers all his cities round his throne —
Who aids the helpless, and appals the base,
Who envies no one, for he reigns supreme;
Who is a mortal, yet an angel too,
Dispensing mercy on the hostile earth.
For the king's throne, which glitters o'er with gold,
Affords a shelter for the destitute;
Power and compassion meet together there,
The guilty tremble, but the just draw near,
And with the guardian lion fearless sport!
The stranger king, who cometh from afar,
Whose fathers' sacred ashes do not lie
Interred among us; can he love our land?
Who was not young among our youth, whose heart
Respondeth not to our familiar words,
Can he be as a father to our sons?
THIB. God save the king and France! We're peaceful
        folk,
Who neither wield the sword, nor rein the steed.
— Let us await the king whom victory crowns;
The fate of battle is the voice of God.
He is our lord who crowns himself at Rheims,
And on his head receives the holy oil.
— Come, now to work! come! and let every one
Think only of the duty of the hour!
Let the earth's great ones for the earth contend,
Untroubled we may view the desolation,
For steadfast stand the acres which we till.
The flames consume our villages, our corn
Is trampled 'neath the tread of warlike steeds;
With the new spring new harvests reappear,
And our light huts are quickly reared again!
        [*They all retire except the maiden.*

SCENE IV.

JOHANNA (*alone*).

Farewell ye mountains, ye beloved glades,
Ye lone and peaceful valleys, fare ye well!
Through you Johanna never more may stray!
For, ay, Johanna bids you now farewell.
Ye meads which I have watered, and ye trees
Which I have planted, still in beauty bloom!
Farewell ye grottos, and ye crystal springs!
Sweet echo, vocal spirit of the vale.
Who sang'st responsive to my simple strain,
Johanna goes, and ne'er returns again.

Ye scenes where all my tranquil joys I knew,
Forever now I leave you far behind!
Poor foldless lambs, no shepherd now have you!
O'er the wide heath stray henceforth unconfined!
For I to danger's field, of crimson hue,
Am summoned hence another flock to find.
Such is to me the spirit's high behest;
No earthly, vain ambition fires my breast.

For who in glory did on Horeb's height
Descend to Moses in the bush of flame,
And bade him go and stand in Pharaoh's sight —
Who once to Israel's pious shepherd came,
And sent him forth, his champion in the fight, —
Who aye hath loved the lowly shepherd train, —
He, from these leafy boughs, thus spake to me,
"Go forth! Thou shalt on earth my witness be.

"Thou in rude armor must thy limbs invest,
A plate of steel upon thy bosom wear;
Vain earthly love may never stir thy breast,
Nor passion's sinful glow be kindled there.
Ne'er with the bride-wreath shall thy locks be dressed,
Nor on thy bosom bloom an infant fair;
But war's triumphant glory shall be thine;
Thy martial fame all women's shall outshine.

"For when in fight the stoutest hearts despair,
When direful ruin threatens France, forlorn,

Then thou aloft my oriflamme shalt bear,
And swiftly as the reaper mows the corn,
Thou shalt lay low the haughty conqueror;
His fortune's wheel thou rapidly shalt turn,
To Gaul's heroic sons deliverance bring,
Relieve beleaguered Rheims, and crown thy king!"

The heavenly spirit promised me a sign;
He sends the helmet, it hath come from him.
Its iron filleth me with strength divine,
I feel the courage of the cherubim;
As with the rushing of a mighty wind
It drives me forth to join the battle's din;
The clanging trumpets sound, the chargers rear,
And the loud war-cry thunders in mine ear.

[*She goes out.*

ACT I.

Scene I.

The royal residence at Chinon.

Dunois *and* Duchatel.

Dunois.   No longer I'll endure it.   I renounce
This recreant monarch who forsakes himself.
My valiant heart doth bleed, and I could rain
Hot tear-drops from mine eyes, that robber-swords
Partition thus the royal realm of France;
That cities, ancient as the monarchy,
Deliver to the foe the rusty keys,
While here in idle and inglorious ease
We lose the precious season of redemption.
Tidings of Orleans' peril reach mine ear,
Hither I sped from distant Normandy,
Thinking, arrayed in panoply of war,
To find the monarch with his marshalled hosts;
And find him — here! begirt with troubadours,
And juggling knaves, engaged in solving riddles,
And planning festivals in Sorel's honor,
As brooded o'er the land profoundest peace!

The Constable hath gone; he will not brook
Longer the spectacle of shame. I, too,
Depart, and leave him to his evil fate.
DUCH.   Here comes the king.

SCENE II.

KING CHARLES. *The same.*

CHAS.   The Constable hath sent us back his sword
And doth renounce our service.   Now, by heaven!
He thus hath rid us of a churlish man,
Who insolently sought to lord it o'er us.
DUNOIS.   A man is precious in such perilous times;
I would not deal thus lightly with his loss.
CHAS.   Thou speakest thus from love of opposition;
While he was here thou never wert his friend.
DUNOIS.   He was a tiresome, proud, vexatious fool,
Who never could resolve.   For once, however,
He hath resolved.   Betimes he goeth hence,
Where honor can no longer be achieved.
CHAS.   Thou'rt in a pleasant humor; undisturbed
I'll leave thee to enjoy it.   Hark, Duchatel!
Ambassadors are here from old King René,
Of tuneful songs the master, far renowned.
Let them as honored guests be entertained,
And unto each present a chain of gold.
                                        [*To the Bastard.*
Why smilest thou, Dunois?
DUNOIS.   That from thy mouth
Thou shakest golden chains.
DUCHATEL.   Alas! my king!
No gold existeth in thy treasury.
CHAS.   Then gold must be procured.   It must not be
That bards unhonored from our court depart.
'Tis they who make our barren sceptre bloom,
'Tis they who wreath around our fruitless crown
Life's joyous branch of never-fading green.
Reigning, they justly rank themselves as kings,
Of gentle wishes they erect their throne,
Their harmless realm existeth not in space;

Hence should the bard accompany the king,
Life's higher sphere the heritage of both!

DUCH. My royal liege! I sought to spare thine ear
So long as aid and counsel could be found;
Now dire necessity doth loose my tongue.
Naught hast thou now in presents to bestow,
Thou hast not wherewithal to live to-morrow!
The spring-tide of thy fortune is run out,
And lowest ebb is in thy treasury!
The soldiers, disappointed of their pay,
With sullen murmurs, threaten to retire.
My counsel faileth, not with royal splendor
But meagerly, to furnish out thy household.

CHAS. My royal customs pledge, and borrow gold
From the Lombardians.

DUCHATEL. Sire, thy revenues,
Thy royal customs are for three years pledged.

DUNOIS. And pledge meanwhile and kingdom both are
lost.

CHAS. Still many rich and beauteous lands are ours.

DUNOIS. So long as God and Talbot's sword permit!
When Orleans falleth into English hands
Then with King René thou may'st tend thy sheep!

CHAS. Still at this king thou lov'st to point thy jest;
Yet 'tis this lackland monarch who to-day
Hath with a princely crown invested me.

DUNOIS. Not, in the name of heaven, with that of Naples,
Which is for sale, I hear, since he kept sheep.

CHAS. It is a sportive festival, a jest,
Wherein he giveth to his fancy play,
To found a world all innocent and pure
In this barbaric, rude reality.
Yet noble — ay, right royal is his aim!
He will again restore the golden age,
When gentle manners reigned, when faithful love
The heroic hearts of valiant knights inspired,
And noble women, whose accomplished taste
Diffuseth grace around, in judgment sat.
The old man dwelleth in those bygone times,
And in our workday world would realize
The dreams of ancient bards, who picture life

'Mid bowers celestial, throned on golden clouds.
He hath established hence a court of love
Where valiant knights may dwell, and homage yield
To noble women, who are there enthroned,
And where pure love and true may find a home.
Me he hath chosen as the prince of love.

DUNOIS.   I am not such a base, degenerate churl
As love's dominion rudely to assail.
I am her son, from her derive my name,
And in her kingdom lies my heritage.
The Prince of Orleans was my sire, and while
No woman's heart was proof against his love,
No hostile fortress could withstand his shock!
Wilt thou, indeed, with honor name thyself
The prince of love — be bravest of the brave!
As I have read in those old chronicles,
Love aye went coupled with heroic deeds,
And valiant heroes, not inglorious shepherds,
So legends tell us, graced King Arthur's board.
The man whose valor is not beauty's shield
Is all unworthy of her golden prize.
Here the arena! combat for the crown,
Thy royal heritage!   With knightly sword
Thy lady's honor and thy realm defend —
And hast thou with hot valor snatched the crown
From streams of hostile blood, — then is the time,
And it would well become thee as a prince,
Love's myrtle chaplet round thy brows to wreathe.

CHARLES (*to a* PAGE, *who enters*).
What is the matter?

PAGE.   Senators from Orleans
Entreat an audience, sire.

CHARLES.   Conduct them hither!
[PAGE *retires.*
Doubtless they succor need; what can I do,
Myself all-succorless!

SCENE III.
The same.   Three SENATORS.

CHAS.   Welcome, my trusty citizens of Orleans!
What tidings bring ye from my faithful town?

Doth she continue with her wonted zeal
Still bravely to withstand the leaguering foe?
SENAT. Ah, sire! the city's peril is extreme;
And giant ruin, waxing hour by hour,
Still onward strides. The bulwarks are destroyed —
The foe at each assault advantage gains;
Bare of defenders are the city walls,
For with rash valor forth our soldiers rush,
While few, alas! return to view their homes,
And famine's scourge impendeth o'er the town.
In this extremity the noble Count
Of Rochepierre, commander of the town,
Hath made a compact with the enemy,
According to old custom, to yield up,
On the twelfth day, the city to the foe,
Unless, meanwhile, before the town appear
A host of magnitude to raise the siege.
  [DUNOIS *manifests the strongest indignation.*
CHAS. The interval is brief.
SENATOR.   We hither come,
Attended by a hostile retinue,
To implore thee, sire, to pity thy poor town,
And to send succor ere the appointed day,
When, if still unrelieved, she must surrender.
DUNOIS. And could Saintrailles consent to give his
  voice
To such a shameful compact?
SENATOR.   Never, sir!
Long as the hero lived, none dared to breathe
A single word of treaty or surrender.
DUNOIS. He then is dead?
SENATOR.   The noble hero fell,
His monarch's cause defending on our walls.
CHAS. What! Saintrailles dead! Oh, in that single man
  A host is foundered!
  [*A Knight enters and speaks apart with* DUNOIS, *who
  starts with surprise.*
DUNOIS.   That too!
CHARLES.   Well? What is it?
DUNOIS. Count Douglass sendeth here. The Scottish
  troops

Revolt, and threaten to retire at once,
Unless their full arrears are paid to-day.
CHAS. Duchatel!
DUCHATEL (*shrugs his shoulders*).
                    Sire! I know not what to counsel.
CHAS. Pledge, promise all, even unto half my realm.
DUCHAT. 'Tis vain! They have been fed with hope too
        often!
CHAS. They are the finest troops of all my host!
    They must not now, not now abandon me!
SENATOR (*throwing himself at the* KING'S *feet*).
    Oh, king, assist us! Think of our distress!
CHARLES (*in despair*).
    How! Can I summon armies from the earth?
    Or grow a cornfield on my open palm?
    Rend me in pieces! Pluck my bleeding heart
    Forth from my breast, and coin it 'stead of gold!
    I've blood for you, but neither coin nor troops.
    [*He sees* SOREL *approach, and hastens towards her with*
        outstretched arms.

SCENE IV.

The same. AGNES SOREL, *a casket in her hand.*

CHAS. My Agnes! Oh, my love! my dearest life!
    Thou comest here to snatch me from despair!
    Refuge I take within thy loving arms;
    Possessing thee I feel that naught is lost.
SOREL. My king, beloved!
            [*Looking round with an anxious, inquiring gaze*
                            Dunois! Say, is it true,
    Duchatel?
DUCHATEL.   'Tis, alas!
SOREL.   So great the need?
    No treasure left? The soldiers will disband?
DUCHAT. Alas! it is too true!
SOREL (*giving him the casket*). Here — here is gold,
    Here too are jewels! Melt my silver down!
    Sell, pledge my castles — on my fair domains
    In Provence, treasure raise — turn all to gold,
    Appease the troops! No time is to be lost!
                        [*She urges him to depart*

CHAS.   Well now, Dunois! Duchatel! Do ye still
  Account me poor, when I possess the crown
  Of womankind? She's nobly born as I;
  The royal blood of Valois not more pure;
  The most exalted throne she would adorn —
  Yet she rejects it with disdain, and claims
  No other title than to be my love.
  No gift more costly will she e'er receive
  Than early flower in winter, or rare fruit!
  No sacrifice on my part she permits,
  Yet sacrificeth all she had to me!
  With generous spirit she doth venture all
  Her wealth and fortune in my sinking bark.
DUNOIS.   Ay, she is mad indeed, my king, as thou;
  She throws her all into a burning house,
  And draweth water in the leaky vessel
  Of the Danaïdes. Thee she will not save,
  And in thy ruin but involve herself.
SOREL.   Believe him not! Full many a time he hath
  Perilled his life for thee, and now, forsooth,
  Chafeth because I risk my worthless gold!
  How? Have I freely sacrificed to thee
  What is esteemed far more than gold and pearls,
  And shall I now hold back the gifts of fortune?
  Oh, come! Let my example challenge thee
  To noble self-denial! Let's at once
  Cast off the needless ornaments of life!
  Thy courtiers metamorphose into soldiers;
  Thy gold transmute to iron; all thou hast,
  With resolute daring, venture for thy crown!
  Peril and want we will participate!
  Let us bestride the war-horse, and expose
  Our tender person to the fiery glow
  Of the hot sun, take for our canopy
  The clouds above, and make the stones our pillow.
  The rudest warrier, when he sees his king
  Bear hardship and privation like the meanest
  Will patiently endure his own hard lot!
CHARLES (*laughing*).
  Ay! now is realized an ancient word
  Of prophesy, once uttered by a nun

Of Clairmont, in prophetic mood, who said,
That through a woman's aid I o'er my foes
Should triumph, and achieve my father's crown.
Far off I sought her in the English camp;
I strove to reconcile a mother's heart;
Here stands the heroine — my guide to Rheims!
My Agnes! I shall triumph through thy love!

SOREL. Thou'lt triumph through the valiant swords of
    friends.

CHAS. And from my foes' dissensions much I hope —
For sure intelligence hath reached mine ear,
That 'twixt these English lords and Burgundy
Things do not stand precisely as they did;
Hence to the duke I have despatched La Hire,
To try if he can lead my angry vassal
Back to his ancient loyalty and faith:
Each moment now I look for his return.

DUCHATEL (*at the window*).
A knight e'en now dismounteth in the court.

CHAS. A welcome messenger! We soon shall learn
Whether we're doomed to conquer or to yield.

SCENE V.

The same. LA HIRE.

CHARLES (*meeting him*).
Hope bringest thou, or not? Be brief, La Hire,
Out with thy tidings! What must we expect?

HIRE. Expect naught, sire, save from thine own good
    sword.

CHAS. The haughty duke will not be reconciled!
Speak! How did he receive my embassy?

HIRE. His first and unconditional demand,
Ere he consent to listen to thine errand,
Is that Duchatel be delivered up,
Whom he doth name the murderer of his sire.

CHAS. This base condition we reject with scorn!

HIRE. Then be the league dissolved ere it commence!

CHAS. Hast thou thereon, as I commanded thee,
Challenged the duke to meet him in fair fight
On Montereau's bridge, whereon his father fell?

HIRE. Before him on the ground I flung thy glove,
And said: "Thou wouldst forget thy majesty,
And like a knight do battle for thy realm."
He scornfully rejoined "He needed not
To fight for that which he possessed already,
But if thou wert so eager for the fray,
Before the walls of Orleans thou wouldst find him,
Whither he purposed going on the morrow;"
Thereon he laughing turned his back upon me.
CHAS. Say, did not justice raise her sacred voice,
Within the precincts of my parliament?
HIRE. The rage of party, sire, hath silenced her.
An edict of the parliament declares
Thee and thy race excluded from the throne.
DUNOIS. These upstart burghers' haughty insolence!
CHAS. Hast thou attempted with my mother aught?
HIRE. With her?
CHARLES.   Ay! How did she demean herself?
LA HIRE (*after a few moments' reflection*).
I chanced to step within St. Denis' walls
Precisely at the royal coronation.
The crowds were dressed as for a festival;
Triumphal arches rose in every street
Through which the English monarch was to pass.
The way was strewed with flowers, and with huzzas,
As France some brilliant conquest had achieved,
The people thronged around the royal car.
SOREL. They could huzza — huzza, while trampling thus
Upon a gracious sovereign's loving heart!
HIRE. I saw young Harry Lancaster — the boy —
On good St. Lewis' regal chair enthroned;
On either side his haughty uncles stood,
Bedford and Gloucester, and before him kneeled,
To render homage for his lands, Duke Philip.
CHAS. Oh, peer dishonored! Oh, unworthy cousin!
HIRE. The child was timid, and his footing lost
As up the steps he mounted towards the throne.
An evil omen! murmured forth the crowd,
And scornful laughter burst on every side.
Then forward stepped Queen Isabel — thy mother,
And — but it angers me to utter it!

CHARLES.   Say on.
HIRE.   Within her arms she clasped the boy,
    And herself placed him on thy father's throne.
CHAS.   Oh, mother! mother!
LA HIRE.   E'en the murderous bands
    Of the Burgundians, at this spectacle,
    Evinced some tokens of indignant shame.
    The queen perceived it, and addressed the crowds,
    Exclaiming with loud voice: " Be grateful, French-
        men,
    That I engraft upon a sickly stock
    A healthy scion, and redeem you from
    The misbegotten son of a mad sire!"
    [*The* KING *hides his face ;* AGNES *hastens towards him*
        and clasps him in her arms; all the bystanders
        express aversion and horror.
DUNOIS.   She-wolf of France!   Rage-breathing Megara!
CHARLES (*after a pause, to the* SENATORS).
    Yourselves have heard the posture of affairs.
    Delay no longer, back return to Orleans,
    And bear this message to my faithful town ;
    I do absolve my subjects from their oath,
    Their own best interests let them now consult,
    And yield them to the Duke of Burgundy ;
    'Yclept the Good, he need must prove humane.
DUNOIS.   What say'st thou, sire?   Thou wilt abandon
        Orleans!
SENATOR (*kneels down*).
    My king!   Abandon not thy faithful town!
    Consign her not to England's harsh control.
    She is a precious jewel in the crown,
    And none hath more inviolate faith maintained
    Towards the kings, thy royal ancestors.
DUNOIS.   Have we been routed?   Is it lawful, sire,
    To leave the English masters of the field,
    Without a single stroke to save the town?
    And thinkest thou, with careless breath, forsooth,
    Ere blood hath flowed, rashly to give away
    The fairest city from the heart of France?
CHAS.   Blood hath been poured forth freely, and in vain!
    The hand of heaven is visibly against me;

In every battle is my host o'erthrown,
I am rejected of my parliament,
My capital, my people, hail me foe,
Those of my blood, — my nearest relatives, —
Forsake me and betray — and my own mother
Doth nurture at her breast the hostile brood.
Beyond the Loire we will retire, and yield
To the o'ermastering hand of destiny
Which sideth with the English.

SOREL.   God forbid
That we in weak despair should quit this realm!
This utterance came not from thy heart, my king,
Thy noble heart, which hath been sorely riven
By the fell deed of thy unnatural mother,
Thou'lt be thyself again, right valiantly
Thou'lt battle with thine adverse destiny,
Which doth oppose thee with relentless ire.

CHARLES (*lost in gloomy thought*).
Is it not true? A dark and ominous doom
Impendeth o'er the heaven-abandoned house
Of Valois — there preside the avenging powers,
To whom a mother's crime unbarred the way.
For thirty years my sire in madness raved;
Already have three elder brothers been
Mowed down by death; 'tis the decree of heaven,
The house of the Sixth Charles is doomed to fall.

SOREL.   In thee 'twill rise with renovated life!
Oh, in thyself have faith! — believe me, king,
Not vainly hath a gracious destiny
Redeemed thee from the ruin of thy house,
And by thy brethren's death exalted thee,
The youngest born, to an unlooked-for throne
Heaven in thy gentle spirit hath prepared
The leech to remedy the thousand ills
By party rage inflicted on the land.
The flames of civil discord thou wilt quench,
And my heart tells me thou'lt establish peace,
And found anew the monarchy of France.

CHAS.   Not I! The rude and storm-vexed times require
A pilot formed by nature to command.
A peaceful nation I could render happy,

A wild, rebellious people not subdue.
I never with the sword could open hearts
Against me closed in hatred's cold reserve.
SOREL. The people's eye is dimmed, an error blinds
          them,
But this delusion will not long endure;
The day is not far distant when the love
Deep rooted in the bosom of the French,
Towards their native monarch, will revive,
Together with the ancient jealousy,
Which forms a barrier 'twixt the hostile nations.
The haughty foe precipitates his doom.
Hence, with rash haste abandon not the field,
With dauntless front contest each foot of ground,
As thine own heart defend the town of Orleans!
Let every boat be sunk beneath the wave,
Each bridge be burned, sooner than carry thee
Across the Loire, the boundary of thy realm,
The Stygian flood, o'er which there's no return.
CHAS. What could be done I have done.   I have
          offered,
In single fight, to combat for the crown.
I was refused.   In vain my people bleed,
In vain my towns are levelled with the dust.
Shall I, like that unnatural mother, see
My child in pieces severed with the sword?
No; I forego my claim, that it may live.
DUNOIS. How, sire!   Is this fit language for a king?
Is a crown thus renounced?   Thy meanest subject.
For his opinion's sake, his hate and love,
Sets property and life upon a cast;
When civil war hangs out her bloody flag,
Each private end is drowned in party zeal.
The husbandman forsakes his plough, the wife
Neglects her distaff ; children, and old men,
Don the rude garb of war; the citizen
Consigns his town to the devouring flames,
The peasant burns the produce of his fields;
And all to injure or advantage thee,
And to achieve the purpose of his heart.
Men show no mercy, and they wish for none,

When they at honor's call maintain the fight,
Or for their idols or their gods contend.
A truce to such effeminate pity, then,
Which is not suited to a monarch's breast.
Thou didst not heedlessly provoke the war;
As it commenced, so let it spend its fury.
It is the law of destiny that nations
Should for their monarchs immolate themselves.
We Frenchmen recognize this sacred law,
Nor would annul it. Base, indeed, the nation
That for its honor ventures not its all.

CHARLES (*to the* SENATORS).
　　You've heard my last resolve; expect no other.
　　May God protect you! I can do no more.

DUNOIS. As thou dost turn thy back upon thy realm,
　　So may the God of battle aye avert
　　His visage from thee. Thou forsak'st thyself,
　　So I forsake thee. Not the power combined
　　Of England and rebellious Burgundy,
　　Thy own mean spirit hurls thee from the throne.
　　Born heroes ever were the kings of France;
　　Thou wert a craven, even from thy birth.
　　　　　　　　　　　　　[*To the* SENATORS.
　　The king abandons you. But I will throw
　　Myself into your town — my father's town —
　　And 'neath its ruins find a soldier's grave.
　　　[*He is about to depart.* AGNES SOREL *detains him.*

SOREL (*to the* KING).
　　Oh, let him not depart in anger from thee!
　　Harsh words his lips have uttered, but his heart
　　Is true as gold. 'Tis he, himself, my king,
　　Who loves thee, and hath often bled for thee.
　　Dunois, confess, the heat of noble wrath
　　Made thee forget thyself; and oh, do thou
　　Forgive a faithful friend's o'erhasty speech!
　　Come, let me quickly reconcile your hearts,
　　Ere anger bursteth forth in quenchless flame.
　　[DUNOIS *looks fixedly at the* KING, *and appears to
　　　　await an answer.*

CHAS. Our way lies over the Loire. Duchatel,
　　See all our equipage embarked.

DUNOIS (*quickly to* SOREL).   Farewell.
> [*He turns quickly round, and goes out. The* SENATORS *follow.*

SOREL (*wringing her hands in despair*).
     Oh, if he goes, we are forsaken quite!
     Follow, La Hire!   Oh, seek to soften him!
> [LA HIRE *goes out.*

SCENE VI.

CHARLES, SOREL, DUCHATEL.

CHAS.   Is, then, the sceptre such a peerless treasure?
     Is it so hard to loose it from our grasp?
     Believe me, 'tis more galling to endure
     The domineering rule of these proud vassals.
     To be dependent on their will and pleasure
     Is, to a noble heart, more bitter far
     Than to submit to fate.
> [*To* DUCHATEL, *who still lingers.*

                 Duchatel, go,
     And do what I commanded.

DUCHATEL (*throws himself at the* KING'S *feet*).
                  Oh, my king!

CHAS.   No more!   Thou'st heard my absolute resolve!

DUCHATEL.   Sire, with the Duke of Burgundy make
         peace!
     'Tis the sole outlet from destruction left!

CHAS.   Thou giv'st this counsel, and thy blood alone
     Can ratify this peace.

DUCHATEL.   Here is my head.
     I oft have risked it for thee in the fight,
     And with a joyful spirit I, for thee,
     Would lay it down upon the block of death.
     Conciliate the duke!   Deliver me
     To the full measure of his wrath, and let
     My flowing blood appease the ancient hate.

CHARLES (*looks at him for some time in silence, and with deep emotion*).
     Can it be true?   Am I, then, sunk so low,
     That even friends, who read my inmost heart,
     Point out for my escape the path of shame?

Yes, now I recognize my abject fall.
My honor is no more confided in.
DUCHATEL.　　Reflect——
CHARLES.　　　　　　　Be silent, and incense me not!
Had I ten realms, on which to turn my back,
With my friend's life I would not purchase them.
Do what I have commanded.　Hence, and see
My equipage embarked.
DUCHATEL.　　　　　　'Twill speedily
Be done.

> [*He stands up and retires.　*AGNES SOREL *weeps passionately.*

SCENE VII.

The royal palace at Chinon.

CHARLES, AGNES SOREL.

CHARLES (*seizing the hand of* AGNES).
　　　　　　My Agnes, be not sorrowful!
Beyond the Loire we still shall find a France;
We are departing to a happier land,
Where laughs a milder, an unclouded sky,
And gales more genial blow; we there shall meet
More gentle manners; song abideth there,
And love and life in richer beauty bloom.
SOREL.　Oh, must I contemplate this day of woe!
The king must roam in banishment! the son
Depart, an exile from his father's house,
And turn his back upon his childhood's home!
Oh, pleasant, happy land that we forsake,
Ne'er shall we tread thee joyously again.

SCENE VIII.

LA HIRE *returns,* CHARLES, SOREL.

SOREL.　You come alone?　You do not bring him back?
　　　　　　　[*Observing him more closely.*
La Hire!　What news?　What does that look announce?
Some new calamity?

LA HIRE. Calamity
Hath spent itself; sunshine is now returned.
SOREL. What is it? I implore you.
LA HIRE (*to the* KING). Summon back
The delegates from Orleans.
CHARLES. Why? What is it?
LA HIRE. Summon them back! Thy fortune is reversed.
A battle has been fought, and thou hast conquered.
SOREL. Conquered! Oh, heavenly music of that word!
CHAS. La Hire! A fabulous report deceives thee;
Conquered! In conquest I believe no more.
LA HIRE. Still greater wonders thou wilt soon believe.
Here cometh the archbishop. To thine arms
He leadeth back Dunois.
SOREL. O beauteous flower
Of victory, which doth the heavenly fruits
Of peace and reconcilement bear at once!

SCENE IX.

The same, ARCHBISHOP OF RHEIMS, DUNOIS, DUCHATEL,
with RAOUL, *a Knight in armor.*

ARCHBISHOP (*leading* DUNOIS *to the* KING, *and joining
their hands*).
Princes, embrace! Let rage and discord cease,
Since Heaven itself hath for our cause declared.
[DUNOIS *embraces the* KING
CHAS. Relieve my wonder and perplexity.
What may this solemn earnestness portend?
Whence this unlooked-for change of fortune?
ARCHBISHOP (*leads the* KNIGHT *forward, and presents him
to the* KING). Speak!
RAOUL. We had assembled sixteen regiments
Of Lotharingian troops to join your host;
And Baudricourt, a knight of Vaucouleurs,
Was our commander. Having gained the heights
By Vermanton, we wound our downward way
Into the valley watered by the Yonne.
There, in the plain before us, lay the foe,
And when we turned, arms glittered in our rear.
We saw ourselves surrounded by two hosts,

And could not hope for conquest or for flight.
Then sank the bravest heart, and in despair
We all prepared to lay our weapons down.
The leaders with each other anxiously
Sought counsel and found none; when to our eyes
A spectacle of wonder showed itself.
For suddenly from forth the thickets' depths
A maiden, on her head a polished helm,
Like a war-goddess, issued; terrible
Yet lovely was her aspect, and her hair
In dusky ringlets round her shoulders fell.
A heavenly radiance shone around the height;
When she upraised her voice and thus addressed us :
" Why be dismayed, brave Frenchmen? On the
    foe !
Were they more numerous than the ocean sands,
God and the holy maiden lead you on "!
Then quickly from the standard-bearer's hand
She snatched the banner, and before our troop
With valiant bearing strode the wond'rous maid.
Silent with awe, scarce knowing what we did,
The banner and the maiden we pursue,
And fired with ardor, rush upon the foe,
Who, much amazed, stand motionless and view
The miracle with fixed and wondering gaze.
Then, as if seized by terror sent from God,
They suddenly betake themselves to flight,
And casting arms and armor to the ground,
Disperse in wild disorder o'er the field.
No leader's call, no signal now avails;
Senseless from terror, without looking back,
Horses and men plunge headlong in the stream,
Where they without resistance are despatched.
It was a slaughter rather than a fight !
Two thousand of the foe bestrewed the field,
Not reckoning numbers swallowed by the flood,
While of our company not one was slain.

CHAS. 'Tis strange, by heaven! most wonderful and
        strange !
SOREL. A maiden worked this miracle, you say?
    Whence did she come ? Who is she ?

RAOUL.   Who she is
   She will reveal to no one but the king!
   She calls herself a seer and prophetess
   Ordained by God, and promises to raise
   The siege of Orleans ere the moon shall change.
   The people credit her, and thirst for war.
   The host she follows — she'll be here anon.
  *[The ringing of bells is heard, together with the clang
    of arms.*
   Hark to the din!   The pealing of the bells!
   'Tis she!   The people greet God's messenger.
CHARLES (*to* DUCHATEL).
   Conduct her thither.   [*To the* ARCHBISHOP.
               What should I believe?
   A maiden brings me conquest even now,
   When naught can save me but a hand divine!
   This is not in the common course of things.
   And dare I here believe a miracle?
MANY VOICES (*behind the scene*).
   Hail to the maiden! — the deliverer!
CHAS.   She comes!   Dunois, now occupy my place!
   We will make trial of this wond'rous maid.
   Is she indeed inspired and sent by God
   She will be able to discern the king.
  *[*DUNOIS *seats himself; the* KING *stands at his right
    hand,* AGNES SOREL *near him; the* ARCHBISHOP *and
    the others opposite; so that the intermediate space
    remains vacant.*

SCENE X.

The same.   JOHANNA, *accompanied by the councillors
and many knights, who occupy the background of the
scene; she advances with noble bearing, and slowly
surveys the company.*

DUNOIS (*after a long and solemn pause*).
   Art thou the wond'rous maiden ——
JOHANNA (*interrupts him, regarding him with dignity*).
   Bastard of Orleans, thou wilt tempt thy God!
   This place abandon, which becomes thee not!
   To this more mighty one the maid is sent.
  [With a firm step she approaches the KING, *bows one*

knee before him, and, rising immediately, steps back.
All present express their astonishment, DUNOIS *for-*
sakes his seat, which is occupied by the KING.

CHAS.   Maiden, thou ne'er hast seen my face before.
    Whence hast thou then this knowledge?
JOHANNA.   Thee I saw
    When none beside, save God in heaven, beheld
        thee.
        [*She approaches the* KING, *and speaks mysteriously.*
    Bethink thee, Dauphin, in the bygone night,
    When all around lay buried in deep sleep,
    Thou from thy couch didst rise and offer up
    An earnest prayer to God.   Let these retire
    And I will name the subject of thy prayer.
CHAS.   What I to Heaven confided need not be
    From men concealed.   Disclose to me my prayer,
    And I shall doubt no more that God inspires thee.
JOHAN.   Three prayers thou offeredst, Dauphin; listen
        now
    Whether I name them to thee!   Thou didst pray
    That if there were appended to this crown
    Unjust possession, or if heavy guilt,
    Not yet atoned for, from thy father's times,
    Occasioned this most lamentable war,
    God would accept thee as a sacrifice,
    Have mercy on thy people, and pour forth
    Upon thy head the chalice of his wrath.
CHARLES (*steps back with awe*).
    Who art thou, mighty one?   Whence comest thou?
                        [*All express their astonishment.*
JOHAN.   To God thou offeredst this second prayer:
    That if it were his will and high decree
    To take away the sceptre from thy race,
    And from thee to withdraw whate'er thy sires,
    The monarchs of this kingdom, once possessed,
    He in his mercy would preserve to thee
    Three priceless treasures — a contented heart,
    Thy friend's affection, and thine Agnes' love.
    [*The* KING *conceals his face: the spectators express*
        their astonishment.   After a pause.
    Thy third petition shall I name to thee?

CHAS.   Enough; I credit thee! This doth surpass
    Mere human knowledge: thou art sent by God!
ARCHB.   Who art thou, wonderful and holy maid?
    What favored region bore thee? What blest pair,
    Beloved of Heaven, may claim thee as their child?
JOHAN.   Most reverend father, I am named Johanna,
    I am a shepherd's lowly daughter, born
    In Dom Remi, a village of my king.
    Included in the diocese of Toul,
    And from a child I kept my father's sheep.
    And much and frequently I heard them tell
    Of the strange islanders, who o'er the sea
    Had come to make us slaves, and on us force
    A foreign lord, who loveth not the people;
    How the great city, Paris, they had seized,
    And had usurped dominion o'er the realm.
    Then earnestly God's Mother I implored
    To save us from the shame of foreign chains,
    And to preserve to us our lawful king.
    Not distant from my native village stands
    An ancient image of the Virgin blest,
    To which the pious pilgrims oft repaired;
    Hard by a holy oak, of blessed power,
    Standeth, far-famed through wonders manifold.
    Beneath the oak's broad shade I loved to sit
    Tending my flock — my heart still drew me there.
    And if by chance among the desert hills
    A lambkin strayed, 'twas shown me in a dream,
    When in the shadow of this oak I slept.
    And once, when through the night beneath this tree
    In pious adoration I had sat,
    Resisting sleep, the Holy One appeared,
    Bearing a sword and banner, otherwise
    Clad like a shepherdess, and thus she spake:
" 'Tis I; arise, Johanna! leave thy flock,
    The Lord appoints thee to another task!
    Receive this banner! Gird thee with this sword!
    Therewith exterminate my people's foes;
    Conduct to Rheims thy royal master's son,
    And crown him with the kingly diadem!"
    And I made answer: "How may I presume

To undertake such deeds, a tender maid,
Unpractised in the dreadful art of war!"
And she replied: "A maiden pure and chaste
Achieves whate'er on earth is glorious
If she to eartly love ne'er yields her heart.
Look upon me! a virgin, like thyself;
I to the Christ, the Lord divine, gave birth,
And am myself divine!" Mine eyelids then
She touched, and when I upward turned my gaze,
Heaven's wide expanse was filled with angel-boys,
Who bore white lilies in their hands, while tones
Of sweetest music floated through the air.
And thus on three successive nights appeared
The Holy One, and cried, — "Arise, Johanna!
The Lord appoints thee to another task!"
And when the third night she revealed herself,
Wrathful she seemed, and chiding spake these words
"Obedience, woman's duty here on earth;
Severe endurance is her heavy doom;
She must be purified through discipline;
Who serveth here, is glorified above!"
While thus she spake, she let her shepherd garb
Fail from her, and as Queen of Heaven stood forth
Enshrined in radiant light, while golden clouds
Upbore her slowly to the realms of bliss.
[*All are moved;* AGNES SOREL *weeping, hides her face
on the bosom of the* KING.
ARCHBISHOP (*after a long pause*).
Before divine credentials such as these
Each doubt of earthly prudence must subside,
Her deeds attest the truth of what she speaks,
For God alone such wonders can achieve.
DUNOIS. I credit not her wonders, but her eyes
Which beam with innocence and purity.
CHAS. Am I, a sinner, worthy of such favor?
Infallible, All-searching eye, thou seest
Mine inmost heart, my deep humility!
JOHAN. Humility shines brightly in the skies;
Thou art abased, hence God exalteth thee.
CHAS. Shall I indeed withstand mine enemies?
JOHAN. France I will lay submissive at thy feet!

CHAS. And Orleans, say'st thou, will not be surrendered?
JOHAN. The Loire shall sooner roll its waters back.
CHAS. Shall I in triumph enter into Rheims?
JOHAN. I through ten thousand foes will lead thee there.
[*The knights make a noise with their lances and shields,*
and evince signs of courage.
DUNOIS. Appoint the maiden to command the host!
We follow blindly whereso'er she leads!
The Holy One's prophetic eye shall guide,
And this brave sword from danger shall protect
her!
HIRE. A universe in arms we will not fear,
If she, the mighty one, precede our troops.
The God of battle walketh by her side;
Let her conduct us on to victory!
[*The knights clang their arms and step forward.*
CHAS. Yes, holy maiden, do thou lead mine host;
My chiefs and warriors shall submit to thee.
This sword of matchless temper, proved in war,
Sent back in anger by the Constable,
Hath found a hand more worthy. Prophetess,
Do thou receive it, and henceforward be ——
JOHAN. No, noble Dauphin! conquest to my liege
Is not accorded through this instrument
Of earthly might. I know another sword
Wherewith I am to conquer, which to thee,
I, as the Spirit taught, will indicate;
Let it be hither brought.
CHARLES. Name it, Johanna.
JOHAN. Send to the ancient town of Fierbois;
There in Saint Catherine's churchyard is a vault
Where lie in heaps the spoils of bygone war.
Among them is the sword which I must use.
It by three golden lilies may be known,
Upon the blade impressed. Let it be brought,
For thou, my liege, shalt conquer through this sword.
CHAS. Perform what she commands.
JOHANNA. And a white banner,
Edged with a purple border, let me bear.
Upon this banner let the Queen of Heaven
Be pictured, with the beauteous Jesus child

THE MAID OF ORLEANS. 165

Floating in glory o'er this earthly ball.
For so the Holy Mother showed it me.
CHAS. So be it as thou sayest.
JOHANNA (*to the* ARCHBISHOP). Reverend bishop;
Lay on my head thy consecrated hands!
Pronounce a blessing, Father, on thy child!
                                    [*She kneels down.*
ARCH. Not blessings to receive, but to dispense
Art thou appointed. Go, with power divine!
But we are sinners all and most unworthy.
                              [*She rises: a* PAGE *enters.*
PAGE. A herald from the English generals.
JOHAN. Let him appear, for he is sent by God!
        [*The* KING *motions to the* PAGE, *who retires.*

SCENE XI.

The HERALD. *The same.*

CHAS. Thy tidings, herald? What thy message!
        Speak!
HER. Who is it, who for Charles of Valois,
The Count of Pointhieu, in this presence speaks?
DUNOIS. Unworthy herald! base, insulting knave!
Dost thou presume the monarch of the French
Thus in his own dominions to deny?
Thou art protected by thine office, else ——
HER. One king alone is recognized by France,
And he resideth in the English camp.
CHAS. Peace, peace, good cousin! Speak thy message,
        herald!
HER. My noble general laments the blood
Which hath already flowed, and still must flow.
Hence, in the scabbard holding back the sword,
Before by storm the town of Orleans falls,
He offers thee an amicable treaty.
CHAS. Proceed!
JOHANNA (*stepping forward*).
                        Permit me, Dauphin, in thy stead,
To parley with this herald.
CHARLES.   Do so, maid!
Determine thou, for peace, or bloody war.

JOHANNA (*to the* HERALD).   [mouth?
    Who sendeth thee?   Who speaketh through thy
HER.   The Earl of Salisbury; the British chief.
JOHAN.   Herald, 'tis false!   The earl speaks not through
        thee.
    Only the living speak, the dead are silent.
HER.   The earl is well, and full of lusty strength;
    He lives to bring down ruin on your heads.
JOHAN.   When thou didst quit the British camp he lived.
    This morn, while gazing from Le Tournelle's tower,
    A ball from Orleans struck him to the ground.
    Smilest thou that I discern what is remote?
    Not to my words give credence; but believe
    The witness of thine eyes! his funeral train
    Thou shalt encounter as thou goest hence!
    Now, herald, speak, and do thine errand here.
HER.   If what is hidden thou canst thus reveal,
    Thou knowest mine errand ere I tell it thee.
JOHAN.   It boots me not to know it.   But do thou
    Give ear unto my words!   This message bear
    In answer to the lords who sent thee here.
    Monarch of England, and ye haughty dukes,
    Bedford and Gloucester, regents of this realm!
    To heaven's high King ye are accountable
    For all the blood that hath been shed!   Restore
    The keys of all the cities ta'en by force
    In opposition to God's holy law!
    The maiden cometh from the King of Heaven
    And offers you or peace or bloody war.
    Choose ye! for this I say, that ye may know it:
    To you this beauteous realm is not assigned
    By Mary's son; — but God hath given it
    To Charles, my lord and Dauphin, who ere long
    Will enter Paris with a monarch's pomp,
    Attended by the great ones of his realm.
    Now, herald, go, and speedily depart,
    For ere thou canst attain the British camp
    And do thine errand, is the maiden there,
    To plant the sign of victory at Orleans.
[*She retires.   In the midst of a general movement, the
    curtain falls.*

ACT II.

Landscape, bounded by rocks.

SCENE I.

TALBOT *and* LIONEL, *English generals*, PHILIP, DUKE OF BURGUNDY, FASTOLFE, *and* CHATILLON, *with soldiers and banners.*

TALBOT. Here let us make a halt beneath these rocks,
And pitch our camp, in case our scattered troops,
Dispersed in panic fear, again should rally.
Choose trusty sentinels, and guard the heights!
'Tis true the darkness shields us from pursuit,
And sure I am, unless the foe have wings,
We need not fear surprisal.   Still 'tis well
To practice caution, for we have to do
With a bold foe, and have sustained defeat.
                    [FASTOLFE *goes out with the soldiers.*
LIONEL. Defeat!   My general, do not speak that word.
It stings me to the quick to think the French
To-day have seen the backs of Englishmen.
Oh, Orleans! Orleans! Grave of England's glory!
Our honor lies upon thy fatal plains
Defeat most ignominious and burlesque!
Who will in future years believe the tale!
The victors of Poictiers and Agincourt,
Cressy's bold heroes, routed by a woman?
BURG.   That must console us.   Not by mortal power,
But by the devil have we been o'erthrown!
TALBOT.   The devil of our own stupidity!
How, Burgundy?   Do princes quake and fear
Before the phantom which appals the vulgar?
Credulity is but a sorry cloak
For cowardice.   Your people first took flight.
BURG.   None stood their ground. The flight was general.
TALBOT.   'Tis false!   Your wing fled first.   You wildly broke
Into our camp, exclaiming: "Hell is loose,
The devil combats on the side of France!"
And thus you brought confusion 'mong our troops.
LIONEL.   You can't deny it.   Your wing yielded first.

BURG. Because the brunt of battle there commenced.
TALBOT. The maiden knew the weakness of our camp;
    She rightly judged where fear was to be found.
BURG. How? Shall the blame of our disaster rest
    With Burgundy?
LIONEL.   By heaven! were we alone,
    We English, never had we Orleans lost!
BURG. No, truly! for ye ne'er had Orleans seen!
    Who opened you a way into this realm,
    And reached you forth a kind and friendly hand
    When you descended on this hostile coast?
    Who was it crowned your Henry at Paris,
    And unto him subdued the people's hearts?
    Had this Burgundian arm not guided you
    Into this realm, by heaven you ne'er had seen
    The smoke ascending from a single hearth!
LIONEL. Were conquests with big words effected, duke
    You, doubtless, would have conquered France alone
BURG. The loss of Orleans angers you, and now
    You vent your gall on me, your friend and ally.
    What lost us Orleans but your avarice?
    The city was prepared to yield to me,
    Your envy was the sole impediment.
TALBOT. We did not undertake the siege for you.
BURG. How would it stand with you if I withdrew
    With all my host?
LIONEL.   We should not be worse off
    Than when, at Agincourt, we proved a match
    For you and all the banded power of France.
BURG. Yet much you stood in need of our alliance;
    The regent purchased it at heavy cost.
TALBOT. Most dearly, with the forfeit of our honor,
    At Orleans have we paid for it to-day.
BURG. Urge me no further, lords. Ye may repent it!
    Did I forsake the banners of my king,
    Draw down upon my head the traitor's name,
    To be insulted thus by foreigners?
    Why am I here to combat against France?
    If I must needs endure ingratitude,
    Let it come rather from my native king!
TALBOT. You're in communication with the Dauphin,

We know it well, but we soon shall find means
To guard ourselves 'gainst treason.
BURGUNDY.   Death and hell!
    Am I encountered thus? Chatillon, hark!
    Let all my troops prepare to quit the camp.
    We will retire into our own domain.
                    [CHATILLON *goes out.*
LIONEL. God speed you there! Never did Britain's fame
    More brightly shine than when she stood alone,
    Confiding solely in her own good sword.
    Let each one fight his battle for himself,
    For 'tis eternal truth that English blood
    Cannot, with honor, blend with blood of France.

SCENE II.

The same. QUEEN ISABEL, *attended by a* PAGE.

ISABEL. What must I hear? This fatal strife forbear!
    What brain-bewildering planet o'er your minds
    Sheds dire perplexity? When unity
    Alone can save you, will you part in hate,
    And, warring 'mong yourselves, prepare your doom?
    — I do entreat you, noble duke, recall
    Your hasty order. You, renowned Talbot,
    Seek to appease an irritated friend!
    Come, Lionel, aid me to reconcile
    These haughty spirits and establish peace.
LIONEL. Not I, madame. It is all one to me.
    'Tis my belief, when things are misallied,
    The sooner they part company the better.
ISABEL. How? Do the arts of hell, which on the field
    Wrought such disastrous ruin, even here
    Bewilder and befool us? Who began
    This fatal quarrel? Speak! Lord-general!
    Your own advantage did you so forget,
    As to offend your worthy friend and ally?
    What could you do without his powerful arm?
    'Twas he who placed your monarch on the throne,
    He holds him there, and he can hurl him thence;
    His army strengthens you — still more his name.
    Were England all her citizens to pour

Upon our coasts, she never o'er this realm
Would gain dominion did she stand alone;
No! France can only be subdued by France!
TALBOT. A faithful friend we honor as we ought;
Discretion warns us to beware the false.
BURG. The liar's brazen front beseemeth him
Who would absolve himself from gratitude.
ISABEL. How, noble duke? Could you so far renounce
Your princely honor, and your sense of shame,
As clasp the hand of him who slew your sire?
Are you so mad to entertain the thought
Of cordial reconcilement with the Dauphin,
Whom you yourself have hurled to ruin's brink?
His overthrow you have well nigh achieved,
And madly now would you renounce your work?
Here stand your allies. Your salvation lies
In an indissoluble bond with England?
BURG. Far is my thought from treaty with the Dauphin;
But the contempt and insolent demeanor
Of haughty England I will not endure.
ISABEL. Come, noble duke? Excuse a hasty word.
Heavy the grief which bows the general down,
And well you know misfortune makes unjust.
Come! come! embrace; let me this fatal breach
Repair at once, ere it becomes eternal.
TALBOT. What think you, Burgundy? A noble heart,
By reason vanquished, doth confess its fault.
A wise and prudent word the queen hath spoken;
Come, let my hand with friendly pressure heal
The wound inflicted by my angry tongue.
BURG. Discreet the counsel offered by the queen!
My just wrath yieldeth to necessity.
ISABEL. 'Tis well! Now, with a brotherly embrace
Confirm and seal the new-established bond;
And may the winds disperse what hath been spoken.
                    [BURGUNDY *and* TALBOT *embrace.*
LIONEL (*contemplating the group aside*).
Hail to an union by the furies planned!
ISABEL. Fate hath proved adverse, we have lost a battle,
But do not, therefore, let your courage sink.
The Dauphin, in despair of heavenly aid,

Doth make alliance with the powers of hell;
Vainly his soul he forfeits to the devil,
For hell itself cannot deliver him.
A conquering maiden leads the hostile force;
Yours, I myself will lead; to you I'll stand
In place of maiden or of prophetess.

LIONEL. Madame, return to Paris! We desire
To war with trusty weapons, not with women.

TALBOT. Go! go! Since your arrival in the camp,
Fortune hath fled our banners, and our course
Hath still been retrograde.

BURGUNDY.   Depart at once!
Your presence here doth scandalize the host.

ISABEL (*looks from one to the other with astonishment*).
This, Burgundy, from you? Do you take part
Against me with these thankless English lords?

BURG. Go! go! The thought of combating for you
Unnerves the courage of the bravest men.

ISABEL. I scarce among you have established peace,
And you already form a league against me!

TALBOT. Go, in God's name. When you have left the
camp
No devil will again appal our troops.

ISABEL. Say, am I not your true confederate?
Are we not banded in a common cause?

TALBOT. Thank God! your cause of quarrel is not ours.
We combat in an honorable strife.

BURG. A father's bloody murder I avenge.
Stern filial duty consecrates my arms.

TALBOT. Confess at once. Your conduct towards the
Dauphin
Is an offence alike to God and man.

ISABEL. Curses blast him and his posterity!
The shameless son who sins against his mother!

BURG. Ay! to avenge a husband and a father!

ISABEL. To judge his mother's conduct he presumed!

LIONEL. That was, indeed, irreverent in a son!

ISABEL. And me, forsooth, he banished from the realm.

TALBOT. Urged to the measure by the public voice.

ISABEL. A curse light on him if I e'er forgive him!
Rather than see him on his father's throne——

TALBOT.   His mother's honor you would sacrifice!
ISABEL.   Your feeble natures cannot comprehend
  The vengance of an outraged mother's heart.
  Who pleasures me, I love; who wrongs, I hate.
  If he who wrongs me chance to be my son,
  All the more worthy is he of my hate.
  The life I gave I will again take back
  From him who doth, with ruthless violence,
  The bosom rend which bore and nourished him.
  Ye, who do thus make war upon the Dauphin,
  What rightful cause have ye to plunder him?
  What crime hath he committed against you?
  What insult are you called on to avenge?
  Ambition, paltry envy, goad you on;
  I have a right to hate him — he's my son.
TALBOT.   He feels his mother in her dire revenge!
ISABEL.   Mean hypocrites! I hate you and despise.
  Together with the world, you cheat yourselves!
  With robber-hands you English seek to clutch
  This realm of France, where you have no just right
  Nor equitable claim, to so much earth
  As could be covered by your charger's hoof.
  — This duke, too, whom the people style the Good,
  Doth to a foreign lord, his country's foe,
  For gold betray the birthland of his sires.
  And yet is justice ever on your tongue.
  — Hypocrisy I scorn.   Such as I am,
  So let the world behold me!
BURGUNDY.   It is true!
  Your reputation you have well maintained.
ISABEL.   I've passions and warm blood, and as a queen
  Came to this realm to live, and not to seem.
  Should I have lingered out a joyless life
  Because the curse of adverse destiny
  To a mad consort joined my blooming youth?
  More than my life I prize my liberty.
  And who assails me here —— But why should I
  Stoop to dispute with you about my rights?
  Your sluggish blood flows slowly in your veins!
  Strangers to pleasure, ye know only rage!
  This duke, too — who, throughout his whole career,

Hath wavered to and fro, 'twixt good and ill —
Can neither love or hate with his whole heart.
— I go to Melun. Let this gentleman,
[*Pointing to* LIONEL.
Who doth my fancy please, attend me there,
To cheer my solitude, and you may work
Your own good pleasure ! I'll inquire no more
Concerning the Burgundians or the English.
[*She beckons to her* PAGE, *and is about to retire.*
LIONEL. Rely upon us, we will send to Melun
The fairest youths whom we in battle take.
[*Coming back.*
ISABEL. Skilful your arm to wield the sword of death,
The French alone can round the polished phrase.
[*She goes out.*

SCENE III.

TALBOT, BURGUNDY, LIONEL.

TALBOT. Heavens ! What a woman !
LIONEL.   Now, brave generals,
Your counsel ! Shall we prosecute our flight,
Or turn, and with a bold and sudden stroke
Wipe out the foul dishonor of to-day ?
BURG. We are too weak, our soldiers are dispersed,
The recent terror still unnerves the host.
TALBOT. Blind terror, sudden impulse of a moment,
Alone occasioned our disastrous rout.
This phantom of the terror-stricken brain,
More closely viewed will vanish into air.
My counsel, therefore, is, at break of day,
To lead the army back, across the stream,
To meet the enemy.
BURGUNDY.   Consider well ——
LIONEL. Your pardon ! Here is nothing to consider
What we have lost we must at once retrieve,
Or look to be eternally disgraced.
TALBOT. It is resolved. To-morrow morn we fight,
This dread-inspiring phantom to destroy,
Which thus doth blind and terrify the host
Let us in fight encounter this she-devil.

If she oppose her person to our sword,
Trust me, she never will molest us more;
If she avoid our stroke — and be assured
She will not stand the hazard of a battle —
Then is the dire enchantment at an end?

LIONEL.   So be it!   And to me, my general, leave
This easy, bloodless combat, for I hope
Alive to take this ghost, and in my arms,
Before the Bastard's eyes — her paramour —
To bear her over to the English camp,
To be the sport and mockery of the host.

BURG.   Make not too sure.

TALBOT.   If she encounter me,
I shall not give her such a soft embrace.
Come now, exhausted nature to restore
Through gentle sleep.   At daybreak we set forth.
                                    [*They go out*

SCENE IV.

JOHANNA *with her banner, in a helmet and breastplate,
otherwise attired as a woman.*   DUNOIS, LA HIRE,
*knights and soldiers, appear above upon the rocky path,
pass silently over, and appear immediately after on the
scene.*

JOHANNA (*to the knights who surround her while the pro-
cession continues above.*)
The wall is scaled and we are in the camp!
Now fling aside the mantle of still night,
Which hitherto hath veiled your silent march,
And your dread presence to the foe proclaim
By your loud battle-cry — God and the maiden!

ALL (*exclaim aloud, amidst the loud clang of arms*).
God and the maiden!   [*Drums and trumpets.*

SENTINELS (*behind the scene*). The foe! The foe! The foe!

JOHAN.   Ho! torches here!   Hurl fire into the tents!
Let the devouring flames augment the horror,
While threatening death doth compass them around!
                [*Soldiers hasten on, she is about to follow.*

DUNOIS (*holding her back*).
Thy part thou hast accomplished now, Johanna!
Into the camp thou hast conducted us,

The foe thou hast delivered in our hands,
Now from the rush of war remain apart!
The bloody consummation leave to us.

HIRE. Point out the path of conquest to the host;
Before us, in pure hand, the banner bear.
But wield the fatal weapon not thyself;
Tempt not the treacherous god of battle, for
He rageth blindly. and he spareth not.

JOHAN. Who dares impede my progress? Who presume
The spirit to control which guideth me?
Still must the arrow wing its destined flight!
Where danger is, there must Johanna be;
Nor now, nor here, am I foredoomed to fall;
Our monarch's royal brow I first must see
Invested with the round of sovereignty.
No hostile power can rob me of my life,
Till I've accomplished the commands of God.
[*She goes out.*

HIRE. Come, let us follow after her, Dunois,
And let our valiant bosoms be her shield! [*Exit.*

SCENE V.

ENGLISH SOLDIERS *hurry over the stage. Afterwards*
TALBOT.

1 SOL. The maiden in the camp!

2 SOLDIER. Impossible!
It cannot be! How came she in the camp?

3 SOL. Why, through the air! The devil aided her!

4 AND 5 SOLDIERS.
Fly! fly! We are dead men!

TALBOT (*enters*).
They heed me not! They stay not at my call!
The sacred bands of discipline are loosed!
As hell had poured her damned legions forth,
A wild, distracting impulse whirls along,
In one mad throng, the cowardly and brave.
I cannot rally e'en the smallest troop
To form a bulwark 'gainst the hostile flood,
Whose raging billows press into our camp!
Do I alone retain my sober senses,

While all around in wild delirium rave?
To fly before these weak, degenerate Frenchmen
Whom we in twenty battles have overthrown?
Who is she then — the irresistible —
The dread-inspiring goddess, who doth turn
At once the tide of battle, and transform
To lions bold a herd of timid deer?
A juggling minx, who plays the well-learned part
Of heroine, thus to appal the brave?
A woman snatch from me all martial fame?

SOLDIER (*rushes in*).

The maiden comes! Fly, general! fly! fly!

TALBOT (*strikes him down*).

Fly thou, thyself, to hell! This sword shall pierce
Who talks to me of fear, or coward flight!

                       [*He goes out.*

SCENE VI.

The prospect opens. The English camp is seen in flames.
Drums, flight, and pursuit. After a while MONT-
GOMERY *enters.*

MONTGOMERY (*alone*).

Where shall I flee? Foes all around and death!
    Lo! here
The furious general who, with threatening sword,
    prevents
Escape, and drives us back into the jaws of death.
The dreadful maiden there — the terrible — who, like
Devouring flame, destruction spreads; while all
    around
Appears no bush wherein to hide — no sheltering
    cave!
Oh, would that o'er the sea I never had come here!
Me miserable! Empty dreams deluded me —
Cheap glory to achieve on Gallia's martial fields.
And I am guided by malignant destiny
Into this murderous flight. Oh, were I far, far hence.
Still in my peaceful home, on Severn's flowery banks,
Where in my father's house, in sorrow and in tears,
I left my mother and my fair young bride.

               [JOHANNA *appears in the distance.*

Wo's me! What do I see! The dreadful form appears!
Arrayed in lurid light, she from the raging fire
Issues, as from the jaws of hell, a midnight ghost.
Where shall I go? where flee? Already from afar
She seizes on me with her eye of fire, and flings
Her fatal and unerring coil, whose magic folds
With ever-tightening pressure, bind my feet and make
Escape impossible! Howe'er my heart rebels,
I am compelled to follow with my gaze that form
Of dread!

[JOHANNA *advances towards him some steps; and again remains standing.*

She comes! I will not passively await
Her furious onset! Imploringly I'll clasp
Her knees! I'll sue to her for life. She is a woman.
I may perchance to pity move her by my tears!

[*While he is on the point of approaching her she draws near.*

SCENE VII.

JOHANNA, MONTGOMERY.

JOHAN. Prepare to die! A British mother bore thee!
MONTGOMERY (*falls at her feet*).
Fall back, terrific one! Forbear to strike
An unprotected foe! My sword and shield
I've flung aside, and supplicating fall
Defenceless at thy feet. A ransom take!
Extinguish not the precious light of life!
With fair possessions crowned, my father dwells
In Wales' fair land, where among verdant meads
The winding Severn rolls his silver tide,
And fifty villages confess his sway.
With heavy gold he will redeem his son,
When he shall hear I'm in the camp of France.
JOHAN. Deluded mortal! to destruction doomed!
Thou'rt fallen in the maiden's hand, from which
Redemption or deliverance there is none.
Had adverse fortune given thee a prey
To the fierce tiger or the crocodile —

Hadst robbed the lion mother of her brood —
Compassion thou might'st hope to find and pity ;
But to encounter me is certain death.
For my dread compact with the spirit realm —
The stern inviolable — bindeth me,
To slay each living thing whom battle's God,
Full charged with doom, delivers to my sword.

MONT. Thy speech is fearful, but thy look is mild ;
Not dreadful art thou to contemplate near ;
My heart is drawn towards thy lovely form.
Oh ! by the mildness of thy gentle sex,
Attend my prayer. Compassionate my youth.

JOHAN. Name me not woman ! Speak not of my sex !
Like to the bodiless spirits, who know naught
Of earth's humanities, I own no sex ;
Beneath this vest of steel there beats no heart.

MONT. Oh ! by love's sacred, all-pervading power,
To whom all hearts yield homage, I conjure thee.
At home I left behind a gentle bride,
Beauteous as thou, and rich in blooming grace :
Weeping she waiteth her betrothed's return.
Oh ! if thyself dost ever hope to love,
If in thy love thou hopest to be happy,
Then ruthless sever not two gentle hearts,
Together linked in love's most holy bond !

JOHAN. Thou dost appeal to earthly, unknown gods,
To whom I yield no homage. Of love's bond,
By which thou dost conjure me, I know naught,
Nor ever will I know his empty service.
Defend thy life, for death doth summon thee.

MONT. Take pity on my sorrowing parents, whom
I left at home. Doubtless thou, too, hast left
Parents, who feel disquietude for thee.

JOHAN. Unhappy man ! thou dost remember me
How many mothers of this land your arms
Have rendered childless and disconsolate ;
How many gentle children fatherless ;
How many fair young brides dejected widows !
Let England's mothers now be taught despair,
And learn to weep the bitter tear oft shed
By the bereaved and sorrowing wives of France.

MONT. 'Tis hard in foreign lands to die unwept.
JOHAN. Who called you over to this foreign land,
  To waste the blooming culture of our fields,
  To chase the peasant from his household hearth,
  And in our cities' peaceful sanctuary
  To hurl the direful thunderbolt of war?
  In the delusion of your hearts ye thought
  To plunge in servitude the freeborn French,
  And to attach their fair and goodly realm,
  Like a small boat, to your proud English bark!
  Ye fools! The royal arms of France are hung
  Fast by the throne of God; and ye as soon
  From the bright wain of heaven might snatch a star
  As rend a single village from this realm,
  Which shall remain inviolate forever!
  The day of vengeance is at length arrived;
  Not living shall ye measure back the sea,
  The sacred sea — the boundary set by God
  Betwixt our hostile nations — and the which
  Ye ventured impiously to overpass.
MONTGOMERY (*lets go her hands*).
  Oh, I must die! I feel the grasp of death!
JOHAN. Die, friend! Why tremble at the approach of
      death?
  Of mortals the irrevocable doom?
  Look upon me! I'm born a shepherd maid;
  This hand, accustomed to the peaceful crook,
  Is all unused to wield the sword of death.
  Yet, snatched away from childhood's peaceful haunts,
  From the fond love of father and of sisters,
  Urged by no idle dream of earthly glory,
  But heaven-appointed to achieve your ruin,
  Like a destroying angel I must roam,
  Spreading dire havoc around me, and at length
  Myself must fall a sacrifice to death!
  Never again shall I behold my home!
  Still, many of your people I must slay,
  Still, many widows make, but I at length
  Myself shall perish, and fulfil my doom.
  Now thine fulfil. Arise! resume thy sword,
  And let us fight for the sweet prize of life.

MONTGOMERY (*stands up*).
Now, if thou art a mortal like myself,
Can weapons wound thee, it may be assigned
To this good arm to end my country's woe,
Thee sending, sorceress, to the depths of hell.
In God's most gracious hands I leave my fate.
Accursed one! to thine assistance call
The fiends of hell!   Now combat for thy life!
[*He seizes his sword and shield, and rushes upon her;
martial music is heard in the distance.   After a
short conflict* MONTGOMERY *falls.*

SCENE VIII.

JOHANNA (*alone*).
To death thy foot did bear thee — fare thee well!
[*She steps away from him and remains absorbed in
thought.*
Virgin, thou workest mightily in me!
My feeble arm thou dost endue with strength,
And steep'st my woman's heart in cruelty.
In pity melts the soul and the hand trembles,
As it did violate some sacred fane,
To mar the goodly person of the foe.
Once I did shudder at the polished sheath,
But when 'tis needed, I'm possessed with strength,
And as it were itself a thing of life,
The fatal weapon, in my trembling grasp,
Self-swayed, inflicteth the unerring stroke.

SCENE IX.

A KNIGHT *with closed visor*, JOHANNA.

KNIGHT.   Accursed one! thy hour of death has come!
Long have I sought thee on the battle-field,
Fatal delusion! get thee back to hell,
Whence thou didst issue forth.
JOHANNA.   Say, who art thou,
Whom his bad genius sendeth in my way?
Princely thy port, no Briton dost thou seem,
For the Burgundian colors stripe thy shield,
Before the which my sword inclines its point.

KNIGHT. Vile castaway! Thou all unworthy art
To fall beneath a prince's noble hand.
The hangman's axe should thy accursed head
Cleave from thy trunk, unfit for such vile use
The royal Duke of Burgundy's brave sword.
JOHAN. Art thou indeed that noble duke himself?
KNIGHT (*raises his visor*).
I'm he, vile creature, tremble and despair!
The arts of hell shall not protect thee more.
Thou hast till now weak dastards overcome;
Now thou dost meet a man.

SCENE X.

DUNOIS *and* LA HIRE. *The same.*

DUNOIS. Hold, Burgundy!
Turn! combat now with men, and not with maids.
HIRE. We will defend the holy prophetess;
First must thy weapon penetrate this breast.
BURG. I fear not this seducing Circe; no,
Nor you, whom she hath changed so shamefully!
Oh, blush, Dunois! and do thou blush, La Hire!
To stoop thy valor to these hellish arts —
To be shield-bearer to a sorceress!
Come one — come all! He only who despairs
Of heaven's protection seeks the aid of hell.
[*They prepare for combat*, JOHANNA *steps between.*
JOHAN. Forbear!
BURGUNDY. Dost tremble for thy lover? Thus
Before thine eyes he shall ——
[*He makes a thrust at* DUNOIS.
JOHANNA. Dunois, forbear!
Part them, La Hire! no blood of France must flow:
Not hostile weapons must this strife decide,
Above the stars 'tis otherwise decreed,
Fall back! I say. Attend and venerate
The Spirit which hath seized, which speaks through
me!
DUNOIS. Why, maiden, now hold back my upraised arm?
Why check the just decision of the sword?

My weapon pants to deal the fatal blow
Which shall avenge and heal the woes of France.
[*She places herself in the midst and separates the
parties.*
JOHAN.   Fall back, Dunois!   Stand where thou art, La
Hire!
Somewhat I have to say to Burgundy.
[*When all is quiet.*
What wouldst thou, Burgundy?   Who is the foe
Whom eagerly thy murderous glances seek?
This prince is, like thyself, a son of France, —
This hero is thy countryman, thy friend;
I am a daughter of thy fatherland.
We all, whom thou art eager to destroy,
Are of thy friends; — our longing arms prepare
To clasp, our bending knees to honor thee.
Our sword 'gainst thee is pointless, and that face
E'en in a hostile helm is dear to us,
For there we trace the features of our king.
BURG.   What, syren! wilt thou with seducing words
Allure thy victim?   Cunning sorceress,
Me thou deludest not.   Mine ears are closed
Against thy treacherous words; and vainly dart
Thy fiery glances 'gainst this mail of proof.
To arms, Dunois!
With weapons let us fight, and not with words.
DUNOIS.   First words, then weapons, Burgundy!   Do
words
With dread inspire thee?   'Tis a coward's fear,
And the betrayer of an evil cause.
JOHAN.   'Tis not imperious necessity
Which throws us at thy feet!   We do not come
As suppliants before thee.   Look around!
The English tents are level with the ground,
And all the field is covered with your slain.
Hark! the war-trumpets of the French resound;
God hath decided — ours the victory!
Our new-culled laurel garland with our friend
We fain would share.   Come, noble fugitive!
Oh, come where justice and where victory dwell!
Even I, the messenger of heaven, extend

A sister's hand to thee. I fain would save
And draw thee over to our righteous cause!
Heaven hath declared for France! Angelic powers,
Unseen by thee, do battle for our king;
With lilies are the holy ones adorned,
Pure as this radiant banner is our cause;
Its blessed symbol is the queen of heaven.

BURG. Falsehood's fallacious words are full of guile,
But hers are pure and simple as a child's.
If evil spirits borrow this disguise,
They copy innocence triumphantly.
I'll hear no more. To arms, Dunois! to arms!
Mine ear, I feel, is weaker than mine arm.

JOHAN. You call me an enchantress, and accuse
Of hellish arts. Is it the work of hell
To heal dissension and to foster peace?
Comes holy concord from the depths below?
Say, what is holy, innocent, and good,
If not to combat for our fatherland?
Since when hath nature been so self-opposed
That heaven forsakes the just and righteous cause,
While hell protects it? If my words are true,
Whence could I draw them but from heaven above?
Who ever sought me in my shepherd-walks,
To teach the humble maid affairs of state?
I ne'er have stood with princes, to these lips
Unknown the arts of eloquence. Yet now,
When I have need of it to touch thy heart,
Insight and varied knowledge I possess;
The fate of empires and the doom of kings
Lie clearly spread before my childish mind,
And words of thunder issue from my mouth.

BURGUNDY (*greatly moved, looks at her with emotion and astonishment*).
How is it with me? Doth some heavenly power
Thus strangely stir my spirit's inmost depths?
This pure, this gentle creature cannot lie!
No, if enchantment blinds me, 'tis from heaven.
My spirit tells me she is sent from God.

JOHAN. Oh, he is moved! I have not prayed in vain,
Wrath's thunder-cloud dissolves in gentle tears,

And leaves his brow, while mercy's golden beams
Break from his eyes and gently promise peace.
Away with arms, now clasp him to your hearts,
He weeps — he's conquered, he is ours once more!
[*Her sword and banner fall; she hastens to him with
outstretched arms, and embraces him in great agi-
tation.* La Hire *and* Dunois *throw down their
swords, and hasten also to embrace him.*

ACT III.

Residence of the King *at Chalons on the Marne.*

Scene I.

Dunois, La Hire.

Dunois.   We have been true heart-friends, brothers in
            arms,
Still have we battled in a common cause,
And held together amid toil and death.
Let not the love of woman rend the bond
Which hath resisted every stroke of fate.
Hire.   Hear me, my prince!
Dunois.   You love the wondrous maid,
And well I know the purpose of your heart.
You think without delay to seek the king,
And to entreat him to bestow on you
Her hand in marriage. Of your bravery
The well-earned guerdon he cannot refuse
But know, — ere I behold her in the arms
Of any other ——
La Hire.   Listen to me, prince!
Dunois.   'Tis not the fleeting passion of the eye
Attracts me to her. My unconquered sense
Had set at naught the fiery shafts of love
Till I beheld this wondrous maiden, sent
By a divine appointment to become
The savior of this kingdom, and my wife;
And on the instant in my heart I vowed
A sacred oath, to bear her home, my bride.

For she alone who is endowed with strength
Can be the strong man's friend. This glowing heart
Longs to repose upon a kindred breast,
Which can sustain and comprehend its strength.

HIRE. How dare I venture, prince, my poor deserts
To measure with your name's heroic fame!
When Count Dunois appeareth in the lists,
Each humbler suitor must forsake the field;
Still it doth ill become a shepherd maid
To stand as consort by your princely side.
The royal current in your veins would scorn
To mix with blood of baser quality.

DUNOIS. She, like myself, is holy Nature's child,
A child divine — hence we by birth are equal.
She bring dishonor on a prince's hand,
Who is the holy angel's bride, whose head
Is by a heavenly glory circled round,
Whose radiance far outshineth earthly crowns,
Who seeth lying far beneath her feet
All that is greatest, highest of this earth!
For thrones on thrones, ascending to the stars,
Would fail to reach the height where she abides
In angel majesty!

HIRE. Our monarch must decide.

DUNOIS.   Not so! she must
Decide! Free hath she made this realm of France,
And she herself must freely give her heart.

HIRE. Here comes the king!

SCENE II.

CHARLES, AGNES, SOREL, DUCHATEL, *and* CHATILLON.
The same.

CHARLES (*to* CHATILLON).
He comes! My title he will recognize,
And do me homage as his sovereign liege?

CHATIL. Here, in his royal town of Chalons, sire,
The duke, my master, will fall down before thee.
He did command me, as my lord and king,
To give thee greeting. He'll be here anon.

SOREL. He comes! Hail beauteous and auspicious day,
Which bringeth joy, and peace, and reconcilement!

CHATIL. The duke, attended by two hundred knights,
    Will hither come; he at thy feet will kneel;
    But he expecteth not that thou to him
    Should yield the cordial greeting of a kinsman.
CHAS. I long to clasp him to my throbbing heart.
CHATIL. The duke entreats that at this interview,
    No word be spoken of the ancient strife!
CHAS. In Lethe be the past forever sunk!
    The smiling future now invites our gaze.
CHATIL. All who have combated for Burgundy
    Shall be included in the amnesty.
CHAS. So shall my realm be doubled in extent!
CHATIL. Queen Isabel, if she consent thereto,
    Shall also be included in the peace.
CHAS. She maketh war on me, not I on her.
    With her alone it rests to end our quarrel.
CHATIL. Twelve knights shall answer for thy royal word.
CHAS. My word is sacred.
CHATILLON.   The archbishop shall
    Between you break the consecrated host,
    As pledge and seal of cordial reconcilement.
CHAS. Let my eternal weal be forfeited,
    If my hand's friendly grasp belie my heart.
    What other surety doth the duke require?
CHATILLON (*glancing at* DUCHATEL).
    I see one standing here, whose presence, sire,
    Perchance might poison the first interview.
                    [DUCHATEL *retires in silence.*
CHAS. Depart, Duchatel, and remain concealed
    Until the duke can bear thee in his sight.
    [*He follows him with his eye, then hastens after and
    embraces him.*
    True-hearted friend! Thou wouldst far more than this
    Have done for my repose!   [*Exit* DUCHATEL.
CHATIL. This instrument doth name the other points.
CHARLES (*to the* ARCHBISHOP).
    Let it be settled. We agree to all.
    We count no price too high to gain a friend.
    Go now, Dunois, and with a hundred knights,
    Give courteous conduct to the noble duke.
    Let the troops, garlanded with verdant boughs,

Receive their comrades with a joyous welcome.
Be the whole town arrayed in festive pomp,
And let the bells with joyous peal, proclaim
That France and Burgundy are reconciled.

[A PAGE *enters.   Trumpets sound.*
Hark !   What importeth that loud trumpet's call ?
PAGE.   The Duke of Burgundy hath stayed his march.

[Exit.
DUNOIS.   Up! forth to meet him !

[Exit with LA HIRE *and* CHATILLON.
CHARLES (*to* SOREL).
My Agnes! thou dost weep!   Even my strength
Doth almost fail me at this interview.
How many victims have been doomed to fall
Ere we could meet in peace and reconcilement !
But every storm at length suspends its rage,
Day follows on the murkiest night; and still
When comes the hour, the latest fruits mature!
ARCHBISHOP (*at the window*).
The thronging crowds impede the duke's advance ;
He scarce can free himself.   They lift him now
From off his horse ; they kiss his spurs, his mantle.
CHAS.   They're a good people, in whom love flames forth
As suddenly as wrath.   In how brief space
They do forget that 'tis this very duke
Who slew, in fight, their fathers and their sons;
The moment swallows up the whole of life !
Be tranquil, Sorel.   E'en thy passionate joy
Perchance might to his conscience prove a thorn.
Nothing should either shame or grieve him here.

SCENE   III.

The DUKE OF BURGUNDY, DUNOIS, LA HIRE, CHATILLON,
and two other knights of the DUKE'S *train.   The* DUKE
remains standing at the door; the KING *inclines
towards him ;* BURGUNDY *immediately advances, and
in the moment when he is about to throw himself upon
his knees, the* KING *receives him in his arms.*

CHAS.   You have surprised us ; it was our intent
To fetch you hither, but your steeds are fleet.

BURG.   They bore me to my duty.
　　　　　　[*He embraces* SOREL, *and kisses her brow.*
　　　　　　　　　　　　　With your leave!
　　At Arras, niece, it is our privilege,
　　And no fair damsel may exemption claim.
CHAS.   Rumor doth speak your court the seat of love,
　　The mart where all that's beautiful must tarry.
BURG.   We are a traffic-loving people, sire;
　　Whate'er of costly earth's wide realms produce,
　　For show and for enjoyment, is displayed
　　Upon our mart at Bruges; but above all
　　There woman's beauty is pre-eminent.
SOREL.   More precious far is woman's truth; but it
　　Appeareth not upon the public mart.
CHAS.   Kinsman, 'tis rumored to your prejudice
　　That woman's fairest virtue you despise.
BURG.   The heresy inflicteth on itself
　　The heaviest penalty.   'Tis well for you,
　　From your own heart, my king, you learned betimes
　　What a wild life hath late revealed to me.
　　　　[*He perceives the* ARCHBISHOP, *and extends his hand.*
　　Most reverend minister of God! your blessing!
　　You still are to be found on duty's path,
　　Where those must walk who would encounter you.
ARCHB.   Now let my Master call me when he will;
　　My heart is full, I can with joy depart,
　　Since that mine eyes have seen this day!
BURGUNDY (*to* SOREL).　　　　　　　　　'Tis said
　　That of your precious stones you robbed yourself,
　　Therefrom to forge 'gainst me the tools of war!
　　Bear you a soul so martial?　Were you then
　　So resolute to work my overthrow?
　　Well, now our strife is over; what was lost
　　Will in due season all be found again.
　　Even your jewels have returned to you.
　　Against me to make war they were designed;
　　Receive them from me as a pledge of peace.
　　　　[*He receives a casket from one of the attendants, and
　　　　presents it to her open.*   SOREL, *embarrassed, looks
　　　　at the* KING.
CHAS.   Receive this present; 'tis a twofold pledge
　　Of reconcilement and of fairest love.

BURGUNDY (*placing a diamond rose in her hair*).
Why, is it not the diadem of France?
With full as glad a spirit I would place
The golden circle on this lovely brow.
                    [*Taking her hand significantly.*
And count on me if, at some future time
You should require a friend.
[AGNES SOREL *bursts into tears, and steps aside.* THE
    KING *struggles with his feelings. The bystanders
    contemplate the two princes with emotion.*
BURGUNDY (*after gazing round the circle, throws himself
into the* KING's *arms*).   Oh, my king!
[*At the same moment the three Burgundian knights
    hasten to* DUNOIS, LA HIRE, *and the* ARCHBISHOP.
    They embrace each other. The two PRINCES *remain
    for a time speechless in each other's arms.*
I could renounce you! I could bear your hate!
CHAS. Hush! hush! No further!
BURGUNDY.   I this English king
Could crown! Swear fealty to this foreigner!
And you, my sovereign, into ruin plunge!
CHAS. Forget it! Everything's forgiven now!
This single moment doth obliterate all.
'Twas a malignant star! A destiny!
BURGUNDY (*grasps his hand*).
Believe me, sire, I'll make amends for all.
Your bitter sorrow I will compensate;
You shall receive your kingdom back entire,
A solitary village shall not fail!
CHAS. We are united. Now I fear no foe.
BURG. Trust me, it was not with a joyous spirit
That I bore arms against you. Did you know?
Oh, wherefore sent you not this messenger?
                    [*Pointing to* SOREL.
I must have yielded to her gentle tears.
Henceforth, since breast to breast we have embraced,
No power of hell again shall sever us!
My erring course ends here. His sovereign's heart
Is the true resting-place for Burgundy.
ARCHBISHOP (*steps between them*).
Ye are united, princes! France doth rise

A renovated phœnix from its ashes.
The auspicious future greets us with a smile.
The country's bleeding wounds will heal again,
The villages, the desolated towns,
Rise in new splendor from their ruined heaps,
The fields array themselves in beauteous green;
But those who, victims of your quarrel, fell,
The dead, rise not again; the bitter tears,
Caused by your strife, remain forever wept!
One generation hath been doomed to woe;
On their descendants dawns a brighter day;
The gladness of the son wakes not the sire.
This the dire fruitage of your brother-strife!
Oh, princes, learn from hence to pause with dread
Ere from its scabbard ye unsheath the sword.
The man of power lets loose the god of war,
But not, obedient, as from fields of air
Returns the falcon to the sportsman's hand,
Doth the wild deity obey the call
Of mortal voice; nor will the Saviour's hand
A second time forth issue from the clouds.

BURG.   Oh, sire! an angel walketh by your side.
Where is she?   Why do I behold her not?

CHAS.   Where is Johanna?   Wherefore faileth she
To grace the festival we owe to her?

ARCHB.   She loves not, sire, the idless of the court,
And when the heavenly mandate calls her not
Forth to the world's observance, she retires,
And doth avoid the notice of the crowd.
Doubtless, unless the welfare of the realm
Claims her regard, she communes with her God,
For still a blessing on her steps attends.

Scene IV.

The same.

JOHANNA *enters.*   *She is clad in armor, and wears a
garland in her hair.*

CHAS.   Thou comest as a priestess decked, Johanna,
To consecrate the union formed by thee!

BURG. How dreadful was the maiden in the fight!
How lovely circled by the beams of peace!
My word, Johanna, have I now fulfilled?
Art thou contented? Have I thine applause?
JOHAN. The greatest favor thou hast shown thyself.
Arrayed in blessed light thou shinest now,
Who didst erewhile with bloody, ominous ray,
Hang like a moon of terror in the heavens.
                                    [*Looking round.*
Many brave knights I find assembled here,
And joy's glad radiance beams in every eye;
One mourner, one alone I have encountered;
He must conceal himself, where all rejoice.
BURG. And who is conscious of such heavy guilt,
That of our favor he must needs despair?
JOHAN. May he approach? Oh, tell me that he may;
Complete thy merit. Void the reconcilement
That frees not the whole heart. A drop of hate
Remaining in the cup of joy converts
The blessed draught to poison. Let there be
No deed so stained with blood that Burgundy
Cannot forgive it on this day of joy.
BURG. Ha! now I understand!
JOHANNA.   And thou'lt forgive?
Thou wilt indeed forgive? Come in, Duchatel!
[*She opens the door and leads in* DUCHATEL, *who
  remains standing at a distance.* ·
The duke is reconciled to all his foes,
And he is so to thee.
[DUCHATEL *approaches a few steps nearer, and tries to
  read the countenance of the* DUKE.
BURGUNDY.   What makest thou
Of me, Johanna? Know'st thou what thou askest?
JOHAN. A gracious sovereign throws his portals wide,
Admitting every guest, excluding none;
As freely as the firmament the world,
So mercy must encircle friend and foe.
Impartially the sun pours forth his beams
Through all the regions of infinity;
The heaven's reviving dew falls everywhere,
And brings refreshment to each thirsty plant;

Whate'er is good, and cometh from on high,
Is universal, and without reserve;
But in the heart's recesses darkness dwells!
BURG.   Oh, she can mould me to her wish; my heart
Is in her forming hand like melted wax.
— Duchatel, I forgive thee — come, embrace me!
Shade of my sire! oh, not with wrathful eye
Behold me clasp the hand that shed thy blood.
Ye death-gods, reckon not to my account,
That my dread oath of vengeance I abjure.
With you, in yon drear realm of endless night,
There beats no human heart, and all remains
Eternal, steadfast, and immovable.
Here in the light of day 'tis otherwise.
Man, living, feeling man, is aye the sport
Of the o'ermastering present.
CHARLES (to JOHANNA).   Lofty maid!
What owe I not to thee! How truly now
Hast thou fulfilled thy word, — how rapidly
Reversed my destiny! Thou hast appeased
My friends, and in the dust o'erwhelmed my foes;
From foreign yoke redeemed my cities. Thou
Hast all achieved. Speak, how can I reward thee?
JOHAN.   Sire, in prosperity be still humane,
As in misfortune thou hast ever been;
And on the height of greatness ne'er forget —
The value of a friend in times of need;
Thou hast approved it in adversity.
Refuse not to the lowest of thy people
The claims of justice and humanity,
For thy deliverer from the fold was called.
Beneath thy royal sceptre thou shalt gather
The realm entire of France. Thou shalt become
The root and ancestor of mighty kings;
Succeeding monarchs, in their regal state,
Shall those outshine, who filled the throne before
Thy stock, in majesty shall bloom so long
As it stands rooted in the people's love.
Pride only can achieve its overthrow,
And from the lowly station, whence to-day
God summoned thy deliverer, ruin dire
Obscurely threats thy crime-polluted sons!

BURG. Exalted maid! Possessed with sacred fire!
   If thou canst look into the gulf of time,
   Speak also of my race! Shall coming years
   With ampler honors crown my princely line!
JOHAN. High as the throne, thou, Burgundy, hast built
   Thy seat of power, and thy aspiring heart
   Would raise still higher, even to the clouds,
   The lofty edifice. But from on high
   A hand omnipotent shall check its rise.
   Fear thou not hence the downfall of thy house!
   Its glory in a maiden shall survive;
   Upon her breast shall sceptre-bearing kings,
   The people's shepherds, bloom. Their ample sway
   Shall o'er two realms extend, they shall ordain
   Laws to control the known world, and the new,
   Which God still veils behind the pathless waves.
CHAS. Oh, if the Spirit doth reveal it, speak;
   Shall this alliance which we now renew
   In distant ages still unite our sons?
JOHANNA (*after a pause*).
   Sovereigns and kings! disunion shun with dread!
   Wake not contention from the murky cave
   Where he doth lie asleep, for once aroused
   He cannot soon be quelled? He doth beget
   An iron brood, a ruthless progeny;
   Wildly the sweeping conflagration spreads.
   — Be satisfied! Seek not to question further!
   In the glad present let your hearts rejoice,
   The future let me shroud!
SOREL.   Exalted maid!
   Thou canst explore my heart, thou readest there
   If after worldly greatness it aspires,
   To me to give a joyous oracle.
JOHAN. Of empires only I discern the doom;
   In thine own bosom lies thy destiny!
DUNOIS. What, holy maid, will be thy destiny?
   Doubtless, for thee, who art beloved of heaven,
   The fairest earthly happiness shall bloom,
   For thou art pure and holy.
JOHANNA.   Happiness
   Abideth yonder, with our God, in heaven.

CHAS. Thy fortune be henceforth thy monarch's care!
For I will glorify thy name in France,
And the remotest age shall call thee blest.
Thus I fulfil my word. Kneel down!
   [*He draws his sword and touches her with it*
          And rise
  A noble! I, thy monarch, from the dust
Of thy mean birth exalt thee. In the grave
Thy fathers I ennoble — thou shalt bear
Upon thy shield the *fleur-de-lis,* and be
Of equal lineage with the best in France.
Only the royal blood of Valois shall
Be nobler than thine own! The highest peer
Shall feel himself exalted by thy hand;
To wed thee nobly, maid, shall be my care.
DUNOIS (*advancing*).
My heart made choice of her when she was lowly.
The recent honor which encircles her,
Neither exalts her merit nor my love.
Here in my sovereign's presence, and before
This holy bishop, maid, I tender thee
My hand, and take thee as my princely wife,
If thou esteem me worthy to be thine.
CHAS. Resistless maiden! wonder thou dost add
To wonder! Yes, I now believe that naught's
Impossible to thee. Thou hast subdued
This haughty heart, which still hath scoffed till now
At love's omnipotence.
LA HIRE (*advancing*). If I have read
Aright Johanna's soul, her modest heart's
Her fairest jewel. She deserveth well
The homage of the great, but her desires
Soar not so high. She striveth not to reach
A giddy eminence; an honest heart's
True love contents her, and the quiet lot
Which with this hand I humbly proffer her.
CHAS. Thou, too, La Hire! two brave competitors, —
Peers in heroic virtue and renown!
—Wilt thou, who hast appeased mine enemies,
My realms united, part my dearest friends?
One only can possess her; I esteem

Each to be justly worthy such a prize.
Speak, maid! thy heart alone must here decide.
SOREL. The noble maiden is surprised, her cheek
Is crimsoned over with a modest blush.
Let her have leisure to consult her heart,
And in confiding friendship to unseal
Her long-closed bosom. Now the hour is come
When, with a sister's love, I also may
Approach the maid severe, and offer her
This silent, faithful breast. Permit us women
Alone to weigh this womanly affair;
Do you await the issue.
CHARLES (*about to retire*). Be it so!
JOHAN. No, sire, not so! the crimson on my cheek
Is not the blush of bashful modesty.
Naught have I for this noble lady's ear
Which in this presence I may not proclaim.
The choice of these brave knights much honors
me,
But I did not forsake my shepherd-walks,
To chase vain worldly splendor, nor array
My tender frame in panoply of war,
To twine the bridal garland in my hair.
Far other labor is assigned to me,
Which a pure maiden can alone achieve.
I am the soldier of the Lord of Hosts,
And to no mortal man can I be wife.
ARCHB. To be a fond companion unto man
Is woman born — when nature she obeys,
Most wisely she fulfils high heaven's decree!
When His behest who called thee to the field
Shall be accomplished, thou'lt resign thy arms,
And once again rejoin the softer sex,
Whose gentle nature thou dost now forego,
And which from war's stern duties is exempt.
JOHAN. Most reverend sir! as yet I cannot say
What work the Spirit will enjoin on me.
But when the time comes round, his guiding voice
Will not be mute, and it I will obey.
Now he commands me to complete my task;
My royal master's brow is still uncrowned,

    Still unanointed is his sacred head;
    My sovereign cannot yet be called a king.
CHAS. We are advancing on the way to Rheims.
JOHAN. Let us not linger, for the enemy
    Is planning how to intercept thy course:
    I will conduct thee through the midst of them!
DUNOIS. And when thy holy mission is fulfilled,
    When we in triumph shall have entered Rheims,
    Wilt thou not then permit me, sacred maid ——
JOHAN. If heaven ordain that from the strife of death,
    Crowned with the wreath of conquest, I return,
    My task will be accomplished — and the maid
    Hath thenceforth in the palace naught to do.
CHARLES (*taking her hand*).
    It is the Spirit's voice impels thee now;
    Love in thy bosom, heaven-inspired, is mute;
    'Twill not be ever so; believe me, maid!
    Our weapons will repose, and victory
    Will by the hand lead forward gentle peace.
    Joy will again return to every breast,
    And softer feelings rest in every heart, —
    They will awaken also in thy breast,
    And tears of gentle longing thou wilt weep,
    Such as thine eye hath never shed before;
    — This heart, which heaven now occupies alone,
    Will fondly open to an earthly friend —
    Thousands thou hast till now redeemed and blessed
    Thou wilt at length conclude by blessing one!
JOHAN. Art weary, Dauphin, of the heavenly vision,
    That thou its vessel wouldst annihilate?
    The holy maiden, sent to thee by God,
    Degrade, reducing her to common dust?
    Ye blind of heart! Oh ye of little faith!
    God's glory shines around you; to your gaze
    He doth reveal his wonders, and ye see
    Naught but a woman in me. Dare a woman
    In iron panoply array herself,
    And boldly mingle in the strife of men?
    Woe, woe is me! if e'er my hand should wield
    The avenging sword of God, and my vain heart
    Cherish affection to a mortal man!

'Twere better for me I had ne'er been born!
Henceforth no more of this, unless ye would
Provoke the Spirit's wrath who in me dwells!
The eye of man, regarding me with love,
To me is horror and profanity.

CHAS.   Forbear! It is in vain to urge her further.

JOHAN.   Command the trumpets of the war to sound!
This stillness doth perplex and harass me;
An inward impulse drives me from repose,
It still impels me to achieve my work,
And sternly beckons me to meet my doom.

SCENE V.

A KNIGHT, *entering hastily.*

CHAS.   What tidings? Speak!

KNIGHT.   The foe has crossed the Marne,
And marshalleth his army for the fight.

JOHANNA (*inspired*).
Battle and tumult! Now my soul is free.
Arm, warriors, arm! while I prepare the troops.
                              [*She goes out.*

CHAS.   Follow, La Hire! E'en at the gates of Rheims
They will compel us to dispute the crown!

DUNOIS.   No genuine courage prompts them. This
          essay
Is the last effort of enraged despair.

CHAS.   I do not urge you, duke. To-day's the time
To compensate the errors of the past.

BURG.   You shall be satisfied with me.

CHARLES.   Myself
Will march before you on the path of fame;
Here, with my royal town of Rheims in view,
I'll fight, and gallantry achieve the crown.
Thy knight, my Agnes, bids thee now farewell!

AGNES (*embracing him*).
I do not weep, I do not tremble for thee;
My faith, unshaken, cleaveth unto God!
Heaven, were we doomed to failure, had not given
So many gracious pledges of success!

My heart doth whisper me that, victory-crowned,
In conquered Rheims, I shall embrace my king.
[*Trumpets sound with a spirited tone, and while the
scene is changing pass into a wild martial strain.
When the scene opens, the orchestra joins in, accom-
panied by warlike instruments behind the scene.*

SCENE VI.

*The scene changes to an open country skirted with trees.
During the music soldiers are seen retreating hastily
across the background.*

TALBOT, *leaning on* FASTOLFE, *and accompanied by
soldiers. Soon after,* LIONEL.

TALBOT. Here lay me down beneath the trees, and then
Betake you back, with speed, unto the fight ;
I need no aid to die.
FASTOLFE.   Oh, woful day ! [LIONEL *enters.*
Behold what sign awaits you, Lionel !
Here lies our general wounded unto death.
LIONEL. Now, God forbid ! My noble lord, arise !
No moment this to falter and to sink.
Yield not to death. By your all-powerful will
Command your ebbing spirit still to live.
TALBOT. In vain ! The day of destiny is come,
Which will o'erthrow the English power in France.
In desperate combat I have vainly risked
The remnant of our force to ward it off.
Struck by the thunderbolt I prostrate lie,
Never to rise again. Rheims now is lost,
Hasten to succor Paris !
LIONEL. Paris is with the Dauphin reconciled ;
A courier even now has brought the news.
TALBOT (*tearing off his bandages*).
Then freely flow, ye currents of my blood,
For Talbot now is weary of the sun !
LIONEL. I may no longer tarry : Fastolfe, haste !
Convey our leader to a place of safety.
No longer now can we maintain this post ;
Our flying troops disperse on every side,
On, with resistless might, the maiden comes.

TALBOT.   Folly, thou conquerest, and I must yield!
  Against stupidity the very gods
  Themselves contend in vain.   Exalted reason,
  Resplendent daughter of the head divine,
  Wise foundress of the system of the world,
  Guide of the stars, who art thou then if thou,
  Bound to the tail of folly's uncurbed steed,
  Must, vainly shrieking with the drunken crowd,
  Eyes open, plunge down headlong in the abyss.
  Accursed, who striveth after noble ends,
  And with deliberate wisdom forms his plans!
  To the fool-king belongs the world.
LIONEL.   My lord,
  But for a few brief moments can you live —
  Think of your Maker!
TALBOT.   Had we, like brave men,
  Been vanquished by the brave, we might, indeed,
  Console ourselves that 'twas the common lot;
  For fickle fortune aye revolves her wheel.
  But to be baffled by such juggling arts!
  Deserved our earnest and laborious life
  Not a more earnest issue?
LIONEL (*extends his hand to him*).   Fare you well!
  The debt of honest tears I will discharge
  After the battle — if I then survive.
  Now Fate doth call me hence, where on the field
  Her web she waveth, and dispenseth doom.
  We in another world shall meet again;
  For our long friendship, this a brief farewell.   [*Exit.*
TALBOT.   Soon is the struggle past, and to the earth,
  To the eternal sun, I render back
  These atoms, joined in me for pain and pleasure.
  And of the mighty Talbot, who the world
  Filled with his martial glory, there remains
  Naught save a modicum of senseless dust.
  Such is the end of man — the only spoil
  We carry with us from life's battle-field,
  Is but an insight into nothingness,
  And utter scorn of all which once appeared
  To us exalted and desirable.

Scene VII.

Charles, Burgundy, Dunois, Duchatel, *and Soldiers.*

Burg. The trench is stormed!

Dunois.   The victory is ours!

Charles *(perceiving Talbot.)*
  Look! Who is he, who yonder of the sun
  Taketh reluctant, sorrowful farewell?
  His armor indicates no common man;
  Go, succor him, if aid may yet avail.
          [*Soldiers of the King's retinue step forward.*

Fastol. Back! Stand apart! Respect the mighty dead,
  Whom ye in life ne'er ventured to approach!

Burg. What do I see? Lord Talbot in his blood!
  [*He approaches him. Talbot gazes fixedly at him, and
  dies.*

Fastol. Traitor, avaunt! Let not the sight of thee
  Poison the dying hero's parting glance.

Dunois. Resistless hero! Dread-inspiring Talbot!
  Does such a narrow space suffice thee now,
  And this vast kingdom could not satisfy
  The large ambition of thy giant soul!
  Now first I can salute you, sire, as king:
  The diadem but tottered on your brow,
  While yet a spirit tenanted this clay.

Charles *(after contemplating the body in silence).*
  A higher power hath vanquished him, not we!
  He lies upon the soil of France, as lies
  The hero on the shield he would not quit.
  Well, peace be with his ashes! Bear him hence!
          [*Soldiers take up the body and carry it away.*
  Here in the heart of France, where his career
  Of conquest ended, let his relics lie!
  So far no hostile sword attained before.
  A fitting tomb shall memorize his name;
  His epitaph the spot whereon he fell.

Fastolfe *(yielding his sword).*
  I am your prisoner, sir.

Charles *(returning his sword).* Not so! Rude war
  Respects each pious office; you are free

To render the last honors to the dead,
Go now, Duchatel — still my Agnes trembles —
Hasten to snatch her from anxiety —
Bring her the tidings of our victory,
And usher her in triumph into Rheims !
[*Exit* DUCHATEL.

SCENE VIII.

The same. LA HIRE.

DUNOIS. La Hire, where is the maiden ?
LA HIRE. That I ask
Of you ; I left her fighting by your side.
DUNOIS. I thought she was protected by your arm,
When I departed to assist the king.
BURG. Not long ago I saw her banner wave
Amidst the thickest of the hostile ranks.
DUNOIS. Alas ! where is she ? Evil I forebode ?
Come, let us haste to rescue her. I fear
Her daring soul hath led her on too far ;
Alone she combats in the midst of foes,
And without succor yieldeth to the crowd.
CHAS. Haste to her rescue !
LA HIRE. Come !
BURGUNDY. We follow all ! [*Exit.*
[*They retire in haste.*

*A deserted part of the battle-field. In the distance are seen
the towers of Rheims illumined by the sun.*

SCENE IX.

A KNIGHT *in black armor, with closed visor.* JOHANNA
*follows him to the front of the stage, where he stops and
awaits her.*

JOHAN. Deluder ! now I see thy stratagem !
Thou hast deceitfully, through seeming flight,
Allured me from the battle, doom and death
Averting thus from many a British head.
Destruction now doth overtake thyself,
KNIGHT. Why dost thou follow after me and track

My steps with quenchless rage? I am not doomed
To perish by thy hand.

JOHANNA.   Deep in my soul
I hate thee as the night, which is thy color;
To blot thee out from the fair light of day
An irresistible desire impels me.
Who art thou? Raise thy visor. I had said
That thou wert Talbot had I not myself
Seen warlike Talbot in the battle fall.

KNIGHT.   Is the divining-spirit mute in thee?

JOHAN.   His voice speaks loudly in my spirit's depth
The near approach of woe.

BLACK KNIGHT.   Johanna D'Arc!
Borne on the wings of conquest, thou hast reached
The gates of Rheims. Let thy achieved renown
Content thee. Fortune, like thy slave, till now
Hath followed thee; dismiss her, ere in wrath
She free herself; fidelity she hates;
She serveth none with constancy till death.

JOHAN.   Why check me in the midst of my career?
Why bid me falter and forsake my work?
I will complete it and fulfil my vow!

KNIGHT.   Nothing can thee, thou mighty one, withstand;
In battle thou art aye invincible.
But henceforth shun the fight; attend my warning.

JOHAN.   Not from my hand will I resign this sword
Till haughty England's prostrate in the dust.

KNIGHT.   Behold! there Rheims ariseth with its towers,
The goal and end of thy career. Thou seest
The lofty minster's sun-illumined dome;
Thou in triumphal pomp wouldst enter there,
Thy monarch crown, and ratify thy vow.
Enter not there! Return! Attend my warning!

JOHAN.   What art thou, double-tongued, deceitful being,
Who wouldst bewilder and appal me? Speak!
By what authority dost thou presume
To greet me with fallacious oracles?

[*The* BLACK KNIGHT *is about to depart, she steps in his
    way.*
No, thou shalt speak, or perish by my hand!
                                [*She endeavors to strike him.*

BLACK KNIGHT (*touches her with his hand, she remains motionless*).

Slay what is mortal!

[*Darkness, thunder and lightning. The* KNIGHT *sinks into the earth.*

JOHANNA (*stands at first in amazement, but soon recovers herself*).

'Twas nothing living. 'Twas a base delusion,
An instrument of hell, a juggling fiend,
Uprisen hither from the fiery pool
To shake and terrify my steadfast heart.
Wielding the sword of God, whom should I fear!
I will triumphantly achieve my work.
My courage should not waver, should not fail
Were hell itself to champion me to fight!

[*She is about to depart.*

SCENE X.

LIONEL, JOHANNA.

LIONEL. Accursed one, prepare thee for the fight!
Not both of us shall quit this field alive.
Thou hast destroyed the bravest of our host:
The noble Talbot hath his mighty soul
Breathed forth upon my bosom. I'll avenge
The hero, or participate his doom.
And wouldst thou know who brings thee glory now,
Whether he live or die, — I'm Lionel,
The sole survivor of the English chiefs,
And still unconquered is this valiant arm.

[*He rushes upon her; after a short combat she strikes the sword out of his hand.*

Perfidious fortune!

[*He wrestles with her.* JOHANNA *seizes him by the crest and tears open his helmet; his face is thus exposed; at the same time she draws her sword with her right hand.*

JOHANNA. Suffer what thou soughtest!

The Virgin sacrifices thee through me!

[*At this moment she gazes in his face. His aspect softens her, she remains motionless and slowly lets her arm sink.*

LIONEL.   Why linger, why withhold the stroke of death?
My glory thou hast taken — take my life!
I want no mercy, I am in thy power.
           [*She makes him a sign with her hand to fly.*
How! shall I fly and owe my life to thee?
No, I would rather die.
JOHANNA (*with averted face*).   I will not know
That ever thou didst owe thy life to me.
LIONEL.   I hate alike thee and thy proffered gift.
I want no mercy — kill thine enemy
Who loathes and would have slain thee.
JOHANNA.   Slay me, then,
And fly!
LIONEL.   Ha! What is this?
JOHANNA (*hiding her face*).   Woe's me!
LIONEL (*approaching her*).   'Tis said
Thou killest all the English whom thy sword
Subdues in battle — why spare me alone?
JOHANNA (*raises her sword with a rapid movement as if
to strike him, but lets it fall quickly when she gazes on
his face*).
Oh, Holy Virgin!
LIONEL.   Wherefore namest thou
The Holy Virgin? she knows naught of thee;
Heaven hath no part in thee.
JOHANNA (*in the greatest anxiety*).   What have I done?
Alas! I have broke my vow!
                    [*She wrings her hands in despair.*
LIONEL (*looks at her with sympathy and approaches her*).
                              Unhappy maid!
I pity thee! Thy sorrow touches me;
Thou hast shown mercy unto me alone,
My hatred yielded unto sympathy!
Who art thou, and whence comest thou?
JOHANNA.   Away!
LIONEL.   Thy youth, thy beauty, move my soul to pity!
Thy look sinks in my heart. I fain would save thee!
How may I do so? tell me. Come! oh, come!
Renounce this fearful league — throw down these
           arms!
JOHAN.   I am unworthy now to carry them!

LIONEL. Then throw them from thee — quick! come,
    follow me!

JOHANNA (*with horror*).
    How! follow thee!

LIONEL.   Thou may'st be saved. Oh, come!
    I will deliver thee, but linger not.
    Strange sorrow for thy sake doth seize my heart,
    Unspeakable desire to rescue thee ——
                        [*He seizes her arm.*

JOHAN. The Bastard comes! 'Tis they! They seek
    for me!
    If they should find thee ——

LIONEL.   I'll defend thee, maid.

JOHAN. I die if thou shouldst perish by their hands!

LIONEL. Am I then dear to thee?

JOHANNA.   Ye heavenly powers!

LIONEL. Shall I again behold thee — hear from thee?

JOHAN. No! never!

LIONEL.   Thus this sword I seize in pledge
    That I again behold thee!
                  [*He snatches her sword.*

JOHANNA.   Madman, hold!
    Thou darest?

LIONEL.   Now I yield to force — again
    I'll see thee!   [*He retires.*

SCENE XI.

JOHANNA, DUNOIS, LA HIRE.

LA HIRE.   It is she! The maiden lives!

DUNOIS. Fear not, Johanna! friends are at thy side.

HIRE. Is not that Lionel who yonder flies?

DUNOIS. Let him escape! Maiden, the righteous cause
    Hath triumphed now. Rheims opens wide its gates;
    The joyous crowds pour forth to meet their king.

HIRE. What ails thee, maiden? She grows pale — she
    sinks!
    [*JOHANNA grows dizzy, and is about to fall.*

DUNOIS. She's wounded — rend her breastplate — 'tis
    her arm!
    The wound is not severe.

La Hire.   Her blood doth flow.
Johan.   Oh, that my life would stream forth with my
        blood !   [*She lies senseless in* La Hire's *arms.*

ACT IV.

A hall adorned as for a festival; the columns are hung
with garlands; behind the scene flutes and hautboys.

Scene I.

Johan.   Hushed is the din of arms, war's storms sub-
        side,
  Glad songs and dance succeed the bloody fray,
  Through all the streets joy echoes far and wide,
  Altar and church are decked in rich array,
  Triumphal arches rise in vernal pride,
  Wreathes round the columns wind their flowery way,
  Wide Rheims cannot contain the mighty throng,
  Which to the joyous pageant rolls along.

  One thought alone doth every heart possess,
  One rapt'rous feeling o'er each breast preside.
  And those to-day are linked in happiness
  Whom bloody hatred did erewhile divide.
  All who themselves of Gallic race confess
  The name of Frenchman own with conscious pride,
  France sees the splendor of her ancient crown,
  And to her monarch's son bows humbly down.

  Yet I, the author of this wide delight,
  The joy, myself created, cannot share;
  My heart is changed, in sad and dreary plight
  It flies the festive pageant in despair;
  Still to the British camp it taketh flight,
  Against my will my gaze still wanders there,
  And from the throng I steal, with grief oppressed,
  To hide the guilt which weighs upon my breast.

  What! I permit a human form
  To haunt my bosom's sacred cell?

And there, where heavenly radiance shone,
Doth earthly love presume to dwell?
The savior of my country, I,
The warrior of God most high,
Burn for my country's foeman?   Dare I name
Heaven's holy light, nor feel o'erwhelmed with
    shame?
[*The music behind the scene passes into a soft and*
moving melody.

Woe is me !   Those melting tones !
    They distract my 'wildered brain !
Every note, his voice recalling,
    Conjures up his form again !

Would that spears were whizzing round !
    Would that battle's thunder roared !
Midst the wild tumultuous sound
    My former strength were then restored.

These sweet tones, these melting voices,
    With seductive power are fraught !
They dissolve, in gentle longing,
    Every feeling, every thought,
Waking tears of plaintive sadness.

[*After a pause, with more energy.*
Should I have killed him?   Could I, when I gazed
Upon his face?   Killed him?   Oh, rather far
Would I have turned my weapon 'gainst myself !
And am I culpable because humane?
Is pity sinful?   Pity !   Didst thou hear
The voice of pity and humanity
When others fell the victims of thy sword?
Why was she silent when the gentle youth
From Wales entreated thee to spare his life?
Oh, cunning heart !   Thou liest before high heaven !
It is not pity's voice impels thee now !
Why was I doomed to look into his eyes !
To mark his noble features !   With that glance,
Thy crime, thy woe commenced.   Unhappy one !

A sightless instrument thy God demands,
Blindly thou must accomplish his behest!
When thou didst see, God's shield abandoned thee,
And the dire snares of hell around thee pressed!
Flutes are again heard, and she subsides into a quiet
melancholy.

Harmless staff! Oh, that I ne'er
   Had for the sword abandoned thee!
Had voices never reached mine ear,
   From thy branches, sacred tree!
High queen of heaven! Oh, would that thou
   Hadst ne'er revealed thyself to me!
Take back — I dare not claim it now —
   Take back thy crown, 'tis not for me!

I saw the heavens open wide,
   I gazed upon that face of love!
Yet here on earth my hopes abide,
   They do not dwell in heaven above!
Why, Holy One, on me impose
   This dread vocation? Could I steel,
And to each soft emotion close
   This heart, by nature formed to feel?

Wouldst thou proclaim thy high command,
   Make choice of those who, free from sin,
In thy eternal mansions stand;
   Send forth thy flaming cherubim!
Immortal ones, thy law they keep,
They do not feel, they do not weep!
Choose not a tender woman's aid,
Not the frail soul of shepherd maid!

Was I concerned with warlike things,
With battles or the strife of kings?
In innocence I led my sheep
Adown the mountain's silent steep,
But thou didst send me into life,
'Midst princely halls and scenes of strife,
To lose my spirit's tender bloom:
Alas, I did not seek my doom!

Scene II.

Agnes Sorel, Johanna.

Sorel (*advances joyfully. When she perceives* Johanna *she hastens to her and falls upon her neck ; then suddenly recollecting herself, she relinquishes her hold, and falls down before her*).

No! no! not so! Before thee in the dust——
Johanna (*trying to raise her*).

 Arise! Thou dost forget thyself and me.
Sorel. Forbid me not! 'tis the excess of joy
  Which throws me at thy feet — I must pour forth
  My o'ercharged heart in gratitude to God ;   .
  I worship the Invisible in thee.
  Thou art the angel who has led my lord
  To Rheims, to crown him with the royal crown.
  What I ne'er dreamed to see is realized !
  The coronation march will soon set forth ;
  Arrayed in festal pomp the monarch stands ;
  Assembled are the nobles of the realm,
  The mighty peers to bear the insignia ;
  To the cathedral rolls the billowy crowd ;
  Glad songs resound, the bells unite their peal :
  Oh, this excess of joy I cannot bear !

[Johanna *gently raises her.* Agnes Sorel *pauses a moment, and surveys the* Maiden *more narrowly.*
  Yet thou remainest ever grave and stern ;
  Thou canst create delight, yet share it not.
  Thy heart is cold, thou feelest not our joy,
  Thou hast beheld the glories of the skies ;
  No earthly interest moveth thy pure breast.

[Johanna *seizes her hand passionately, but soon lets it fall again.*
  Oh, couldst thou own a woman's feeling heart !
  Put off this armor, war is over now,
  Confess thy union with the softer sex !
  My loving heart shrinks timidly from thee,
  While thus thou wearest Pallas' brow severe.
Johan. What wouldst thou have me do?
Sorel.   Unarm thyself!
  Put off this coat of mail ! The God of Love

Fears to approach a bosom clad in steel.
Oh, be a woman, thou wilt feel his power!
JOHAN.   What, now unarm myself?   Midst battle's roar
I'll bare my bosom to the stroke of death!
Not now!   Would that a sevenfold wall of brass
Could hide me from your revels, from myself!
SOREL.   Thou'rt loved by Count Dunois.   His noble heart,
Which virtue and renown alone inspire,
With pure and holy passion glows for thee.
Oh, it is sweet to know oneself beloved
By such a hero — sweeter still to love him!
                    [JOHANNA *turns away with aversion.*
Thou hatest him? — no, no, thou only canst
Not love him : — how could hatred stir thy breast!
Those who would tear us from the one we love,
We hate alone ; but none can claim thy love.
Thy heart is tranquil — if it could but feel ——
JOHAN.   Oh, pity me!   Lament my hapless fate!
SOREL.   What can be wanting to complete thy joy?
Thou hast fulfilled thy promise, France is free,
To Rheims, in triumph, thou hast led the king,
Thy mighty deeds have gained thee high renown,
A happy people praise and worship thee ;
Thy name, the honored theme of every tongue;
Thou art the goddess of this festival ;
The monarch, with his crown and regal state,
Shines not with greater majesty than thou!
JOHAN.   Oh, could I hide me in the depths of earth!
SOREL.   Why this emotion?   Whence this strange dis-
      tress?
Who may to-day look up without a fear,
If thou dost cast thine eyes upon the ground!
It is for me to blush, me, who near thee
Feel all my littleness ; I cannot reach
Thy lofty virtue, thy heroic strength!
For — all my weakness shall I own to thee?
Not the renown of France, my Fatherland,
Not the new splendor of the monarch's crown,
Not the triumphant gladness of the crowds,
Engage this woman's heart.   One only form
Is in its depths enshrined ; it hath not room

For any feeling save for one alone:
He is the idol, him the people bless,
Him they extol, for him they strew these flowers,
And he is mine, he is my own true love!

JOHAN. Oh, thou art happy! thou art blessed indeed!
Thou lovest, where all love. Thou may'st, unblamed
Pour forth thy rapture, and thine inmost heart,
Fearless discover to the gaze of man!
Thy country's triumph is thy lover's too.
The vast, innumerable multitudes,
Who, rolling onward, crowd within these walls,
Participate thy joy, they hallow it;
Thee they salute, for thee they twine the wreath,
Thou art a portion of the general joy;
Thou lovest the all-inspiring soul, the sun,
And what thou seest is thy lover's glory!

SOREL (_falling on her neck_).
Thou dost delight me, thou canst read my heart!
I did thee wrong, thou knowest what love is,
Thou tell'st my feelings with a voice of power.
My heart forgets its fear and its reserve,
And seeks confidingly to blend with thine——

JOHANNA (_tearing herself from her with violence_).
Forsake me! Turn away! Do not pollute
Thyself by longer intercourse with me!
Be happy! go — and in the deepest night
Leave me to hide my infamy, my woe!

SOREL. Thou frighten'st me, I understand thee not,
I ne'er have understood thee — for from me
Thy dark mysterious being still was veiled.
Who may divine what thus disturbs thy heart,
Thus terrifies thy pure and sacred soul!

JOHAN. Thou art the pure, the holy one! Couldst thou
Behold mine inmost heart, thou, shuddering,
Wouldst fly the traitoress, the enemy!

SCENE III.

DUNOIS, DUCHATEL, _and_ LA HIRE, _with the banner of_
JOHANNA.

DUNOIS. Johanna, thee we seek. All is prepared;
The king hath sent us, 'tis his royal will

That thou before him shouldst thy banner bear,
The company of princes thou shalt join,
And march immediately before the king:
For he doth not deny it, and the world
Shall witness, maiden, that to thee alone
He doth ascribe the honor of this day.
HIRE.   Here is the banner.   Take it, noble maiden
Thou'rt stayed for by the princes and the people.
JOHAN.   I march before him?   I the banner bear?
DUNOIS.   Whom   else   would   it   become?   What   other
      hand
Is pure enough to bear the sacred ensign!
Amid the battle thou hast waved it oft;
To grace our glad procession bear it now.
      [LA HIRE *presents the banner to her, she draws back,*
      shuddering.
JOHAN.   Away! away!
LA HIRE.   How!   Art thou terrified
At thine own banner, maiden?   Look at it!
                                    [*He displays the banner·*
It is the same thou didst in conquest wave.
Imaged upon it is the queen of heaven,
Floating in glory o'er this earthly ball;
For so the Holy Mother showed it thee.
                      [JOHANNA *gazing upon it with horror.*
'Tis she herself! so she appeared to me.
See, how she looks at me and knits her brow,
And anger flashes from her threatening eye!
SOREL.   Alas, she raveth!   Maiden, be composed!
Collect thyself!   Thou seest nothing real!
That is her pictured image; she herself
Wanders above, amid the angelic choir!
JOHAN.   Thou comest, fearful one, to punish me?
Destroy, o'erwhelm, thine arrowy lightnings hurl
And let them fall upon my guilty head.
Alas, my vow I've broken!   I've profaned
And desecrated thy most holy name!
DUNOIS.   Woe's us!   What may this mean?   What un-
      blest words?
LA HIRE (*in astonishment, to* DUCHATEL).
This strange emotion canst thou comprehend?

DUCHAT. That which I see, I see — I long have feared it.
DUNOIS. What sayest thou?
DUCHATEL.   I dare not speak my thoughts.
     I would to heaven that the king were crowned!
HIRE.   How! hath the awe this banner doth inspire
     Turned back upon thyself? before this sign
     Let Britons tremble; to the foes of France
     'Tis fearful, but to all true citizens
     It is auspicious.
JOHANNA.   Yes, thou sayest truly!
     To friends 'tis gracious! but to enemies
     It causeth horror!
               [*The Coronation march is heard.*
DUNOIS.   Take thy banner, then!
     The march begins — no time is to be lost!
     [*They press the banner upon her; she seizes it with evi-*
     dent emotion, and retires; the others follow.
     [*The scene changes to an open place before the Cathedral.*

SCENE IV.

Spectators occupy the background; BERTRAND, CLAUDE
    MARIE, *and* ÉTIENNE *come forward; then* MARGOT *and*
    LOUISON.   *The Coronation march is heard in the dis-*
    tance.

BERT.   Hark to the music! They approach already!
     What had we better do? Shall we mount up
     Upon the platform, or press through the crowd,
     That we may nothing lose of the procession?
ETIEN.   It is not to be thought of. All the streets
     Are thronged with horsemen and with carriages.
     Beside these houses let us take our stand
     Here we without annoyance may behold
     The train as it goes by.
CLAUDE MARIE.   Almost it seems
     As were the half of France assembled here
     So mighty is the flood that it hath reached
     Even our distant Lotharingian land
     And borne us thither!
BERTRAND.   Who would sit at home
     When great events are stirring in the land!

It hath cost plenty, both of sweat and blood,
Ere the crown rested on its rightful head!
Nor shall our lawful king, to whom we give
The crown, be worse accompanied than he
Whom the Parisians in St. Denis crowned!
He is no loyal, honest-minded man
Who doth absent him from this festival,
And joins not in the cry: "God save the King"!

Scene V.

Margot and Louison join them.

Louis.   We shall again behold our sister, Margot!
How my heart beats!

Margot.   In majesty and pomp
We shall behold her, saying to ourselves:
It is our sister, it is our Johanna!

Louis.   Till I have seen her, I can scarce believe
That she, whom men the Maid of Orleans name,
The mighty warrior, is indeed Johanna,
Our sister whom we lost!

                    [*The music draws nearer.*

Margot.   Thou doubtest still!
Thou wilt thyself behold her!

Bertrand.   See, they come!

Scene VI.

Musicians, with flutes and hautboys, open the procession. Children follow, dressed in white, with branches in their hands; behind them two heralds. Then a procession of halberdiers, followed by magistrates in their robes. Then two marshals with their staves; the Duke *of* Burgundy, *bearing the sword;* Dunois *with the sceptre, other nobles with the regalia; others with sacrificial offerings. Behind these,* Knights *with the ornaments of their order; choristers with incense; two* Bishops *with the ampulla; the* Archbishop *with the crucifix.* Johanna *follows, with her banner, she walks with downcast head and wavering steps; her sisters, on beholding her, express their astonishment and joy. Behind her comes the* King *under a canopy, supported by four barons; courtiers follow, soldiers conclude the procession; as soon as it has entered the church the music ceases.*

Scene VII.

Louison, Margot, Claude Marie, Etienne, Bertrand.

Marg.   Saw you our sister?
Claude Marie.   She in golden armor,
    Who with the banner walked before the king?
Marg.   It was Johanna.   It was she, our sister!
Louis.   She recognized us not!   She did not feel
    That we, her sisters, were so near to her.
    She looked upon the ground, and seemed so pale,
    And trembled so beneath her banner's weight —
    When I beheld her, I could not rejoice.
Marg.   So now, arrayed in splendor and in pomp,
    I have beheld our sister — who in dreams
    Would ever have imagined or conceived,
    When on our native hills she drove the flock,
    That we should see her in such majesty?
Louis.   Our father's dream is realized, that we
    In Rheims before our sister should bow down.
    That is the church, which in his dream he saw
    And each particular is now fulfilled.
    But images of woe he also saw!
    Alas! I'm grieved to see her raised so high!
Bert.   Why stand we idly here?   Let's to the church
    To view the coronation!
Margot.   Yes! perchance
    We there may meet our sister; let us go!
Louis.   We have beheld her.   Let us now return
    Back to our village.
Margot.   How?   Ere we with her
    Have interchanged a word?
Louison.   She doth belong
    To us no longer; she with princes stands
    And monarchs.   Who are we, that we should seek
    With foolish vanity to near her state?
    She was a stranger while she dwelt with us!
Marg.   Will she despise, and treat us with contempt?
Bert.   The king himself is not ashamed of us,
    He kindly greets the meanest of the crowd.

How high soever she may be exalted,
The king is raised still higher!
[*Trumpets and kettle-drums are heard from the church.*
CLAUDE MARIE.   Let's to the church!
[*They hasten to the background, where they are lost among the crowd.*

SCENE VIII.

THIBAUT *enters, clad in black.* RAIMOND *follows him, and tries to hold him back.*

RAIM. Stay, father Thibaut! Do not join the crowds!
Here, at this joyous festival you meet
None but the happy, whom your grief offends.
Come! Let us quit the town with hasty steps.
THIB. Hast thou beheld my child? My wretched child?
Didst thou observe her?
RAIMOND.   I entreat you, fly!
THIB. Didst mark her tottering and uncertain steps,
Her countenance, so pallid and disturbed?
She feels her dreadful state; the hour is come
To save my child, and I will not neglect it.
                              [*He is about to retire.*
RAIM. What would you do?
THIBAUT.   Surprise her, hurl her down
From her vain happiness, and forcibly
Restore her to the God whom she denies.
RAIM. Oh, do not work the ruin of your child!
THIB. If her soul lives, her mortal part may die.
[JOHANNA *rushes out of the church, without her banner. The people press around her, worship her, and kiss her garments. She is detained in the background by the crowd.*
She comes! 'tis she! She rushes from the church.
Her troubled conscience drives her from the fane!
'Tis visibly the judgment of her God!
RAIM. Farewell! Require not my attendance further!
Hopeful I came, and sorrowful depart.
Your daughter once again I have beheld,
And feel again that she is lost to me!
[*He goes out.* THIBAUT *retires on the opposite side.*

Scene IX.

JOHANNA, *People.* *Afterwards her Sisters.*

JOHANNA (*she has freed herself from the crowd and comes forward*).
 Remain I cannot — spirits chase me forth!
 The organ's pealing tones like thunder sound,
 The dome's arched roof threatens to overwhelm me!
 I must escape and seek heaven's wide expanse!
 I left my banner in the sanctuary,
 Never, oh, never, will I touch it more!
 It seemed to me as if I had beheld
 My sisters pass before me like a dream.
 'Twas only a delusion! — they, alas!
 Are far, far distant — inaccessible —
 E'en as my childhood, as mine innocence!
MARGOT (*stepping forward*).
 'Tis she! It is Johanna!
LOUISON (*hastening toward her*). Oh, my sister!
JOHAN. Then it was no delusion — you are here —
 Thee I embrace, Louison! Thee, my Margot?
 Here in this strange and crowded solitude,
 I clasp once more my sisters' faithful breasts!
MARG. She knows us still, she is our own kind sister.
JOHAN. Your love hath led you to me here so far!
 So very far! You are not wroth with her
 Who left her home without one parting word!
LOUIS. God's unseen providence conducted thee.
MARG. Thy great renown, which agitates the world,
 Which makes thy name the theme of every tongue,
 Hath in our quiet village wakened us,
 And led us hither to this festival.
 To witness all thy glory we are come;
 And we are not alone!
JOHANNA (*quickly*).   Our father's here!
 Where is he? Why doth he conceal himself?
MARG. Our father is not with us.
JOHANNA.   Not with you?
 He will not see me, then! You do not bring
 His blessing for his child?

LOUISON.   He knoweth not
    That we are here.
JOHANNA.   Not know it!   Wherefore not?
    You are embarrassed, and you do not speak;
    You look upon the ground!   Where is our father?
MARG.   Since thou hast left——
LOUISON (*making a sign to* MARGOT). Margot!
MARGOT.   Our father hath
    Become dejected.
JOHANNA.   Ah!
LOUISON.   Console thyself!
    Our sire's foreboding spirit well thou knowest!
    He will collect himself, and be composed,
    When he shall learn from us that thou art happy.
MARG.   And thou art happy?   Yes, it must be so,
    For thou art great and honored!
JOHANNA.   I am so,
    Now I again behold you, once again
    Your voices hear, whose fond, familiar tones
    Bring to my mind my dear paternal fields.
    When on my native hills I drove my herd,
    Then I was happy as in paradise —
    I ne'er can be so more, no, never more!
    [*She hides her face on* LOUISON'S *bosom.* CLAUDE
       MARIE, ETIENNE, *and* BERTRAND *appear, and re-*
       main timidly standing in the distance.
MARG.   Come, Bertrand!   Claude Marie!   come, Etienne!
    Our sister is not proud : she is so gentle,
    And speaks so kindly, — more so than of yore,
    When in our village she abode with us.
    [*They draw near, and hold out their hands;* JOHANNA
       gazes on them fixedly, and appears amazed.
JOHAN.   Where am I?   Tell me!   Was it all a dream,
    A long, long dream?   And am I now awake?
    Am I away from Dom Remi ?   Is't so ?
    I fell asleep beneath the Druid tree,
    And I am now awake ; and round me stand
    The kind, familiar forms?   I only dreamed
    Of all these battles, kings, and deeds of war, —
    They were but shadows which before me passed ;
    For dreams are always vivid 'neath that tree.

How did you come to Rheims? How came I here?
No, I have never quitted Dom Remi!
Confess it to me, and rejoice my heart.
LOUIS.	We are at Rheims.	Thou hast not merely
	dreamed
Of these great deeds — thou hast achieved them all.
Come to thyself, Johanna! Look around —
Thy splendid armor feel, of burnished gold!
[JOHANNA *lays her hand upon her breast, recollects herself, and shrinks back.*
BERT.	Out of my hand thou didst receive this helm.
MARIE.	No wonder thou shouldst think it all a dream;
For nothing in a dream could come to pass
More wonderful than what thou hast achieved.
JOHANNA (*quickly*).
	Come, let us fly! I will return with you
Back to our village, to our father's bosom.
LOUIS.	Oh, come! Return with us!
JOHANNA.				The people here
Exalt me far above what I deserve.
You have beheld me weak and like a child;
You love me, but you do not worship me.
MARG.	Thou wilt abandon this magnificence.
JOHAN.	I will throw off the hated ornaments
Which were a barrier 'twixt my heart and yours,
And I will be a shepherdess again,
And like a humble maiden I will serve you,
And will with bitter penitence atone,
That I above you vainly raised myself.
				[*Trumpets sound.*

SCENE X.

The KING *comes forth from the church. He is in the coronation robes.* AGNES SOREL, ARCHBISHOP, BURGUNDY, DUNOIS, LA HIRE, DUCHATEL, KNIGHTS, COURTIERS, *and* PEOPLE.

Many voices shout repeatedly, while the KING *advances, —*
	Long live the king! Long live King Charles the
		Seventh!
[*The trumpets sound. Upon a signal from the* KING,
	the HERALDS *with their staves command silence.*

KING.   Thanks, my good people! Thank you for your
           love!
The crown which God hath placed upon our brow
Hath with our valiant swords been hardly won :
With noble blood 'tis wetted ; but henceforth
The peaceful olive branch shall round it twine.
Let those who fought for us receive our thanks ;
Our pardon, those who joined the hostile ranks,
For God hath shown us mercy in our need,
And our first royal word shall now be, mercy!

PEOPLE.   Long live the king! Long live King Charles
           the good !

KING.   From God alone, the highest potentate,
           The monarchs of the French receive the crown ;
           But visibly from his Almighty hand
           Have we received it.   [*Turning to the* MAIDEN.
           Here stands the holy delegate of heaven,
           Who hath restored to you your rightful king,
           And rent the yoke of foreign tyranny.
           Her name shall equal that of holy Denis,
           The guardian and protector of this realm,
           And to her fame an altar shall be reared.

PEOPLE.   Hail to the maiden, the deliverer !   [*Trumpets.*

KING (*to* JOHANNA).
           If thou art born of woman, like ourselves,
           Name aught that can augment thy happiness.
           But if thy fatherland is there above,
           If in this virgin form thou dost conceal
           The radiant glory of a heavenly nature,
           From our deluded sense remove the veil,
           And let us see thee in thy form of light
           As thou art seen in heaven, that in the dust
           We may bow down before thee.
   [*A general silence ; every eye is fixed upon the* MAIDEN.

JOHANNA (*with a sudden cry*).   God ! my father !

SCENE XI.

THIBAUT *comes forth from the crowd, and stands opposite
           to her.   Many voices exclaim,* —
           Her father !

THIBAUT.   Yes, her miserable father,

Who did beget her, and whom God impels
Now to accuse his daughter.
BURGUNDY.   Ha! What's this?
DUCHAT.   Now will the fearful truth appear!
THIBAUT (*to the* KING).   Thou think'st
That thou art rescued through the power of God?
Deluded prince! Deluded multitude!
Ye have been rescued through the arts of hell!
                    [*All step back with horror.*
DUNOIS.   Is this man mad?
THIBAUT.   Not I, but thou art mad.
And this wise bishop, and these noble lords,
Who think that through a weak and sinful maid
The God of heaven would reveal himself.
Come, let us see if to her father's face
She will maintain the specious, juggling arts
Wherewith she hath deluded king and people.
Now, in the name of the blest Trinity,
Belong'st thou to the pure and holy ones?
[*A general silence; all eyes are fixed upon her; she
    remains motionless.*
SOREL.   God! she is dumb!
THIBAUT.   Before that awful name,
Which even in the depths of hell is feared,
She must be silent! She a holy one,
By God commissioned? On a cursed spot
It was conceived; beneath the Druid tree
Where evil spirits have from olden time
Their sabbath held. There her immortal soul
She bartered with the enemy of man
For transient, worldly glory. Let her bare
Her arm, and ye will see impressed thereon
The fatal marks of hell!
BURGUNDY.   Most horrible!
Yet we must needs believe a father's words
Who 'gainst his daughter gives his evidence.
DUNOIS.   The madman cannot be believed
Who in his child brings shame upon himself.
SOREL (*to* JOHANNA).
Oh, maiden, speak! this fatal silence break!
We firmly trust thee! we believe in thee!

One syllable from thee, one single word
Shall be sufficient. Speak! annihilate
This horrid accusation. But declare
Thine innocence, and we will all believe thee.

[JOHANNA *remains motionless;* AGNES *steps back with*
horror.

HIRE. She's frightened. Horror and astonishment
Impede her utterance. Before a charge
So horrible e'en innocence must tremble.

[*He approaches her.*

Collect thyself, Johanna! innocence
Hath a triumphant look, whose lightning flash
Strikes slander to the earth! In noble wrath
Arise! look up, and punish this base doubt,
An insult to thy holy innocence.

[JOHANNA *remains motionless;* LA HIRE *steps back;*
the excitement increases.

DUNOIS. Why do the people fear, the princes tremble?
I'll stake my honor on her innocence!
Here on the ground I throw my knightly gage;
Who now will venture to maintain her guilt?

[*A loud clap of thunder; all are horror-struck.*

THIB. Answer, by Him whose thunders roll above!
Give me the lie! Proclaim thine innocence;
Say that the enemy hath not thy heart!

[*Another clap of thunder, louder than the first; the*
people fly on all sides.

BURG. God guard and save us! What appalling signs!
DUCHATEL (*to the* KING).

Come, come, my king! Forsake this fearful place!
ARCHBISHOP (*to* JOHANNA).

I ask thee in God's name. Art thou thus silent
From consciousness of innocence or guilt?
If in thy favor the dread thunder speaks,
Touch with thy hand this cross, and give a sign!

[JOHANNA *remains motionless. More violent peals of*
thunder. The KING, AGNES SOREL, *the* ARCHBISHOP,
BURGUNDY, LA HIRE, DUCHATEL *retire.*

Scene XII.

Dunois, Johanna.

Dunois. Thou art my wife; I have believed in thee
From the first glance, and I am still unchanged.
In thee I have more faith than in these signs,
Than in the thunder's voice, which speaks above.
In noble anger thou art silent thus;
Enveloped in thy holy innocence,
Thou scornest to refute so base a charge.
Still scorn it, maiden, but confide in me;
I never doubted of thine innocence.
Speak not one word; only extend thy hand
In pledge and token that thou wilt confide
In my protection and thine own good cause.
[*He extends his hand to her; she turns from him with
a convulsive motion; he remains transfixed with
horror.*

Scene XIII.

Johanna, Duchatel, Dunois, *afterwards* Raimond.

Duchatel (*returning*).
Johanna d'Arc! uninjured from the town
The king permits you to depart. The gates
Stand open to you. Fear no injury, —
You are protected by the royal word.
Come follow me, Dunois! You cannot here
Longer abide with honor. What an issue!
[*He retires.* Dunois *recovers from his stupor, casts
one look upon* Johanna, *and retires. She remains
standing for a moment quite alone. At length*
Raimond *appears; he regards her for a time with
silent sorrow, and then approaching takes her hand.*
Raim. Embrace this opportunity. The streets
Are empty now. Your hand! I will conduct you.
[*On perceiving him, she gives the first sign of con-
sciousness. She gazes on him fixedly, and looks up
to heaven; then taking his hand she retires.*

ACT V.

*A wild wood: charcoal-burners' huts in the distance.   It
is quite dark ; violent thunder and lightning ; firing
heard at intervals.*

Scene I.

Charcoal-Burner *and his* Wife.

Ch. B.   This is a fearful storm, the heavens seem
As they would vent themselves in streams of fire ;
So thick the darkness which usurps the day,
That one might see the stars.   The angry winds
Bluster and howl like spirits loosed from hell.
The firm earth trembles, and the aged elms,
Groaning, bow down their venerable tops
Yet this terrific tumult, o'er our heads,
Which teacheth gentleness to savage beasts,
So that they seek the shelter of their caves,
Appeaseth not the bloody strife of men —
Amidst the raging of the wind and storm
At intervals is heard the cannon's roar;
So near the hostile armaments approach,
The wood alone doth part them ; any hour
May see them mingle in the shock of battle.
Wife.   May God protect us then !   Our enemies,
Not long ago, were vanquished and dispersed.
How comes it that they trouble us again?
Ch. B.   Because they now no longer fear the king.
Since that the maid turned out to be a witch
At Rheims, the devil aideth us no longer,
And things have gone against us.
Wife.   Who comes here?

Scene II.

Raimond *and* Johanna *enter.*

Raim.   See ! here are cottages ; in them at least
We may find shelter from the raging storm.
You are not able longer to endure it.
Three days already you have wandered on,
Shunning the eye of man — wild herbs and roots

Your only nourishment. Come, enter in.
These are kind-hearted cottagers.
    [The storm subsides ; the air grows bright and clear.
CHARCOAL-BURNER.   You seem
To need refreshment and repose — you're welcome
To what our humble roof can offer you !
WIFE.   What has a tender maid to do with arms?
Yet truly ! these are rude and troublous times
When even women don the coat of mail !
The queen herself, proud Isabel, 'tis said,
Appears in armor in the hostile camp ;
And a young maid, a shepherd's lowly daughter,
Has led the armies of our lord the king.
CH. B.   What sayest thou ?   Enter the hut, and bring
A goblet of refreshment for the damsel.
                      [She enters the hut.
RAIMOND (*to* JOHANNA).
All men, you see, are not so cruel ; here
E'en in the wilderness are gentle hearts.
Cheer up ! the pelting storm hath spent its rage,
And, beaming peacefully, the sun declines.
CH. B.   I fancy, as you travel thus in arms,
You seek the army of the king.   Take heed !
Not far remote the English are encamped,
Their troops are roaming idly through the wood.
RAIM.   Alas for us ! how then can we escape ?
CH. B.   Stay here till from the town my boy returns.
He shall conduct you safe by secret paths.
You need not fear — we know each hidden way.
RAIMOND (*to* JOHANNA).
Put off your helmet and your coat-of-mail,
They will not now protect you, but betray.
                [JOHANNA shakes her head.
CH. B.   The maid seems very sad — hush ! who comes
here ?

SCENE III.

CHARCOAL-BURNER'S WIFE *comes out of the hut with
a bowl.* A BOY.

WIFE.   It is our boy whom we expected back.
                     [To JOHANNA.
Drink, noble maiden ! may God bless it to you !

CHARCOAL-BURNER (*to his son*).
Art come, Anet?   What news?
[*The boy looks at* JOHANNA, *who is just raising the
    bowl to her lips ; he recognizes her, steps forward,
    and snatches it from her.*
BOY.   Oh, mother! mother!
Whom do you entertain?   This is the witch
Of Orleans!
CHARCOAL-BURNER (*and his* WIFE).
                  God be gracious to our souls!
                  [*They cross themselves and fly.*

SCENE IV.

RAIMOND, JOHANNA.

JOHANNA (*calmly and gently*)
Thou seest, I am followed by the curse,
And all fly from me.   Do thou leave me, too;
Seek safety for thyself.
RAIMOND.   I leave thee! now!
Alas, who then would bear thee company?
JOHAN.   I am not unaccompanied.   Thou hast
Heard the loud thunder rolling o'er my head —
My destiny conducts me.   Do not fear;
Without my seeking I shall reach the goal.
RAIM.   And whither wouldst thou go?   Here stand our
         foes,
Who have against thee bloody vengeance sworn —
There stand our people who have banished thee.
JOHAN.   Naught will befall me but what heaven ordains.
RAIM.   Who will provide thee food? and who protect
         thee
From savage beasts, and still more savage men?
Who cherish thee in sickness and in grief?
JOHAN.   I know all roots and healing herbs ; my sheep
Taught me to know the poisonous from the whole-
         some.
I understand the movements of the stars,
And the clouds' flight; I also hear the sound
Of hidden springs.   Man hath not many wants,
And nature richly ministers to life.

RAIMOND (*seizing her hand*).
　Wilt thou not look within? Oh, wilt thou not
　Repent thy sin, be reconciled to God,
　And to the bosom of the church return?
JOHAN. Thou hold'st me guilty of this heavy sin?
RAIM. Needs must I — thou didst silently confess ——
JOHAN. Thou, who hast followed me in misery,
　The only being who continued true,
　Who clave to me when all the world forsook,
　Thou also hold'st me for a reprobate
　Who hath renounced her God ——
　　　　　　　　　　　[RAIMOND *is silent.*
　　　　　　　　　　　Oh, this is hard!
RAIMOND (*in astonishment*).
　And thou wert really then no sorceress?
JOHAN. A sorceress!
RAIMOND. 　　　　　And all these miracles
　Thou hast accomplished through the power of God
　And of his holy saints?
JOHANNA. 　　　　　Through whom besides?
RAIM. And thou wert silent to that fearful charge?
　Thou speakest now, and yet before the king,
　When words would have availed thee, thou wert
　　dumb!
JOHAN. I silently submitted to the doom
　Which God, my lord and master, o'er me hung.
RAIM. Thou couldst not to thy father aught reply?
JOHAN. Coming from him, methought it came from God;
　And fatherly the chastisement will prove.
RAIM. The heavens themselves bore witness to thy guilt!
JOHAN. The heavens spoke, and therefore I was silent.
RAIM. Thou with one word couldst clear thyself, and
　　hast
　In this unhappy error left the world?
JOHAN. It was no error — 'twas the will of heaven.
RAIM. Thou innocently sufferedst this shame,
　And no complaint proceeded from thy lips!
　—I am amazed at thee, I stand o'erwhelmed.
　My heart is troubled in its inmost depths.
　Most gladly I receive the word as truth,
　For to believe thy guilt was hard indeed.

But could I ever dream a human heart
Would meet in silence such a fearful doom!
JOHAN.   Should I deserve to be heaven's messenger
Unless the Master's will I blindly honored?
And I am not so wretched as thou thinkest.
I feel privation — this in humble life
Is no misfortune; I'm a fugitive,—
But in the waste I learned to know myself.
When honor's dazzling radiance round me shone,
There was a painful struggle in my breast;
I was most wretched, when to all I seemed
Most worthy to be envied.   Now my mind
Is healed once more, and this fierce storm in nature
Which threatened your destruction, was my friend
It purified alike the world and me!
I feel an inward peace — and, come what may,
Of no more weakness am I conscious now!
RAIM.   Oh, let us hasten! come, let us proclaim
Thine innocence aloud to all the world!
JOHAN.   He who sent this delusion will dispel it!
The fruit of fate falls only when 'tis ripe!
A day is coming that will clear my name,
When those who now condemn and banish me,
Will see their error and will weep my doom.
RAIM.   And shall I wait in silence, until chance ——
JOHANNA (*gently taking his hand*).
Thy sense is shrouded by an earthly veil,
And dwelleth only on external things.
Mine eye hath gazed on the invisible!
— Without permission from our God no hair
Falls from the head of man.   Seest thou the sun
Declining to the west?   So certainly
As morn returneth in her radiant light,
Infallibly the day of truth shall come!

SCENE V.

QUEEN ISABEL, *with soldiers, appears in the background.*

ISABEL (*behind the scene*).
This is the way toward the English camp!

RAIM. Alas! the foe!

[*The soldiers advance, and perceiving* JOHANNA *fall back in terror.*

ISABEL. What now obstructs the march?

SOLD. May God protect us!

ISABEL. Do ye see a spirit?

How! Are ye soldiers! Ye are cowards all!

[*She presses forward, but starts back on beholding the* MAIDEN.

What do I see!

[*She collects herself quickly and approaches her.*

Submit thyself! Thou art

My prisoner!

JOHANNA. I am. [RAIMOND *flies in despair.*

ISABEL (*to the soldiers*). Lay her in chains!

[*The soldiers timidly approach the* MAIDEN; *she extends her arms and is chained.*

Is this the mighty, the terrific one,

Who chased your warriors like a flock of lambs,

Who, powerless now, cannot protect herself?

Doth she work miracles with credulous fools,

And lose her influence when she meets a man?

[*To the* MAIDEN.

Why didst thou leave the army? Where's Dunois,

Thy knight and thy protector.

JOHANNA. I am banished.

[ISABEL, *stepping back astonished.*

ISABEL. What say'st thou? Thou art banished? By the Dauphin?

JOHAN. Inquire no further! I am in thy power,

Decide my fate.

ISABEL. Banished, because thou hast

Snatched him from ruin, placed upon his brow

The crown at Rheims, and made him King of France?

Banished! Therein I recognize my son!

— Conduct her to the camp, and let the host

Behold the phantom before whom they trembled!

She a magician? Her sole magic lies

In your delusion and your cowardice!

She is a fool who sacrificed herself

To save her king, and reapeth for her pains

A king's reward. Bear her to Lionel.
The fortune of the French I send him bound;
I'll follow anon.

JOHANNA.   To Lionel?

Slay me at once, ere send me unto him.

ISABEL (*to the soldiers*).

Obey your orders, soldiers! Bear her hence. [*Exit*

SCENE VI.

JOHANNA, SOLDIERS.

JOHANNA (*to the soldiers*).

Ye English, suffer not that I escape
Alive out of your hands! Revenge yourselves!
Unsheath your weapons, plunge them in my heart,
And drag me lifeless to your general's feet!
Remember it was I who slew your heroes,
Who never showed compassion, who poured forth
Torrents of English blood, who from your sons
Snatched the sweet pleasure of returning home!
Take now a bloody vengance! Murder me!
I now aim in your power; I may perchance
Not always be so weak.

CONDUCTOR OF THE SOLDIERS. Obey the queen!

JOHAN. Must I be yet more wretched than I was!
Unpitying Virgin! Heavy is thy hand!
Hast thou completely thrust me from thy favor?
No God appears, no angel shows himself;
Closed are heaven's portals, miracles have ceased.

[*She follows the* SOLDIERS

SCENE VII.

The French Camp.

DUNOIS, *between the* ARCHBISHOP *and* DUCHATEL.

ARCH. Conquer your sullen indignation, prince!
Return with us! Come back unto your king!
In this emergency abandon not
The general cause, when we are sorely pressed,
And stand in need of your heroic arm.

DUNOIS. Why are ye sorely pressed? Why doth the foe
Again exalt himself? all was achieved; —
France was triumphant — war was at an end; —
The savior you have banished; you henceforth
May save yourselves; I'll not again behold
The camp wherein the maid abideth not.

DUCHAT. Think better of it, prince! Dismiss us not
With such an answer!

DUNOIS. Silence, Duchatel!
You're hateful to me; I'll hear naught from you;
You were the first who doubted of her truth.

ARCH. Who had not wavered on that fatal day,
And been bewildered, when so many signs
Bore evidence against her! We were stunned,
Our hearts were crushed beneath the sudden blow.
— Who in that hour of dread could weigh the proofs?
Our calmer judgment now returns to us,
We see the maid as when she walked with us,
Nor have we any fault to charge her with.
We are perplexed — we fear that we have done
A grievous wrong. The king is penitent,
The duke remorseful, comfortless La Hire,
And every heart doth shroud itself in woe.

DUNOIS. She a deluder? If celestial truth
Would clothe herself in a corporeal form,
She needs must choose the features of the maiden.
If purity of heart, faith, innocence,
Dwell anywhere on earth, upon her lips
And in her eyes' clear depths they find their home.

ARCH. May the Almighty, through a miracle,
Shed light upon this awful mystery,
Which baffles human insight. Howsoe'er
This sad perplexity may be resolved,
One of two grievous sins we have committed!
Either in fight we have availed ourselves
Of hellish arms, or banished hence a saint!
And both call down upon this wretched land
The vengeance and the punishment of heaven!

SCENE VIII.

The same, a NOBLEMAN, *afterwards* RAIMOND.

NOBLE.   A shepherd youth inquires after your highness,
 He urgently entreats an interview,
 He says he cometh from the maiden ——
DUNOIS.   Haste!
 Conduct him hither!   He doth come from her!
 [*The* NOBLEMAN *opens the door to* RAIMOND, DUNOIS
   hastens to meet him.
 Where is she?   Where is the maid?
RAIMOND.   Hail! noble prince!
 And blessed am I that I find with you
 This holy man, the shield of the oppressed,
 The father of the poor and destitute!
DUNOIS.   Where is the maiden?
ARCH.   Speak, my son, inform us!
RAIM.   She is not, sir, a wicked sorceress!
 To God and all his saints I make appeal.
 An error blinds the people.   You've cast forth
 God's messenger, you've banished innocence!
DUNOIS.   Where is she?
RAIMOND.   I accompanied her flight
 Towards the woods of Ardennes; there she hath
 Revealed to me her spirit's inmost depths.
 In torture I'll expire, and will resign
 My hopes of everlasting happiness,
 If she's not guiltless, sir, of every sin!
DUNOIS.   The sun in heaven is not more pure than she!
 Where is she?   Speak!
RAIMOND.   If God hath turned your hearts,
 Oh hasten, I entreat you — rescue her —
 She is a prisoner in the English camp.
DUNOIS.   A prisoner say you?
ARCHBISHOP.   Poor unfortunate!
RAIM.   There in the forest as we sought for shelter,
 We were encountered by Queen Isabel,
 Who seized and sent her to the English host.
 Oh, from a cruel death deliver her
 Who hath full many a time delivered you!
DUNOIS.   Sound an alarm!   to arms!   up!   beat the drums.

Forth to the field! Let France appear in arms!
The crown and the palladium are at stake!
Our honor is in pledge! risk blood and life!
She must be rescued ere the day is done!   [*Exit.*

Scene IX.

A watch-tower — an opening above.

Johanna *and* Lionel.

Fastolfe (*entering hastily*).
  The people can no longer be restrained.
  With fury they demand the maiden's death.
  In vain your opposition. Let her die
  And throw her head down from the battlements!
  Her blood alone will satisfy the host.

Isabel (*coming in*).
  With ladders they begin to scale the walls.
  Appease the angry people! Will you wait
  Till in blind fury they o'erthrow the tower,
  And we beneath its towers are destroyed?
  Protect her here you cannot. Give her up!

Lionel. Let them storm on. In fury let them rage!
  Firm is this castle, and beneath its ruins
  I will be buried ere I yield to them.
  —Johanna, answer me! only be mine,
  And I will shield thee 'gainst a world in arms.

Isabel. Are you a man?

Lionel.   Thy friends have cast thee off.
  To thy ungrateful country thou dost owe
  Duty and faith no longer. The false cowards
  Who sought thy hand, forsake thee in thy need.
  They for thy honor venture not the fight,
  But I, against my people and 'gainst thine,
  Will be thy champion. Once thou didst confess
  My life was dear to thee; in combat then
  I stood before thee as thine enemy —
  Thou hast not now a single friend but me.

Johan. Thou art my people's enemy and mine.
  Between us there can be no fellowship.
  Thee I can never love, but if thy heart
  Cherish affection for me, let it bring

A blessing on my people. Lead thy troops
Far from the borders of my fatherland;
Give up the keys of all the captured towns,
Restore the booty, set the captives free,
Send hostages the compact to confirm,
And peace I offer thee in my king's name.

ISABEL. Wilt thou, a captive, dictate laws to us?

JOHAN. It must be done; 'tis useless to delay.
Never, oh never, will this land endure
The English yoke; sooner will France become
A mighty sepulchre for England's hosts.
Fallen in battle are your bravest chiefs.
Think how you may achieve a safe retreat;
Your fame is forfeited, your power is lost.

ISABEL. Can you endure her raving insolence?

SCENE X.

A CAPTAIN *enters hastily.*

CAPT. Haste, general! Prepare the host for battle.
The French with flying banners come this way,
Their shining weapons glitter in the vale.

JOHANNA (*with enthusiasm*).
My people come this way! Proud England now
Forth in the field! now boldly must you fight!

FASTOL. Deluded woman, moderate your joy!
You will not see the issue of this day.

JOHAN. My friends will win the fight and I shall die!
The gallant heroes need my arm no more.

LIONEL. These dastard enemies I scorn. They have
In twenty battles fled before our arms,
Ere this heroic maiden fought for them.
All the whole nation I despise, save one,
And this one they have banished. Come, Fastolfe,
We soon will give them such another day
As that of Poictiers and of Agincourt
Do you remain with the fortress, queen,
And guard the maiden till the fight is o'er.
I leave for your protection fifty knights.

FASTOL. How! general, shall we march against the foe
And leave this raging fury in our rear?

JOHAN. What! can a fettered woman frighten thee?

LIONEL. Promise, Johanna, not to free thyself.

JOHAN. To free myself is now my only wish.

ISABEL. Bind her with triple chains. I pledged my life
    That she shall not escape.
                         [*She is bound with heavy chains.*

LIONEL (*to* JOHANNA).   Thou will'st it so!
    Thou dost compel us! still it rests with thee!
    Renounce the French — the English banner bear,
    And thou art free, and these rude, savage men
    Who now desire thy blood shall do thy will.

FASTOLFE (*urgently*).
    Away, away, my general!

JOHANNA.   Spare thy words,
    The French are drawing near. Defend thyself!
            [*Trumpets sound,* LIONEL *hastens forth.*

FASTOL. You know your duty, queen! if fate declares
    Against us, should you see our people fly.

ISABEL (*showing a dagger*).
    Fear not. She shall not live to see our fall.

FASTOLFE (*to* JOHANNA).
    Thou knowest what awaits thee, now implore
    A blessing on the weapons of thy people.   [*Exit.*

SCENE XI.

ISABEL, JOHANNA, SOLDIERS.

JOHAN. Ay! that I will! no power can hinder me.
    Hark to that sound, the war-march of my people!
    How its triumphant notes inspire my heart!
    Ruin to England! victory to France!
    Up, valiant countrymen! The maid is near;
    She cannot, as of yore, before you bear
    Her banner — she is bound with heavy chains;
    But freely from her prison soars her soul,
    Upon the pinions of your battle-song.

ISABEL (*to a* SOLDIER).
    Ascend the watch-tower which commands the field,
    And thence report the progress of the fight.
                         [SOLDIER *ascends.*

JOHAN. Courage, my people! 'Tis the final struggle —
    Another victory, and the foe lies low!

ISABEL. What see'st thou?

SOLDIER.   They're already in close fight.
A furious warrior on a Barbary steed,
  In tiger's skin, leads forward the gens d'armes.
JOHAN.   That's Count Dunois! on, gallant warrior!
  Conquest goes with thee.
SOLDIER.   The Burgundian duke
  Attacks the bridge.
ISABEL.   Would that ten hostile spears
  Might his perfidious heart transfix, the traitor!
SOLD.   Lord Fastolfe gallantly opposes him.
  Now they dismount — they combat man to man
  Our people and the troops of Burgundy.
ISABEL.   Behold'st thou not the Dauphin? See'st thou not
  The royal wave?
SOLDIER.   A cloud of dust
  Shrouds everything.   I can distinguish naught.
JOHAN.   Had he my eyes, or stood I there aloft,
  The smallest speck would not elude my gaze!
  The wild fowl I can number on the wing,
  And mark the falcon in his towering flight.
SOLD.   There is a fearful tumult near the trench;
  The chiefs, it seems, the nobles, combat there.
ISABEL.   Still doth our banner wave?
SOLDIER.   It proudly floats.
JOHAN.   Could I look through the loopholes of the wall,
  I with my glance the battle would control.
SOLD.   Alas! What do I see? Our general's
  Surrounded by the foe!
ISABEL (*points the dagger at* JOHANNA). Die, wretch!
SOLDIER (*quickly*).   He's free!
  The gallant Fastolfe in the rear attacks
  The enemy — he breaks their serried ranks.
ISABEL (*withdrawing the dagger*).
  There spoke thy angel!
SOLDIER.   Victory! They fly.
ISABEL.   Who fly?
SOLDIER.   The French and the Burgundians fly;
  The field is covered o'er with fugitives.
JOHAN.   My God! Thou wilt not thus abandon me!
SOLD.   Yonder they lead a sorely wounded knight;
  The people rush to aid him — he's a prince.

ISABEL. One of our country, or a son of France?

SOLD. They loose his helmet — it is Count Dunois.

JOHANNA (*seizes her fetters with convulsive violence*).
  And I am nothing but a fettered woman!

SOLD. Look yonder! Who the azure mantle wears
  Bordered with gold?

JOHANNA.   That is my lord, the king.

SOLD. His horse is restive, plunges, rears and falls —
  He struggles hard to extricate himself.

  [JOHANNA *accompanies these words with passionate
    movements.*

  Our troops are pressing on in full career,
  They near him, reach him — they surround him now.

JOHAN. Oh, have the heavens above no angels more!

ISABEL (*laughing scornfully*).
  Now is the time, deliverer — now deliver!

JOHANNA (*throws herself upon her knees, and prays with
  passionate violence*).
  Hear me, O God, in my extremity!
  In fervent supplication up to Thee,
  Up to thy heaven above I send my soul.
  The fragile texture of a spider's web,
  As a ship's cable, thou canst render strong;
  Easy it is to thine omnipotence
  To change these fetters into spider's webs —
  Command it, and these massy chains shall fall,
  And these thick walls be rent, Thou, Lord of old,
  Didst strengthen Samson, when enchained and blind
  He bore the bitter scorn of his proud foes.
  Trusting in thee, he seized with mighty power
  The pillars of his prison, bowed himself,
  And overthrew the structure.

SOLDIER.   Triumph!

ISABEL.   How?

SOLD. The king is taken!

JOHANNA (*springing up*). Then God be gracious to me!
  [*She seizes her chains violently with both hands, and
    breaks them asunder. At the same moment rushing
    upon the nearest soldier, she seizes his sword and
    hurries out. All gaze after her, transfixed with as-
    tonishment.*

Scene XII.

The same, without Johanna.

Isabel (*after a long pause*).
How was it? Did I dream? Where is she gone?
How did she break these ponderous iron chains?
A world could not have made me credit it,
If I had not beheld it with these eyes.
Soldier (*from the tower*).
How? Hath she wings? Hath the wind borne her
down?
Isabel. Is she below?
Soldier. She strides amidst the fight:
Her course outspeeds my sight — Now she is here —
Now there — I see her everywhere at once!
— She separates the troops — all yield to her:
The scattered French collect — they form anew!
—Alas! what do I see! Our people cast
Their weapons to the ground, our banners sink ——
Isabel. What! Will she snatch from us the victory?
Sold. She presses forward, right towards the king.
She reaches him — she bears him from the fight —
Lord Fastolfe falls — the general is taken!
Isabel. I'll hear no more. Come down!
Sold. Fly, queen! you will be taken by surprise.
Armed soldiers are advancing tow'rds the tower.
[*He comes down.*
Isabel (*drawing her sword*).
Then fight, ye cowards.

Scene IV.

La Hire *with soldiers. At his entrance the people of the*
Queen *lay down their arms.*

La Hire (*approaching her respectfully*).
Queen, submit yourself —
Your knights have yielded — to resist is vain!
—Accept my proffered services. Command
Where you would be conducted.

ISABEL.   Every place
The same, where I encounter not the Dauphin.
[*She resigns her sword, and follows him with the soldiers.*

The Scene changes to the battle-field.

SCENE XIV.

Soldiers with flying banners occupy the background. Before them the KING *and the* DUKE OF BURGUNDY *appear, bearing* JOHANNA *in their arms; she is mortally wounded, and apparently lifeless. They advance slowly to the front of the stage.* AGNES SOREL *rushes in.*

SOREL (*throwing herself on the bosom of the* KING).
   You're free — you live — I have you back again!
KING.   Yes, I am free — I am so at this price!
                              [*Pointing to* JOHANNA.
SOREL.   Johanna! God! she's dying!
BURGUNDY.   She is gone
   An angel passeth hence! See, how she lies,
   Easy and tranquil, like a sleeping child!
   The peace of heaven around her features plays,
   The breath of life no longer heaves her breast,
   But vital warmth still lingers in her hand.
KING.   She's gone! She never will awaken more,
   Her eye will gaze no more on earthly things.
   She soars on high, a spirit glorified,
   She seeth not our grief, our penitence.
SOREL.   Her eyes unclose — she lives!
BURGUNDY (*in astonishment*).   Can she return
   Back from the grave, triumphant e'en o'er death?
   She riseth up! She standeth!
JOHANNA (*standing up, and looking round*). Where
      am I?
BURG.   With thine own people, maiden — with thy
      friends!
KING.   Supported by thy friend, and by thy king.
JOHANNA (*after looking at him fixedly for some time*).
   No! I am not a sorceress! Indeed
   I am not one.

KING.   Thou'rt holy, as an angel;
    A cloud of error dimmed our mental sight.
JOHANNA (*gazing round her with a joyful smile*).
    And am I really, then, among my friends,
    And am no more rejected and despised ?
    They curse me not — kindly they look on me !
    —Yes, all around me now seems clear again !
    That is my king ! — the banners these of France !
    My banner I behold not — where is it?
    Without my banner I dare not appear;
    To me it was confided by my Lord,
    And I before his throne must lay it down ;
    I there may show it, for I bore it truly.
KING (*averting his face*).   Give her the banner !
    [*It is given to her. She stands quite unsupported, the
    banner in her hand. The heaven is illumined by a
    rosy light.*
JOHAN.   See you the rainbow yonder in the air ?
    Its golden portals heaven doth wide unfold,
    Amid the angel choir she radiant stands,
    The eternal Son she claspeth to her breast,
    Her arms she stretcheth forth to me in love.
    How is it with me?   Light clouds bear me up —
    My ponderous mail becomes a winged robe ;
    I mount — I fly — back rolls the dwindling earth —
    Brief is the sorrow, endless is the joy !
    [*Her banner falls and she sinks lifeless on the ground.
    All remain for some time in speechless sorrow. Upon
    a signal from the* KING, *all the banners are gently
    placed over her, so that she is entirely concealed
    by them.*

USE OF THE CHORUS

IN TRAGEDY.

A POETICAL work must vindicate itself: if the execution be defective, little aid can be derived from commentaries.

On these grounds I might safely leave the chorus to be its own advocate, if we had ever seen it presented in an appropriate manner. But it must be remembered that a dramatic composition first assumes the character of a whole by means of representation on the stage. The poet supplies only the words, to which, in a lyrical tragedy, music and rhythmical motion are essential accessories. It follows, then, that if the chorus is deprived of accompaniments appealing so powerfully to the senses, it will appear a superfluity in the economy of the drama — a mere hinderance to the development of the plot — destructive to the illusion of the scene, and wearisome to the spectators.

To do justice to the chorus, more especially if our aims in poetry be of a grand and elevated character, we must transport ourselves from the actual to a possible stage. It is the privilege of art to furnish for itself whatever is requisite, and the accidental deficiency of auxiliaries ought not to confine the plastic imagination of the poet. He aspires to whatever is most dignified, he labors to realize the ideal in his own mind — though in the execution of his purpose he must needs accommodate himself to circumstances.

The assertion so commonly made that the public degrades art is not well founded. It is the artist that brings the public to the level of his own conceptions; and, in every age in which art has gone to decay, it has fallen through its professors. The people need feeling alone, and feeling they possess. They take their station before the curtain with an unvoiced longing, with a multifarious capacity. They bring with them an aptitude for what is highest — they derive the greatest pleasure from what is judicious and true; and if, with these powers of appreciation, they deign to be satisfied with inferior productions, still, if they have once tasted what is excellent, they will in the end insist on having it supplied to them.

It is sometimes objected that the poet may labor according to an ideal — that the critic may judge from ideas, but that mere executive art is subject to contingencies, and depends for effect on the occasion. Managers will be obstinate; actors are bent on display — the audience is inattentive and unruly. Their object is relaxation, and they are disappointed if mental exertion be required, when they expected only amusement. But if the theatre be made instrumental towards higher objects, the pleasure of the spectator will not be increased, but ennobled. It will be a diversion, but a poetical one. All art is dedicated to pleasure, and there can be no higher and worthier end than to make men happy. The true art is that which provides the highest degree of pleasure; and this consists in the abandonment of the spirit to the free play of all its faculties.

Every one expects from the imaginative arts a certain emancipation from the bounds of reality: we are willing to give a scope to fancy, and recreate ourselves with the possible. The man who expects it the least will nevertheless forget his ordinary pursuits, his everyday existence and individuality, and experience delight from uncommon incidents: — if he be of a serious turn of mind he will acknowledge on the stage that moral government of the

241

world which he fails to discover in real life. But he is, at the same time, perfectly aware that all is an empty show, and that in a true sense he is feeding only on dreams. When he returns from the theatre to the world of realities, he is again compressed within its narrow bounds; he is its denizen as before — for it remains what it was, and in him nothing has been changed. What, then, has he gained beyond a momentary illusive pleasure which vanished with the occasion?

It is because a passing recreation is alone desired that a mere show of truth is thought sufficient. I mean that probability or *vraisemblance* which is so highly esteemed, but which the commonest workers are able to substitute for the true.

Art has for its object not merely to afford a transient pleasure, to excite to a momentary dream of liberty ; its aim is to make us absolutely free ; and this it accomplishes by awakening, exercising, and perfecting in us a power to remove to an objective distance the sensible world ; (which otherwise only burdens us as rugged matter, and presses us down with a brute influence ;) to transform it into the free working of our spirit, and thus acquire a dominion over the material by means of ideas. For the very reason also that true art requires somewhat of the objective and real, it is not satisfied with a show of truth. It rears its ideal edifice on truth itself — on the solid and deep foundations of nature.

But how art can be at once altogether ideal, yet in the strictest sense real; how it can entirely leave the actual, and yet harmonize with nature, is a problem to the multitude ; and hence the distorted views which prevail in regard to poetical and plastic works ; for to ordinary judgments these two requisites seem to counteract each other.

It is commonly supposed that one may be attained by the sacrifice of the other;— the result is a failure to arrive at either. One to whom nature has given a true sensibility, but denied the plastic imaginative power, will be a faithful painter of the real; he will adapt casual appearances, but never catch the spirit of nature. He will only reproduce to us the matter of the world, which, not being our own work, the product of our creative spirit, can never have the beneficent operation of art, of which the essence is freedom. Serious indeed, but unpleasing, is the cast of thought with which such an artist and poet dismisses us ;· we feel ourselves painfully thrust back into the narrow sphere of reality by means of the very art which ought to have emancipated us. On the other hand, a writer endowed with a lively fancy, but destitute of warmth and individuality of feeling, will not concern himself in the least about truth ; he will sport with the stuff of the world, and endeavor to surprise by whimsical combinations ; and as his whole performance is nothing but foam and glitter, he will, it is true, engage the attention for a time, but build up and confirm nothing in the understanding. His playfulness is, like the gravity of the other, thoroughly unpoetical. To string together at will fantastical images is not to travel into the realm of the ideal ; and the imitative reproduction of the actual cannot be called the representation of nature. Both requisites stand so little in contradiction to each other that they are rather one and the same thing ; that art is only true insomuch as it altogether forsakes the actual, and becomes purely ideal. Nature herself is an idea of the mind, and is never presented to the senses. She lies under the veil of appearances, but is herself never apparent. To the art of the ideal alone is lent, or rather absolutely given, the privilege to grasp the spirit of the all and bind it in a corporeal form.

Yet, in truth, even art cannot present it to the senses, but by means of her creative power to the imaginative faculty alone ; and it is thus that she becomes more true than all reality, and more real than all experience. It follows from these premises that the artist can use no single element taken from reality as he finds it — that his work must be ideal in all its parts, if it be designed to have, as it were, an intrinsic reality, and to harmonize with nature.

What is true of art and poetry, in the abstract, holds good as to their various kinds ; and we may apply what has been advanced to the subject of tragedy. In this department it is still necessary to controvert the ordinary notion of the natural, with which poetry is altogether incompatible. A certain ideality has been allowed in painting, though, I fear, on grounds rather conventional than intrinsic ; but in dramatic works what is desired is allusion, which, if it could be accomplished by means of the actual, would be, at best, a paltry deception. All the externals of a theatrical representation are opposed to this notion ; all is merely a symbol of the real. The day itself in a theatre is an artificial one ; the metrical dialogue is itself ideal ; yet the conduct of the play must forsooth be real, and the general effect sacrificed to a part. Thus the French, who have utterly misconceived the spirit of the ancients, adopted on their stage the unities of time and place in the most common and empirical sense ; as though there were any place but the bare ideal one, or any other time than the mere sequence of the incidents.

By the introduction of a metrical dialogue an important progress has been made towards the poetical tragedy. A few lyrical dramas have been successful on the stage, and poetry, by its own living energy, has triumphed over prevailing prejudices. But so long as these erroneous views are entertained little has been done — for it is not enough barely to tolerate as a poetical license that which is, in truth, the essence of all poetry. The introduction of the chorus would be the last and decisive step ; and if it only served this end, namely, to declare open and honorable warfare against naturalism in art, it would be for us a living wall which tragedy had drawn around herself, to guard her from contact with the world of reality, and maintain her own ideal soil, her poetical freedom.

It is well-known that the Greek tragedy had its origin in the chorus ; and though, in process of time it became independent, still it may be said that poetically, and in spirit, the chorus was the source of its existence, and that without these persevering supporters and witnesses of the incident a totally different order of poetry would have grown out of the drama. The abolition of the chorus, and the debasement of this sensibly powerful organ into the characterless substitute of a confidant, is by no means such an improvement in the tragedy as the French, and their imitators, would have it supposed to be.

The old tragedy, which at first only concerned itself with gods, heroes and kings, introduced the chorus as an essential accompaniment. The poets found it in nature, and for that reason employed it. It grew out of the poetical aspect of real life. In the new tragedy it becomes an organ of art, which aids in making the poetry prominent. The modern poet no longer finds the chorus in nature ; he must needs create and introduce it poetically ; that is, he must resolve on such an adaption of his story as will admit of its retrocession to those primitive times and to that simple form of life.

The chorus thus renders more substantial service to the modern dramatist than to the old poet — and for this reason, that it transforms the commonplace actual world into the old poetical one ; that it enables him to dispense with all that is repugnant to poetry, and conducts him back to the most simple, original, and genuine motives of action. The palaces of kings are in these days closed — courts of justice have been transferred from the gates of cities to the interior of buildings ; writing has narrowed the province of speech ; the people itself — the sensibly living mass — when it does not operate as brute force, has become a part of the civil polity, and thereby an abstract idea in our minds ; the deities have returned within the bosoms of mankind. The poet must reopen the palaces — he must place courts of justice beneath the canopy of heaven — restore the gods, reproduce every extreme which the artificial frame of actual life has abolished — throw aside every factitious influence on the mind or condition of man which impedes the manifestation of his inward nature and primitive character, as the statuary rejects modern costume : — and of all external circumstances adopts nothing but what is palpable in the highest of forms — that of humanity.

But precisely as the painter throws around his figures draperies of ample volume, to fill up the space of his picture richly and gracefully, to arrange its several parts in harmonious masses, to give due play to color, which charms and refreshes the eye — and at once to envelop human forms in a spiritual veil, and make them visible — so the tragic poet inlays and entwines his rigidly contracted plot and the strong outlines of his characters with a tissue of lyrical magnificence, in which, as in flowing robes of purple, they move freely and nobly, with a sustained dignity and exalted repose.

In a higher organization, the material, or the elementary, need not be visible ; the chemical color vanishes in the finer tints of the imaginative one. The material, however, has its peculiar effect, and may be included in an artistical composition. But it must deserve its place by animation, fulness and harmony, and give value to the ideal forms which it surrounds, instead of stifling them by its weight.

In respect of the pictorial art, this is obvious to ordinary apprehension, yet in poetry likewise, and in the tragical kind, which is our immediate subject, the same doctrine holds good. Whatever fascinates the senses alone is mere matter, and the rude element of a work of art : — if it takes the lead it will inevitably destroy the poetical — which lies at the exact medium between the ideal and the sensible. But man is so constituted that he is ever impatient to pass from what is fanciful to what is common ; and reflection must, therefore, have its place even in tragedy. But to merit this place it must, by means of delivery, recover what it wants in actual life ; for if the two elements of poetry, the ideal and the sensible, do not operate with an inward mutuality, they must at least act as allies — or poetry is out of the question. If the balance be not intrinsically perfect, the equipoise can only be maintained by an agitation of both scales.

This is what the chorus effects in tragedy. It is, in itself, not an individual but a general conception ; yet it is represented by a palpable body which appeals to the senses with an imposing grandeur. It forsakes the contracted sphere of the incidents to dilate itself over the past and the future, over distant times and nations, and general humanity, to deduce the grand results of life, and pronounce the lessons of wisdom. But all this it does with the full power of fancy — with a bold lyrical freedom which ascends, as with godlike step, to the topmost height of worldly things; and it effects it in conjunction with the whole sensible influence of melody and rhythm, in tones and movements.

The chorus thus exercises a purifying influence on tragic poetry, insomuch as it keeps reflection apart from the incidents, and by this separation arms it with a poetical vigor; as the painter, by means of a rich drapery, changes the ordinary poverty of costume into a charm and an ornament.

But as the painter finds himself obliged to strengthen the tone of color of the living subject, in order to counterbalance the material influences — so the lyrical effusions of the chorus impose upon the poet the necessity of a proportionate elevation of his general diction. It is the chorus alone which entitles the poet to employ this fulness of tone, which at once charms the senses, pervades the spirit, and expands the mind. This one giant form on his canvas obliges him to mount all his figures on the cothurnus, and thus impart a tragical grandeur to his picture. If the chorus be taken away, the diction of the tragedy must generally be lowered, or what is now great and majestic will appear forced and overstrained. The old chorus introduced into the French tragedy would present it in all its poverty, and reduce it to nothing ; yet, without doubt, the same accompaniment would impart to Shakspeare's tragedy its true significance.

As the chorus gives life to the language — so also it gives repose to the action ; but it is that beautiful and lofty repose which is the characteristic of a true work of art. For the mind of the spectator ought to maintain its freedom through the most impassioned scenes ; it should not be the mere prey of impressions, but calmly and severely detach itself from the emotions which it suffers. The commonplace objection made to the chorus, that it disturbs the illusion, and blunts the edge of the feelings, is what constitutes its highest recommendation ; for it is this blind force of the affections which the true artist deprecates — this illusion is what he disdains to excite. If the strokes which tragedy inflicts on our bosoms followed without respite, the passion would overpower the action. We should mix ourselves up with the subject-matter, and no longer stand above it. It is by holding asunder the different parts, and stepping between the passions with its composing views, that the chorus restores to us our freedom, which would else be lost in the tempest. The characters of the drama need this intermission in order to collect themselves ; for they are no real beings who obey the impulse of the moment, and merely represent individuals — but ideal persons and representatives of their species, who enunciate the deep things of humanity.

Thus much on my attempt to revive the old chorus on the tragic stage. It is true that choruses are not unknown to modern tragedy ; but the chorus of the Greek drama, as I have employed it — the chorus, as a single ideal person, furthering and accompanying the whole plot — is of an entirely distinct character ; and when, in discussion on the Greek tragedy, I hear mention made of choruses, I generally suspect the speaker's ignorance of his subject.

In my view the chorus has never been reproduced since the decline of the old tragedy.

I have divided it into two parts, and represented it in contest with itself; but this occurs where it acts as a real person, and as an unthinking multitude. As chorus and an ideal person it is always one and entire. I have also several times dispensed with its presence on the stage. For this liberty I have the example of Æschylus, the creator of tragedy, and Sophocles, the greatest master of his art.

Another license it may be more difficult to excuse. I have blended together the Christian religion and the pagan mythology, and introduced recollections of the Moorish superstition. But the scene of the drama is Messina — where these three religions either exercised a living influence, or appealed to the senses in monumental remains. Besides, I consider it a privilege of poetry to deal with different religions as a collective whole, in which everything that bears an individual character, and expresses a peculiar mode of feeling, has its place. Religion itself, the idea of a Divine Power, lies under the veil of all religions; and it must be permitted to the poet to represent it in the form which appears the most appropriate to his subject.

THE BRIDE OF MESSINA.

DRAMATIS PERSONÆ.

ISABELLA, *Princess of Messina.*
DON MANUEL }
DON CÆSAR } *her Sons.*
BEATRICE.
DIEGO, *an ancient Servant.*

MESSENGERS.
THE ELDERS OF MESSINA, *mute.*
THE CHORUS, *consisting of the Followers of the two Princes.*

SCENE I.

A spacious hall, supported on columns, with entrances on both sides; at the back of the stage a large folding-door leading to a chapel.

DONNA ISABELLA *in mourning; the* ELDERS OF MESSINA.

ISAB. Forth from my silent chamber's deep recesses,
  Gray Fathers of the State, unwillingly
  I come; and, shrinking from your gaze, uplift
  The veil that shades my widowed brows: the light
  And glory of my days is fled forever!
  And best in solitude and kindred gloom
  To hide these sable weeds, this grief-worn frame,
  Beseems the mourner's heart. A mighty voice
  Inexorable — duty's stern command,
  Calls me to light again.
                          Not twice the moon
  Has filled her orb since to the tomb ye bore
  My princely spouse, your city's lord, whose arm
  Against a world of envious foes around
  Hurled fierce defiance! Still his spirit lives
  In his heroic sons, their country's pride:
  Ye marked how sweetly from their childhood's bloom
  They grew in joyous promise to the years
  Of manhood's strength; yet in their secret hearts,

From some mysterious root accursed, upsprung
Unmitigable, deadly hate, that spurned
All kindred ties, all youthful, fond affections,
Still ripening with their thoughtful age; not mine
The sweet accord of family bliss; though each
Awoke a mother's rapture; each alike
Smiled at my nourishing breast! for me alone
Yet lives one mutual thought, of children's love;
In these tempestuous souls discovered else
By mortal strife and thirst of fierce revenge.
    While yet their father reigned, his stern control
Tamed their hot spirits, and with iron yoke
To awful justice bowed their stubborn will:
Obedient to his voice, to outward seeming
They calmed their wrathful mood, nor in array
Ere met, of hostile arms; yet unappeased
Sat brooding malice in their bosoms' depths;
They little reck of hidden springs whose power
Can quell the torrent's fury: scarce their sire
In death had closed his eyes, when, as the spark
That long in smouldering embers sullen lay,
Shoots forth a towering flame; so unconfined
Burst the wild storm of brothers' hate triumphant
O'er nature's holiest bands. Ye saw, my friends,
Your country's bleeding wounds, when princely strife
Woke discord's maddening fires, and ranged her sons
In mutual deadly conflict; all around
Was heard the clash of arms, the din of carnage,
And e'en these halls were stained with kindred gore.
    Torn was the state with civil rage, this heart
With pangs that mothers feel; alas, unmindful
Of aught but public woes, and pitiless
You sought my widow's chamber — there with taunts
And fierce reproaches for your country's ills
From that polluted spring of brother's hate
Derived, invoked a parent's warning voice,
And threatening told of people's discontent
And princes' crimes! "Ill-fated land! now wasted
By thy unnatural sons, ere long the prey
Of foeman's sword! Oh, haste," you cried, "and end
This strife! bring peace again, or soon Messina

Shall bow to other lords." Your stern decree
Prevailed ; this heart, with all a mother's anguish
O'erlabored, owned the weight of public cares.
I flew, and at my children's feet, distracted,
A suppliant lay; till to my prayers and tears
The voice of nature answered in their breasts !
   Here in the palace of their sires, unarmed,
In peaceful guise Messina shall behold
The long inveterate foes; this is the day !
E'en now I wait the messenger that brings
The tidings of my sons' approach : be ready
To give your princes joyful welcome home
With reverence such as vassals may beseem.
Bethink ye to fulfil your subject duties,
And leave to better wisdom weightier cares.
Dire was their strife to them, and to the State
Fruitful of ills; yet, in this happy bond
Of peace united, know that they are mighty
To stand against a world in arms, nor less
Enforce their sovereign will — against yourselves.
[*The* ELDERS *retire in silence ; she beckons to an old*
   attendant, who remains.
                              Diego !
DIEGO.   Honored mistress !
ISAB. Old faithful servant, thou true heart, come near me ;
   Sharer of all a mother's woes, be thine
   The sweet communion of her joys : my treasure
   Shrined in thy heart, my dear and holy secret
   Shall pierce the envious veil, and shine triumphant
   To cheerful day; too long by harsh decrees,
   Silent and overpowered, affection yet
   Shall utterance find in Nature's tones of rapture !
   And this unprisoned heart leap to the embrace
   Of all it holds most dear, returned to glad
   My desolate halls ;
                         So bend thy aged steps
   To the old cloisteresd anctuary that guards
   The darling of my soul, whose innocence
   To thy true love (sweet pledge of happier days) !
   Trusting I gave, and asked from fortune's storm
   A resting-place and shrine.   Oh, in this hour

Of bliss, the dear reward of all thy cares.
Give to my longing arms my child again!
    [*Trumpets are heard in the distance.*
Haste! be thy footsteps winged with joy — I hear
The trumpet's blast, that tells in warlike accents
My sons are near:
[*Exit* DIEGO. *Music is heard in an opposite direction,
 and becomes gradually louder.*
      Messina is awake!
Hark! how the stream of tongues hoarse murmuring
Rolls on the breeze, — 'tis they! my mother's heart
Feels their approach, and beats with mighty throes
Responsive to the loud, resounding march!
They come! they come! my children! oh, my chil-
   dren!   [*Exit.*
    The CHORUS *enters.*

(*It consists of two semi-choruses which enter at the same
time from opposite sides, and after marching round the
stage range themselves in rows, each on the side by which
it entered. One semi-chorus consists of young knights,
the other of older ones, each has its peculiar costume
and ensigns. When the two choruses stand opposite
to each other, the march ceases, and the two leaders
speak.*)*
    First Chorus (CAJETAN).

I greet ye, glittering halls
 Of olden time!
Cradle of kings! Hail! lordly roof,
 In pillared majesty sublime!

 Sheathed be the sword!
 In chains before the portal lies
The fiend with tresses snake-entwined,
 Fell Discord! Gently treat the inviolate floor!
  Peace to this royal dome!
Thus by the Furies' brood we swore,
And all the dark, avenging Deities!

---

* The first chorus consists of Cajetan, Berengar, Manfred, Tristan, and
eight followers of Don Manuel. The second of Bohemund, Roger, Hippolyte,
and nine others of the party of Don Cæsar.

Second Chorus (BOHEMUND).

I rage ! I burn ! and scarce refrain
  To lift the glittering steel on high,
For, lo ! the Gorgon-visaged train
  Of the detested foeman nigh :
Shall I my swelling heart control ?
  To parley deign — or still in mortal strife
The tumult of my soul ?
Dire sister, guardian of the spot, to thee
Awe-struck I bend the knee,
Nor dare with arms profane thy deep tranquillity !

First Chorus (CAJETAN).

  Welcome the peaceful strain !
Together we adore the guardian power
Of these august abodes !
  Sacred the hour
To kindred brotherly ties
And reverend, holy sympathies ; —
Our hearts the genial charm shall own,
And melt awhile at friendship's soothing tone : —
  But when in yonder plain
We meet — then peace away !
Come gleaming arms, and battle's deadly fray !

The whole Chorus.

But when in yonder plain
We meet — then peace away !
Come gleaming arms, and battle's deadly fray !

First Chorus (BERENGAR).

I hate thee not — nor call thee foe,
My brother ! this our native earth,
The land that gave our fathers birth : —
Of chief's behest the slave decreed,
The vassal draws the sword at need,
For chieftain's rage we strike the blow,
For stranger lords our kindred blood must flow.

Second Chorus (BOHEMUND).

Hate fires their souls — we ask not why ; —
At honor's call to fight and die,

Boast of the true and brave !
Unworthy of a soldier's name
Who burns not for his chieftain's fame !

The whole Chorus.

Unworthy of a soldier's name
Who burns not for his chieftain's fame!

One of the Chorus (BERENGAR).

Thus spoke within my bosom's core
  The thought — as hitherward I strayed ;
And pensive 'mid the waving store,
  I mused, of autumn's yellow glade : —
These gifts of nature's bounteous reign, —
The teeming earth, and golden grain,
Yon elms, among whose leaves entwine
The tendrils of the clustering vine ; —
Gay children of our sunny clime, —
Region of spring's eternal prime !
Each charm should woo to love and joy,
No cares the dream of bliss annoy,
And pleasure through life's summer day
Speed every laughing hour away.
We rage in blood, — oh, dire disgrace !
For this usurping, alien race ;
From some far distant land they came,
Beyond the sun's departing flame.
And owned upon our friendly shore
The welcome of our sires of yore.
Alas ! their sons in thraldom pine,
The vassals of this stranger line.

A second (MANFRED).

Yes! pleased, on our land, from his azure way,
The sun ever smiles with unclouded ray.
But never, fair isle, shall thy sons repose
'Mid the sweets which the faithless waves enclose
On their bosom they wafted the corsair bold,
With his dreaded barks to our coast of old.
For thee was thy dower of beauty vain,
'Twas the treasure that lured the spoiler's train.

Oh, ne'er from these smiling vales shall rise
A sword for our vanquished liberties;
'Tis not where the laughing Ceres reigns,
And the jocund lord of the flowery plains : —
Where the iron lies hid in the mountain cave,
Is the cradle of empire — the home of the brave!
[*The folding-doors at the back of the stage are thrown
    open.* DONNA ISABELLA *appears between her sons,*
DON MANUEL *and* DON CÆSAR.

Both Choruses (CAJETAN).

Lift high the notes of praise!
    Behold! where lies the awakening sun,
She comes, and from her queenly brow
    Shoots glad, inspiring rays.
        Mistress, we bend to thee!

First Chorus.

Fair is the moon amid the starry choir
    That twinkle o'er the sky,
    Shining in silvery, mild tranquillity ; —
The mother with her sons more fair!
    See! blooming at her side,
She leads the royal, youthful pair;
    With gentle grace, and soft, maternal pride,
    Attempering sweet their manly fire.

Second Chorus (BERENGAR).

From this fair stem a beauteous tree
    With ever-springing boughs shall smile,
    And with immortal verdure shade our isle ;
    Mother of heroes, joy to thee!
Triumphant as the sun thy kingly race
    Shall spread from clime to clime,
    And give a deathless name to rolling time !

ISABELLA (*comes forward with her* SONS).
    Look down! benignant Queen of Heaven, and still,
This proud tumultuous heart, that in my breast
Swells with a mother's tide of ecstasy,
As blazoned in these noble youths, my image
More perfect shows ; — Oh, blissful hour! the first

That comprehends the fulness of my joy,
When long-constrained affection dares to pour
In unison of transport from my heart,
Unchecked, a parent's undivided love:
Oh! it was ever one — my sons were twain.
Say — shall I revel in the dreams of bliss,
And give my soul to nature's dear emotions?
Is this warm pressure of thy brother's hand
A dagger in thy breast?   [*To* Don Manuel
                              Or when my eyes
Feed on that brow with love's enraptured gaze,
Is it a wrong to thee?   [*To* Don Cæsar.
                          Trembling, I pause,
Lest e'en affection's breath should wake the fires
Of slumbering hate.
            [*After regarding both with inquiring looks*
                  Speak! In your secret hearts
What purpose dwells? Is it the ancient feud
Unreconciled, that in your father's halls
A moment stilled; beyond the castle gates,
Where sits infuriate war, and champs the bit —
Shall rage anew in mortal, bloody conflict?

              Chorus (Bohemund).

Concord or strife — the fate's decree
Is bosomed yet in dark futurity!
What comes, we little heed to know,
Prepared for aught the hour may show!

Isabella (*looking round*).
What mean these arms? this warlike, dread array,
That in the palace of your sires portends
Some fearful issue? needs a mother's heart
Outpoured, this rugged witness of her joys?
Say, in these folding arms shall treason hide
The deadly snare? Oh, these rude, pitiless men,
The ministers of your wrath! — trust not the show
Of seeming friendship; treachery in their breasts
Lurks to betray, and long-dissembled hate.
Ye are a race of other lands; your sires
Profaned their soil; and ne'er the invader's yoke
Was easy — never in the vassal's heart

Languished the hope of sweet revenge; — our sway
Not rooted in a people's love, but owns
Allegiance from their fears; with secret joy —
For conquest's ruthless sword, and thraldom's chains
From age to age, they wait the atoning hour
Of princes' downfall; — thus their bards awake
The patriot strain, and thus from sire to son
Rehearsed, the old traditionary tale
Beguiles the winter's night. False is the world,
My sons, and light are all the specious ties
By fancy twined : friendship — deceitful name !
Its gaudy flowers but deck our summer fortune,
To wither at the first rude breath of autumn !
So happy to whom heaven has given a brother ;
The friend by nature signed — the true and stead-
  fast !
Nature alone is honest — nature only —
When all we trusted strews the wintry shore —
On her eternal anchor lies at rest,
Nor heeds the tempest's rage.

DON MANUEL.   My mother !
DON CÆSAR.   Hear me !
ISABELLA (*taking their hands*).
 Be noble, and forget the fancied wrongs
Of boyhood's age : more godlike is forgiveness
Than victory, and in your father's grave
Should sleep the ancient hate : — Oh, give your days
Renewed henceforth to peace and holy love !
[*She recedes one or two steps, as if to give them space to
 approach each other. Both fix their eyes on the
 ground without regarding one another.*
ISABELLA (*after awaiting for some time, with suppressed
emotion, a demonstration on the part of her sons*).
 I can no more ; my prayers — my tears are vain : —
'Tis well ! obey the demon in your hearts !
Fulfil your dread intent, and stain with blood
The holy altars of your household gods ; —
These halls that gave you birth, the stage where
  murder
Shall hold his festival of mutual carnage
Beneath a mother's eye ! — then, foot to foot,

Close, like the Theban pair, with maddening gripe,
And fold each other in a last embrace!
Each press with vengeful thrust the dagger home,
And " Victory !" be your shriek of death : — nor then
Shall discord rest appeased ; the very flame
That lights your funeral pyre shall tower dissevered
In ruddy columns to the skies, and tell
With horrid image — "thus they lived and died!"
          [*She goes away ; the* BROTHERS *stand as before.*

Chorus (CAJETAN).

How have her words with soft control
Resistless calmed the tempest of my soul!
     No guilt of kindred blood be mine !
Thus with uplifted hands I pray;
Think, brothers, on the awful day,
     And tremble at the wrath divine !

DON CÆSAR (*without taking his eyes from the ground*).
     Thou art my elder — speak — without dishonor
     I yield to thee.
DON MANUEL.   One gracious word, an instant,
     My tongue is rival in the strife of love !
DON C. I am the guiltier — weaker ——
DON MANUEL.   Say not so!
     Who doubts thy noble heart, knows thee not well;
     Thy words were prouder, if thy soul were mean.
DON C. It burns indignant at the thought of wrong —
     But thou — methinks, in passion's fiercest mood,
     'Twas aught but scorn that harbored in thy breast.
DON M. Oh! had I known thy spirit thus to peace
     Inclined, what thousand griefs had never torn
     A mother's heart !
DON CÆSAR.   I find thee just and true :
     Men spoke thee proud of soul.
DON MANUEL.   The curse of greatness !
     Ears ever open to the babbler's tale.
DON C. Thou art too proud to meanness — I to false-
          hood !
DON M. We're deceived, betrayed !
DON CÆSAR.   The sport of frenzy !
DON M. And said my mother true, false is the world ?

Don C. Believe her, false as air.

Don Manuel.   Give me thy hand!

Don C. And thine be ever next my heart!

[*They stand clasping each other's hands, and regard
each other in silence.*

Don Manuel.   I gaze
Upon thy brow, and still behold my mother
In some dear lineament.

Don Cæsar.   Her image looks
From thine, and wondrous in my bosom wakes
Affection's springs.

Don Manuel.   And is it thou? — that smile
Benignant on thy face? — thy lips that charm
With gracious sounds of love and dear forgiveness?

Don C. Is this my brother, this the hated foe?
His mien all gentleness and truth, his voice,
Whose soft prevailing accents breathe of friendship!

[*After a pause.*

Don M. Shall aught divide us?

Don Cæsar.   We are one forever!

[*They rush into each other's arms.*

1st Chorus (*to the Second*).
Why stand we thus, and coldly gaze,
  While Nature's holy transports burn?
No dear embrace of happier days
  The pledge — that discord never shall return!
Brothers are they by kindred band;
We own the ties of home and native land.

[*Both Choruses embrace.*

A Messenger *enters.*

2d Chorus *to* Don Cæsar (Bohemund).
Rejoice, my prince, thy messenger returns:
And mark that beaming smile! the harbinger
Of happy tidings.

Messenger.   Health to me, and health
To this delivered state! Oh sight of bliss,
That lights mine eyes with rapture! I behold
Their hands in sweet accord entwined; the sons
Of my departed lord, the princely pair
Dissevered late by conflict's hottest rage.

DON C. Yes, from the flames of hate, a new-born Phœnix,
  Our love aspires!
MESSENGER.   I bring another joy;
  My staff is green with flourishing shoots.
DON CÆSAR (*taking him aside*).   Oh, tell me
  Thy gladsome message.
MESSENGER.   All is happiness
  On this auspicious day; long sought, the lost one
  Is found.
DON CÆSAR. Discovered! Oh, where is she? Speak!
MESS. Within Messina's walls she lies concealed.
DON MANUEL (*turning to the* 1ST SEMI-CHORUS).
  A ruddy glow mounts in my brother's cheek,
  And pleasure dances in his sparkling eye;
  Whate'er the spring, with sympathy of love
  My inmost heart partakes his joy.
DON CÆSAR (*to the* MESSENGER).   Come, lead me;
  Farewell, Don Manuel; to meet again
  Enfolded in a mother's arms! I fly
  To cares of utmost need.   [*He is about to depart.*
DON MANUEL.   Make no delay;
  And happiness attend thee!
DON CÆSAR (*after a pause of reflection, he returns*).
          How thy looks
  Awake my soul to transport! Yes, my brother,
  We shall be friends indeed! This hour is bright
  With glad presage of ever-springing love,
  That in the enlivening beam shall flourish fair,
  Sweet recompense of wasted years!
DON MANUEL.   The blossom
  Betokens goodly fruit.
DON CÆSAR.   I tear myself
  Reluctant from thy arms, but think not less —
  If thus I break this festal hour — my heart
  Thrills with a holy joy.
DON MANUEL (*with manifest absence of mind*).
          Obey the moment!
  Our lives belong to love.
DON CÆSAR.   What calls me hence ——
DON M. Enough! thou leav'st thy heart.
DON CÆSAR.   No envious secret

Shall part us long ; soon the last darkening fold
Shall vanish from my breast.
                    [*Turning to the* CHORUS.
                    Attend ! Forever
Stilled is our strife; he is my deadliest foe,
Detested as the gates of hell, who dares
To blow the fires of discord ; none may hope
To win my love, that with malicious tales
Encroach upon a brother's ear, and point
With busy zeal of false, officious friendship.
The dart of some rash, angry word, escaped
From passion's heat; it wounds not from the lips,
But, swallowed by suspicion's greedy ear,
Like a rank, poisonous weed, embittered creeps,
And hangs about her with a thousand shoots,
Perplexing nature's ties.
    [*He embraces his brother again, and goes away accom-
    panied by the* 2D CHORUS.
Chorus (CAJETAN).   Wondering, my prince,
    I gaze, for in thy looks some mystery
    Strange-seeming shows : scarce with abstracted mien
    And cold thou answered'st, when with earnest heart
    Thy brother poured the strain of dear affection.
    As in a dream thou stand'st, and lost in thought,
    As though — dissevered from its earthly frame —
    Thy spirit roved afar.   Not thine the breast
    That deaf to nature's voice, ne'er owned the throbs
    Of kindred love : — nay more — like one entranced
    In bliss, thou look'st around, and smiles of rapture
    Play on thy cheek.
DON MANUEL.   How shall my lips declare
    The transports of my swelling heart ? My brother
    Revels in glad surprise, and from his breast
    Instinct with strange new-felt emotions, pours
    The tide of joy ; but mine — no hate came with me,
    Forgot the very spring of mutual strife !
    High o'er this earthly sphere, on rapture's wings,
    My spirit floats ; and in the azure sea,
    Above — beneath — no track of envious night
    Disturbs the deep serene !   I view these halls,
    And picture to my thoughts the timid joy

Of my sweet bride, as through the palace gates,
In pride of queenly state, I lead her home.
She loved alone the loving one, the stranger,
And little deems that on her beauteous brow
Messina's prince shall 'twine the nuptial wreath.
How sweet, with unexpected pomp of greatness,
To glad the darling of my soul ! too long
I brook this dull delay of crowning bliss !
Her beauty's self, that asks no borrowed charm,
Shall shine refulgent, like the diamond's blaze
That wins new lustre from the circling gold !
Chorus (CAJETAN).
Long have I marked thee, prince, with curious eye,
Foreboding of some mystery deep enshrined
Within thy laboring breast.   This day, impatient,
Thy lips have burst the seal; and unconstrained
Confess a lover's joy; — the gladdening chase,
The Olympian coursers, and the falcon's flight
Can charm no more: — soon as the sun declines
Beneath the ruddy west, thou hiest thee quick
To some sequestered path, of mortal eye
Unseen — not one of all our faithful train
Companion of thy solitary way.
Say, why so long concealed the blissful flame?
Stranger to fear — ill-brooked thy princely heart
One thought unuttered.
DON MANUEL.   Ever on the wing
Is mortal joy ; — with silence best we guard
The fickle good ; — but now, so near the goal
Of all my cherished hopes, I dare to speak.
To-morrow's sun shall see her mine ! no power
Of hell can make us twain !   With timid stealth
No longer will I creep at dusky eve,
To taste the golden fruits of Cupid's tree,
And snatch a fearful, fleeting bliss : to-day
With bright to-morrow shall be one !   So smooth
As runs the limpid brook, or silvery sand
That marks the flight of time, our lives shall flow
In continuity of joy !
Chorus (CAJETAN).   Already
Our hearts, my prince, with silent vows have blessed

Thy happy love; and now from every tongue,
For her — the royal, beauteous bride — should sound
The glad acclaim; so tell what nook unseen,
What deep umbrageous solitude, enshrines
The charmer of thy heart?   With magic spells
Almost I deem she mocks our gaze, for oft
In eager chase we scour each rustic path
And forest dell; yet not a trace betrayed
The lover's haunts, ne'er were the footsteps marked
Of this mysterious fair.

DON MANUEL.   The spell is broke!
And all shall be revealed: now list my tale: —
'Tis five months flown, — my father yet controlled
The land, and bowed our necks with iron sway;
Little I knew but the wild joys of arms,
And mimic warfare of the chase; —
                                        One day, —
Long had we tracked the boar with zealous toil
On yonder woody ridge: — it chanced, pursuing
A snow-white hind, far from your train I roved
Amid the forest maze; — the timid beast,
Along the windings of the narrow vale,
Through rocky cleft and thick-entangled brake,
Flew onward, scarce a moment lost, nor distant
Beyond a javelin's throw; nearer I came not,
Nor took an aim; when through a garden's gate,
Sudden she vanished: — from my horse quick spring-
          ing,
I followed: — lo! the poor scared creature lay
Stretched at the feet of a young, beauteous nun,
That strove with fond caress of her fair hands
To still its throbbing heart: wondering, I gazed,
And motionless — my spear, in act to strike,
High poised — while she, with her large piteous eyes
For mercy sued — and thus we stood in silence
Regarding one another.
                              How long the pause
I know not — time itself forgot; — it seemed
Eternity of bliss: her glance of sweetness
Flew to my soul; and quick the subtle flame
Pervaded all my heart: —

                                    But what I spoke,
And how this blessed creature answered, none
May ask; it floats upon my thought, a dream
Of childhood's happy dawn!   Soon as my sense
Returned, I felt her bosom throb responsive
To mine, — then fell melodious on my ear
The sound, as of a convent bell, that called
To vesper song; and, like some shadowy vision
That melts in air, she flitted from my sight,
And was beheld no more.
Chorus (CAJETAN).   Thy story thrills
My breast with pious awe!   Prince, thou hast robbed
The sanctuary, and for the bride of heaven
Burned with unholy passion!   Oh, remember
The cloister's sacred vows!
DON MANUEL.   Thenceforth one path
My footsteps wooed; the fickle train was still
Of young desires — new felt my being's aim,
My soul revealed! and as the pilgrim turns
His wistful gaze, where, from the orient sky,
With gracious lustre beams Redemption's star; —
So to that brightest point of heaven, her presence,
My hopes and longings centred all.   No sun
Sank in the western waves, but smiled farewell
To two united lovers: — thus in stillness
Our hearts were twined, — the all-seeing air above us
Alone the faithful witness of our joys!
Oh, golden hours!   Oh, happy days! nor Heaven
Indignant viewed our bliss; — no vows enchained
Her spotless soul; naught but the link which bound it
Eternally to mine!
Chorus (CAJETAN).   Those hallowed walls,
Perchance the calm retreat of tender youth,
No living grave?
DON MANUEL.   In infant innocence
Consigned a holy pledge, ne'er has she left
Her cloistered home.
Chorus (CAJETAN).   But what her royal line?
The noble only spring from noble stem.
DON M.   A secret to herself, — she ne'er has learned
Her name or fatherland.

Chorus (CAJETAN). And not a trace
Guides to her being's undiscovered springs?
DON M. An old domestic, the sole messenger
Sent by her unknown mother, oft bespeaks her
Of kingly race.
Chorus (CAJETAN). And hast thou won naught else
From her garrulous age?
DON MANUEL. Too much I feared to peril
My secret bliss!
Chorus (CAJETAN). What were his words? What
tidings
He bore — perchance thou know'st.
DON MANUEL. Oft he has cheered her
With promise of a happier time, when all
Shall be revealed.
Chorus (CAJETAN). Oh, say — betokens aught
The time is near?
DON MANUEL. Not distant far the day
That to the arms of kindred love once more
Shall give the long forsaken, orphaned maid —
Thus with mysterious words the aged man
Has shadowed oft what most I dread — for awe
Of change disturbs the soul supremely blest:
Nay, more; but yesterday his message spoke
The end of all my joys — this very dawn,
He told, should smile auspicious on her fate,
And light to other scenes — no precious hour
Delayed my quick resolves — by night I bore her
In secret to Messina.
Chorus (CAJETAN). Rash the deed
Of sacrilegious spoil! forgive, my prince,
The bold rebuke; thus to unthinking youth
Old age may speak in friendship's warning voice.
DON M. Hard by the convent of the Carmelites,
In a sequestered garden's tranquil bound,
And safe from curious eyes, I left her, — hastening
To meet my brother: trembling there she counts
The slow-paced hours, nor deems how soon tri-
umphant
In queenly state, high on the throne of fame,
Messina shall behold my timid bride.

For next, encompassed by your knightly train,
With pomp of greatness in the festal show,
Her lover's form shall meet her wondering gaze!
Thus will I lead her to my mother; thus —
While countless thousands on her passage wait
Amid the loud acclaim — the royal bride
Shall reach my palace gates!

Chorus (CAJETAN).   Command us, prince,
We live but to obey!

DON MANUEL.   I tore myself
Reluctant from her arms; my every thought
Shall still be hers: so come along, my friends,
To where the turbaned merchant spreads his store
Of fabrics gold enwrought with curious art;
And all the gathered wealth of eastern climes.
First choose the well-formed sandals — meet to guard
And grace her delicate feet; then for her robe —
The tissue, pure as Etna's snow that lies
Nearest the sun — light as the wreathy mist
At summer dawn — so playful let it float
About her airy limbs. A girdle next,
Purple with gold embroidered o'er, to bind
With witching grace the tunic that confines
Her bosom's swelling charms: of silk the mantle,
Gorgeous with like empurpled hues, and fixed
With clasp of gold — remember, too, the bracelets
To gird her beauteous arms; nor leave the treasure
Of ocean's pearly deeps and coral caves.
About her locks entwine a diadem
Of purest gems — the ruby's fiery glow
Commingling with the emerald's green. A veil,
From her tiara pendent to her feet,
Like a bright fleecy cloud shall circle round
Her slender form; and let a myrtle wreath
Crown the enchanting whole!

Chorus (CAJETAN).   We haste, my prince.
Amid the Bazar's glittering rows, to cull
Each rich adornment.

DON MANUEL.   From my stables lead
A palfrey, milk-white as the steeds that draw
The chariot of the sun; purple the housings,

The bridle sparkling o'er with precious gems,
For it shall bear my queen! Yourselves be ready
With trumpet's cheerful clang, in martial train
To lead your mistress home : let two attend me,
The rest await my quick return ; and each
Guard well my secret purpose.

[He goes away accompanied by two of the CHORUS.

Chorus (CAJÉTAN).

The princely strife is o'er, and say,
    What sport shall wing the slow-paced hours,
And cheat the tedious day ?
    With hope and fear's enlivening zest
    Disturb the slumber of the breast,
    And wake life's dull, untroubled sea
    With freshening airs of gay variety.

One of the Chorus (MANFRED).

Lovely is peace ! A beauteous boy,
Couched listless by the rivulet's glassy tide,
    'Mid nature's tranquil scene,
He views the lambs that skip with innocent joy,
    And crop the meadow's flowering pride : —
Then with his flute's enchanting sound,
He wakes the mountain echoes round,
    Or slumbers in the sunset's ruddy sheen,
    Lulled by the murmuring melody.
But war for me ! my spirit's treasure,
Its stern delight, and wilder pleasure :
I love the peril and the pain,
And revel in the surge of fortune's boisterous **main** !

A second (BERENGAR).

Is there not love, and beauty's smile
That lures with soft, resistless wile?
'Tis thrilling hope! 'tis rapturous fear
'Tis heaven upon this mortal sphere ;
When at her feet we bend the knee,
And own the glance of kindred ecstasy !
For ever on life's checkered way,
    'Tis love that tints the darkening hues of **care**
With soft benignant ray :

The mirthful daughter of the wave,
  Celestial Venus ever fair,
Enchants our happy spring with fancy's gleam,
And wakes the airy forms of passion's golden dream

First (MANFRED).

To the wild woods away!
Quick let us follow in the train
Of her, chaste huntress of the silver bow;
And from the rocks amain
Track through the forest gloom the bounding roe,
  The war-god's merry bride,
The chase recalls the battle's fray,
  And kindles victory's pride: —
Up with the streaks of early morn,
  We scour with jocund hearts the misty vale,
Loud echoing to the cheerful horn —
  Over mountain — over dale —
And every languid sense repair,
Bathed in the rushing streams of cold, reviving air.

Second (BERENGAR).

Or shall we trust the ever-moving sea,
The azure goddess, blithe and free.
Whose face, the mirror of the cloudless sky,
Lures to her bosom wooingly?
Quick let us build on the dancing waves
A floating castle gay,
And merrily, merrily, swim away!
Who ploughs with venturous keel the brine
Of the ocean crystalline —
His bride is fortune, the world his own,
For him a harvest blooms unsown: —
Here, like the wind that swift careers
  The circling bound of earth and sky,
  Flits ever-changeful destiny!
Of airy chance 'tis the sportive reign,
And hope ever broods on the boundless main!

A third (CAJETAN).

Nor on the watery waste alone
  Of the tumultuous, heaving sea; —

On the firm earth that sleeps secure,
  Based on the pillars of eternity.
Say, when shall mortal joy endure?
New bodings in my anxious breast,
    Waked by this sudden friendship, rise;
Ne'er would I choose my home of rest
  On the stilled lava-stream, that cold
    Beneath the mountain lies:
Not thus was discord's flame controlled—
Too deep the rooted hate — too long
  They brooded in their sullen hearts
O'er unforgotten, treasured wrong.
In warning visions oft dismayed,
  I read the signs of coming woe;
And now from this mysterious maid
  My bosom tells the dreaded ills shall flow:
Unblest, I deem, the bridal chain
  Shall knit their secret loves, accursed
With holy cloisters' spoil profane.
No crooked paths to virtue lead;
Ill fruit has ever sprung from evil seed!

BERENGAR.

And thus to sad unhallowed rites
  Of an ill-omened nuptial tie,
Too well ye know their father bore
  A bride of mournful destiny,
Torn from his sire, whose awful curse has sped
Heaven's vengeance on the impious bed!
This fierce, unnatural rage atones
A parent's crime — decreed by fate,
Their mother's offspring, strife and hate!

[*The scene changes to a garden opening on the sea.*

BEATRICE (*steps forward from an alcove. She walks to
and fro with an agitated air, looking round in every
direction. Suddenly she stands still and listens.*)
  No! 'tis not he: 'twas but the playful wind
  Rustling the pine-tops. To his ocean bed
  The sun declines, and with o'erwearied heart

I count the lagging hours : an icy chill
Creeps through my frame ; the very solitude
And awful silence fright my trembling soul !
Where'er I turnn aught meets my gaze — he leaves
          me
Forsaken and alone !
And like a rushing stream the city's hum
Floats on the breeze, and dull the mighty sea
Rolls murmuring to the rocks : I shrink to nothing
With horrors compassed round ; and like the leaf,
Borne on the autumn blast, am hurried onward
Through boundless space.
                              Alas ! that e'er I left
My peaceful cell — no cares, no fond desires
Disturbed my breast, unruffled as the stream
That glides in sunshine through the verdant mead :
Nor poor in joys.   Now — on the mighty surge
Of fortune, tempest-tossed — the world enfolds me
With giant arms !   Forgot my childhood's ties
I listened to the lover's flattering tale —
Listened, and trusted !   From the sacred dome
Allured — betrayed — for sure some hell-born magic
Enchained my frenzied sense — I fled with him,
The invader of religion's dread abodes !
Where art thou, my beloved ?   Haste — return —
With thy dear presence calm my struggling soul !
                              [*She listens.*
Hark ! the sweet voice !   No ! 'twas the echoing surge
That beats upon the shore ; alas ! he comes not.
More faintly, o'er the distant waves, the sun
Gleams with expiring ray ; a deathlike shudder
Creeps to my heart, and sadder, drearier grows
E'en desolation's self.
                    [*She walks to fro, and then listens again.*
                              Yes ! from the thicket shade
A voice resounds ! 'tis he ! the loved one !
No fond illusion mocks my listening ear.
'Tis louder — nearer : to his arms I fly —
To his breast !
[*She rushes with outstretched arms to the extremity of
     the garden. Don Cæsar meets her.*

Don Cæsar. Beatrice.

Beatrice (*starting back in horror*)
    What do I see?
        [*At the same moment the Chorus comes forward.*
Don Cæsar.   Angelic sweetness! fear not.
            [*To the Chorus.*
    Retire! your gleaming arms and rude array
    Affright the timorous maid.   [*To* Beatrice.
                Fear nothing! beauty
    And virgin shame are sacred in my eyes.
    [*The Chorus steps aside. He approaches and takes her
        hand.*
    Where hast thou been? for sure some envious power
    Has hid thee from my gaze : long have I sought thee :
    E'en from the hour when 'mid the funeral rites
    Of the dead prince, like some angelic vision,
    Lit with celestial brightness, on my sight
    Thou shonest, no other image in my breast
    Waking or dreaming, lives ; nor to thyself
    Unknown thy potent spells ; my glance of fire,
    My faltering accents, and my hand that lay
    Trembling in thine, bespoke my ecstasy!
    Aught else with solemn majesty the rite
    And holy place forbade :
                The bell proclaimed
    The awful sacrifice! With downcast eyes,
    And kneeling I adored : soon as I rose,
    And caught with eager gaze thy form again,
    Sudden it vanished ; yet, with mighty magic
    Of love enchained, my spirit tracked thy presence ;
    Nor ever, with unwearied quest, I cease
    At palace gates, amid the temple's throng,
    In secret paths retired, or public scenes,
    Where beauteous innocence perchance might rove,
    To mark each passing form — in vain ; but, guided
    By some propitious deity this day
    One of my train, with happy vigilance,
    Espied thee in the neighboring church.
    [Beatrice, *who had stood trembling with averted eyes,
        here makes a gesture of terror.*

I see thee
Once more ; and may the spirit from this frame
Be severed ere we part !   Now let me snatch
This glad, auspicious moment, and defy
Or chance, or envious demon's power, to shake
Henceforth my solid bliss ; here I proclaim thee,
Before this listening warlike train my bride,
With pledge of knightly honors !
> [*He shows her to the Chorus.*
Who thou art,
I ask not : thou art mine !   But that thy soul
And birth are pure alike one glance informed
My inmost heart ; and though thy lot were mean,
And poor thy lowly state, yet would I strain thee
With rapture to my arms : no choice remains,
Thou art my love — my wife !   Know too, that lifted
On fortune's height, I spurn control ; my will
Can raise thee to the pinnacle of greatness —
Enough my name — I am Don Cæsar !   None
Is nobler in Messina !

> [BEATRICE *starts back in amazement.   He remarks her*
> *agitation, and after a pause continues.*

What a grace
Lives in thy soft surprise and modest silence !
Yes ! gentle humbleness is beauty's crown —
The beautiful forever hid, and shrinking
From its own lustre : but thy spirit needs
Repose, for aught of strange — e'en sudden joy —
Is terror-fraught.   I leave thee.

> *Turning to the Chorus.*

From this hour
She is your mistress, and my bride ; so teach her
With honors due to entertain the pomp
Of queenly state.   I will return with speed,
And lead her home as fits Messina's princess.

> [*He goes away.*

BEATRICE *and the Chorus.*

Chorus (BOHEMUND).

Fair maiden — hail to thee,
  Thou lovely queen !

Thine is the crown, and thine the victory!
Of heroes to a distant age,
The blooming mother thou shalt shine,
Preserver of this kingly line.

(ROGER).

And thrice I bid thee hail,
Thou happy fair!
Sent in auspicious hour to bless
This favored race — the god's peculiar care.
Here twine the immortal wreaths of fame
And evermore, from sire to son,
Rolls on the sceptered sway,
To heirs of old renown, a race of deathless name!

(BOHEMUND.)

The household gods exultingly
Thy coming wait;
The ancient, honored sires,
That on the portals frown sedate,
Shall smile for thee!
There blooming Hebe shall thy steps attend;
And golden victory, that sits
By Jove's eternal throne, with waving plumes
For conquest ever spread,
To welcome thee from heaven descend.

(ROGER.)

Ne'er from this queenly, bright array
The crown of beauty fades, —
Departing to the realms of day,
Each to the next, as good and fair,
Extends the zone of feminine grace,
And veil of purity: —
Oh, happy race!
What vision glads my raptured eye!
Equal in nature's blooming pride,
I see the mother and the virgin bride.

BEATRICE (*awaking from her reverie*).
Oh, luckless hour!
Alas! ill-fated maid!

Where shall I fly
From these rude warlike men?
Lost and betrayed!
A shudder o'er me came,
When of this race accursed — the brothers twain —
Their hands embrued with kindred gore,
I heard the dreaded name;
Oft told, their strife and serpent hate
With terror thrilled my bosom's core: —
And now — oh, hapless fate!
I tremble, 'mid the rage of discord thrown,
Deserted and alone!

[*She runs into the alcove.*

Chorus (BOHEMUND).

Son of the immortal deities,
And blest is he, the lord of power;
His every joy the world can give;
Of all that mortals prize
He culls the flower.

(ROGER.)

For him from ocean's azure caves
The diver bears each pearl of purest ray;
Whate'er from nature's boundless field
Or toil or art has won,
Obsequious at his feet we lay;
His choice is ever free;
We bow to chance, and fortune's blind decree.

(BOHEMUND.)

But this of princes' lot I deem
The crowning treasure, joy supreme —
Of love the triumph and the prize,
The beauty, star of neighboring eyes!
She blooms for him alone,
He calls the fairest maid his own.

(ROGER).

Armed for the deadly fray,
The corsair bounds upon the strand,

And drags, amid the gloom of night, away,
  The shrieking captive train,
Of wild desires the hapless prey;
  But ne'er his lawless hands profane
The gem — the peerless flower —
Whose charms shall deck the Sultan's bower.

(BOHEMUND.)

Now haste and watch, with curious eye,
  These hallowed precincts round,
That no presumptuous foot come nigh
  The secret, solitary ground:
Guard well the maiden fair,
Your chieftain's brightest jewel owns your care.
      [*The Chorus withdraws to the background.*

[*The scene changes to a chamber in the interior of*
  the palace.

DONNA ISABELLA *between* DON MANUEL *and* DON CÆSAR.

ISAB. The long-expected, festal day is come,
  My children's hearts are twined in one, as thus
  I fold their hands. Oh, blissful hour, when first
  A mother dares to speak in nature's voice,
  And no rude presence checks the tide of love.
  The clang of arms affrights mine ear no more;
  And as the owls, ill-omened brood of night,
  From some old, shattered homestead's ruined walls,
  Their ancient reign, fly forth a dusky swarm,
  Darkening the cheerful day; when absent long,
  The dwellers home return with joyous shouts,
  To build the pile anew; so Hate departs
  With all his grisly train; pale Envy, scowling Malice,
  And hollow-eyed Suspicion; from our gates,
  Hoarse murmuring, to the realms of night; while
      Peace,
  By Concord and fair Friendship led along,
  Comes smiling in his place.   [*She pauses.*
                    But not alone
  This day of joy to each restores a brother;
  It brings a sister! Wonderstruck you gaze!
  Yet now the truth, in silence guarded long,

Bursts from my soul.   Attend!   I have a daughter!
A sister lives, ordained by heaven to bind ye
With ties unknown before.
DON CÆSAR.   We have a sister!
What hast thou said, my mother? never told
Her being till this hour!
DON MANUEL.   In childhood's years,
Oft of a sister we have heard, untimely
Snatched in her cradle by remorseless death;
So ran the tale.
ISABELLA.   She lives!
DON CÆSAR.   And thou wert silent!
ISAB.   Hear how the seed was sown in early time,
That now shall ripen to a joyful harvest.
Ye bloomed in boyhood's tender age; e'en then
By mutual, deadly hate, the bitter spring
Of grief to this torn, anxious heart, dissevered;
Oh, may your strife return no more!   A vision,
Strange and mysterious, in your father's breast
Woke dire presage: it seemed that from his couch,
With branches intertwined, two laurels grew,
And in the midst a lily all in flames,
That, catching swift the boughs and knotted stems,
Burst forth with crackling rage, and o'er the house
Spread in one mighty sea of fire: perplexed
By this terrific dream, my husband sought
An Arab, skilled to read the stars, and long
The trusted oracle, whose counsels swayed
His inmost purpose: thus the boding sage
Spoke Fate's decrees: if I a daughter bore,
Destruction to his sons and all his race
From her should spring.   Soon, by heaven's will, this child
Of dreadful omen saw the light; your sire
Commanded instant in the waves to throw
The new-born innocent; a mother's love
Prevailed, and, aided by a faithful servant,
I snatched the babe from death.
DON CÆSAR.   Blest be the hands
The ministers of thy care!   Oh, ever rich
Of counsels was a parent's love!

ISABELLA.   But more
   Than Nature's mighty voice, a warning dream
   Impelled to save my child: while yet unborn
   She slumbered in my womb, sleeping I saw
   An infant, fair as of celestial kind,
   That played upon the grass; soon from the wood
   A lion rushed, and from his gory jaws,
   Caressing, in the infant's lap let fall
   His prey, new-caught; then through the air down-
      swept
   An eagle, and with fond caress alike
   Dropped from his claws a trembling kid, and both
   Cowered at the infant's feet, a gentle pair.
   A monk, the saintly guide whose counsels poured
   In every earthly need, the balm of heaven
   Upon my troubled soul, my dream resolved.
   Thus spoke the man of God: a daughter, sent
   To knit the warring spirits of my sons
   In bonds of tender love, should recompense
   A mother's pains! Deep in my heart I treasured
   His words, and, reckless of the Pagan seer,
   Preserved the blessed child, ordained of heaven
   To still your growing strife; sweet pledge of hope
   And messenger of peace!
DON MANUEL (*embracing his brother*).
                 There needs no sister
   To join our hearts; she shall but bind them closer.
ISAB. In a lone spot obscure, by stranger hands
   Nurtured, the secret flower has grown; to me
   Denied the joy to mark each infant charm
   And opening grace from that sad hour of parting;
   These arms ne'er clasped my child again! her sire,
   To jealousy's corroding fears a prey,
   And brooding dark suspicion, restless tracked
   Each day my steps.
DON CÆSAR.   Yet three months flown, my father
   Sleeps in the tranquil grave; say, whence delayed
   The joyous tidings? Why so long concealed
   The maid, nor earlier taught our hearts to glow
   With brother's love?
ISABELLA.   The cause, your frenzied hate,

That raging unconfined, e'en on the tomb
Of your scarce buried father, lit the flames
Of mortal strife.   What! could I throw my daughter
Betwixt your gleaming blades?   Or 'mid the storm
Of passion would ye list a woman's counsels?
Could she, sweet pledge of peace, of all our hopes
The last and holy anchor, 'mid the rage
Of discord find a home?   Ye stand as brothers,
So will I give a sister to your arms!
The reconciling angel comes; each hour
I wait my messenger's return; he leads her
From her sequestered cell, to glad once more
A mother's eyes.
DON MANUEL.   Nor her alone this day
Thy arms shall fold; joy pours through all our gates;
Soon shall the desolate halls be full, the seat
Of every blooming grace.   Now hear my secret:
A sister thou hast given; to thee I bring
A daughter; bless thy son!   My heart has found
Its lasting shrine: ere this day's sun has set
Don Manuel to thy feet shall lead his bride,
The partner of his days.
ISABELLA.   And to my breast
With transport will I clasp the chosen maid
That makes my first-born happy.   Joy shall spring
Where'er she treads, and every flower that blooms
Around the path of life smile in her presence!
May bliss reward the son, that for my brows
Has twined the choicest wreath a mother wears.
CÆSAR.   Yet give not all the fulness of thy blessing
To him, thy eldest born.   If love be blest,
I, too, can give thee joy.   I bring a daughter,
Another flower for thy most treasured garland!
The maid that in this ice-cold bosom first
Awoke the rapturous flame!   Ere yonder sun
Declines, Don Cæsar's bride shall call thee mother.
DON M.   Almighty Love! thou godlike power — for well
We call thee sovereign of the breast!   Thy sway
Controls each warring element, and tunes
   To soft accord; naught lives but owns thy great-
      ness.

  Lo! the rude soul that long defied thee melts
At thy command!   [*He embraces* DON CÆSAR.
      Now I can trust thy heart,
And joyful strain thee to a brother's arms!
I doubt thy faith no more, for thou canst love!
ISAB. Thrice blest the day, when every gloomy care
From my o'erlabored breast has flown. I see
On steadfast columns reared our kingly race,
And with contented spirit track the stream
Of measureless time. In these deserted halls,
Sad in my widow's veil, but yesterday
Childless I roamed; and soon, in youthful charms
Arrayed, three blooming daughters at my side
Shall stand! Oh, happiest mother! Chief of women,
In bliss supreme; can aught of earthly joy
O'erbalance thine?
     But say, of royal stem,
What maidens grace our isle? For ne'er my sons
Would stoop to meaner brides.
DON MANUEL.   Seek not to raise
The veil that hides my bliss; another day
Shall tell thee all. Enough — Don Manuel's bride
Is worthy of thy son and thee.
ISABELLA.   Thy sire
Speaks in thy words; thus to himself retired
Forever would he brood o'er counsels dark,
And cloak his secret purpose; — your delay
Be short, my son.   [*Turning to* DON CÆSAR.
     But thou — some royal maid,
Daughter of kings, hath stirred thy soul to love;
So speak — her name ——
DON CÆSAR.   I have no art to veil
My thoughts with mystery's garb — my spirit free
And open as my brows; which thou wouldst know
Concerned me never. What illumes above
Heaven's flaming orb? Himself! On all the world
He shines, and with his beaming glory tells
From light he sprung: — in her pure eyes I gazed,
I looked into her heart of hearts: —the brightness
Revealed the pearl. Her race — her name — my
Ask not of me!   [mother,

ISABELLA.   My son, explain thy words,
    For, like some voice divine, the sudden charm
    Has thralled thy soul: to deeds of rash emprise
    Thy nature prompted, not to fantasies
    Of boyish love :— tell me, what swayed thy choice?
DON C. My choice? my mother! Is it choice when man
    Obeys the might of destiny, that brings
    The awful hour? I sought no beauteous bride,
    No fond delusion stirred my tranquil breast,
    Still as the house of death; for there, unsought,
    I found the treasure of my soul. Thou know'st
    That, heedless ever of the giddy race,
    I looked on beauty's charms with cold disdain,
    Nor deemed of womankind there lived another
    Like thee — whom my idolatrous fancy decked
    With heavenly graces :—
                            'Twas the solemn rite
    Of my dead father's obsequies ; we stood
    Amid the countless throng, with strange attire
    Hid from each other's glance ; for thus ordained
    Thy thoughtful care, lest with outbursting rage,
    E'en by the holy place unawed, our strife
    Should mar the funeral pomp.
                            With sable gauze
    The nave was all o'erhung; the altar round
    Stood twenty giant saints, uplifting each
    A torch; and in the midst reposed on high
    The coffin, with o'erspreading pall, that showed,
    In white, redemption's sign ;— thereon were laid
    The staff of sovereignty, the princely crown,
    The golden spurs of knighthood, and the sword,
    With diamond-studded belt :—
                            And all was hushed
    In silent prayer, when from the lofty choir,
    Unseen, the pealing organ spoke, and loud
    From hundred voices burst the choral strain !
    Then, 'mid the tide of song, the coffin sank
    With the descending floor beneath, forever
    Down to the world below :— but, wide outspread
    Above the yawning grave, the pall upheld
    The gauds of earthly state, nor with the corpse

To darkness fell ; yet on the seraph wings
Of harmony, the enfranchised spirit soared
To heaven and mercy's throne :
                     Thus to thy thought,
My mother, I have waked the scene anew,
And say, if aught of passion in my breast
Profaned the solemn hour ; yet then the beams
Of mighty love — so willed my guiding star —
First lit my soul ; but how it chanced, myself
I ask in vain.

ISABELLA.   I would hear all ; so end
Thy tale.

DON CÆSAR.   What brought her to my side, or whence
She came, I know not : — from her presence quick
Some secret all-pervading inward charm
Awoke ; 'twas not the magic of a smile,
Nor playful Cupid in her cheeks, nor more,
The form of peerless grace ; — 'twas beauty's soul,
The speaking virtue, modesty inborn,
That as with magic spells, impalpable
To sense, my being thralled. We breathed together
The air of heaven : — enough ! — no utterance asked
Of words, our spiritual converse ; — in my heart,
Though strange, yet with familiar ties inwrought
She seemed, and instant spake the thought — 'tis she !
Or none that lives !

DON MANUEL (*interposing with eagerness*).
                    That is the sacred fire
From heaven ! the spark of love — that on the soul
Bursts like the lightning's flash, and mounts in flame,
When kindred bosoms meet ! No choice remains —
Who shall resist ? What mortal break the band
That heaven has knit ? Brother, my blissful fortune
Was echoed in thy tale — well thou hast raised
The veil that shadows yet my secret love.

ISAB. Thus destiny has marked the wayward course
Of my two sons : the mighty torrent sweeps
Down from the precipice ; with rage he wears
His proper bed, nor heeds the channel traced
By art and prudent care. So to the powers
That darkly sway the fortunes of our house,

Trembling I yield. One pledge of hope remains;
Great as their birth — their noble souls.

ISABELLA, DON MANUEL, DON CÆSAR.

DIEGO *is seen at the door.*

ISABELLA. But see,
My faithful messenger returns. Come near me,
Honest Diego. Quick! Where is she? Tell me,
Where is my child? There is no secret here.
Oh, speak! No longer from my eyes conceal her;
Come! we are ready for the height of joy.
[*She is about to lead him towards the door.*
What means this pause? Thou lingerest — thou art
dumb —
Thy looks are terror-fraught — a shudder creeps
Through all my frame — declare thy tidings! —
speak!
Where is she? Where is Beatrice?
[*She is about to rush from the chamber.*
DON MANUEL (*to himself abstractedly*). Beatrice!
DIEGO (*holding back the* PRINCESS). Be still!
ISAB. Where is she? Anguish tears my breast!
DIEGO. She comes not;
I bring no daughter to thy arms.
ISABELLA. Declare
Thy message! Speak! by all the saints!
What has befallen?
DON MANUEL. Where is my sister? Tell us,
Thou harbinger of ill!
DIEGO. The maid is stolen
By corsairs! lost! Oh! that I ne'er had seen
This day of woe!
DON MANUEL. Compose thyself, my mother!
DON C. Be calm; list all this tale.
DIEGO. At thy command
I sought in haste the well-known path that leads
To the old sanctuary: — joy winged my footsteps;
The journey was my last!
DON CÆSAR. Be brief!
DON MANUEL. Proceed!

DIEGO. Soon as I trod the convent's court — impatient —
I ask — " Where is thy daughter?" Terror sate
In every eye; and straight, with horror mute,
I heard the worst.
[ISABELLA *sinks, pale and trembling, upon a chair;*
DON MANUEL *is busied about her.*
DON CÆSAR. Say'st thou by pirates stolen?
Who saw the band? — what tongue relates the spoil?
DIEGO. Not far a Moorish galley was descried,
At anchor in the bay ——
DON CÆSAR. The refuge oft
From tempests' rage; where is the bark?
DIEGO. At dawn,
With favoring breeze she stood to sea.
DON CÆSAR. But never
One prey contents the Moor; say, have they told
Of other spoil?
DIEGO. A herd that pastured near
Was dragged away.
DON CÆSAR. Yet from the convent's bound
How tear the maid unseen?
DIEGO. 'Tis thought with ladders
They scaled the wall.
DON CÆSAR. Thou knowest what jealous care
Enshrines the bride of Heaven; scarce could their steps
Invade the secret cells.
DIEGO. Bound by no vows
The maiden roved at will; oft would she seek
Alone the garden's shade. Alas! this day,
Ne'er to return!
DON CÆSAR. Saidst thou — the prize of corsairs?
Perchance, at other bidding, she forsook
The sheltering dome ——
ISABELLA (*rising suddenly*). 'Twas force! 'twas savage
spoil!
Ne'er has my child, reckless of honor's ties
With vile seducer fled! My sons! Awake!
I thought to give a sister to your arms;
I ask a daughter from your swords! Arise!
Avenge this wrong! To arms! Launch every ship!

Scour all our coasts! From sea to sea pursue them!
Oh, bring my daughter! haste!
DON CÆSAR.   Farewell — I fly
To vengeance!   [*He goes away.*
[DON MANUEL *arouses himself from a state of abstrac-*
tion, and turns, with an air of agitation, to DIEGO.
DON MANUEL.   Speak! within the convent's walls
When first unseen ——
DIEGO.   This day at dawn.
DON MANUEL (*to* ISABELLA).   Her name
Thou say'st is Beatrice?
ISABELLA.   No questions! Fly!
DON M. Yet tell me ——
ISABELLA.   Haste! Begone! Why this delay?
Follow thy brother.
DON MANUEL.   I conjure thee — speak ——
ISABELLA (*dragging him away*).
Behold my tears!
DON MANUEL.   Where was she hid? What region
Concealed my sister?
ISABELLA.   Scarce from curious eyes
In the deep bosom of the earth more safe
My child had been!
DIEGO.   Oh! now a sudden horror
Starts in my breast.
DON MANUEL.   What gives thee fear?
DIEGO.   'Twas I
That guiltless caused this woe!
ISABELLA.   Unhappy man!
What hast thou done?
DIEGO.   To spare thy mother's heart
One anxious pang, my mistress, I concealed
What now my lips shall tell: 'twas on the day
When thy dead husband in the silent tomb
Was laid; from every side the unnumbered throng
Pressed eager to the solemn rites; thy daughter —
For e'en amid the cloistered shade was noised
The funeral pomp, urged me, with ceaseless prayers,
To lead her to the festival of Death.
In evil hour I gave consent; and, shrouded
In sable weeds of mourning, she surveyed

Her father's obsequies. With keen reproach
My bosom tells (for through the veil her charms
Resistless shone), 'twas there, perchance, the spoiler
Lurked to betray.

DON MANUEL (*to himself*). Thrice happy words! I live!
It was another!

ISABELLA (*to* DIEGO). Faithless! Ill betide
Thy treacherous age!

DIEGO. Oh, never have I strayed
From duty's path! My mistress, in her prayers
I heard the voice of Nature; thus from Heaven
Ordained, methought, the secret impulse moves
Of kindred blood, to hallow with her tears
A father's grave: the tender office owned
Thy servant's care, and thus with good intent
I wrought but ill.

DON MANUEL (*to himself*). Why stand I thus a prey
To torturing fears! No longer will I bear
The dread suspense — I will know all!

DON CÆSAR (*who returns*). Forgive me,
I follow thee.

DON MANUEL. Away! Let no man follow. [*Exit.*

DON CÆSAR (*looking after him in surprise*).
What means my brother? Speak ——

ISABELLA. In wonder lost
I gaze; some mystery lurks ——

DON CÆSAR. Thou mark'st, my mother,
My quick return; with eager zeal I flew
At thy command, nor asked one trace to guide
My footsteps to thy daughter. Whence was torn
Thy treasure? Say, what cloistered solitude
Enshrined the beauteous maid?

ISABELLA. 'Tis consecrate
To St. Cecilia; deep in forest shades,
Beyond the woody ridge that slowly climbs
Toward's Etna's towering throne, it seems a refuge
Of parted souls!

DON CÆSAR. Have courage, trust thy sons;
She shall be thine, though with unwearied quest
O'er every land and sea I track her presence
To earth's extremest bounds: one thought alone

Disturbs, — in stranger hands my timorous bride
Waits my return; to thy protecting arms
I give the pledge of all my joy! She comes;
Soon on her faithful bosom thou shalt rest
In sweet oblivion of thy cares.   [*Exit.*

ISAB. When will the ancient curse be stilled that weighs
Upon our house? Some mocking demon sports
With every new-formed hope, nor envious leaves
One hour of joy. So near the haven smiled —
So smooth the treacherous main — secure I deemed
My happiness: the storm was lulled; and bright
In evening's lustre gleamed the sunny shore!
Then through the placid air the tempest sweeps,
And bears me to the roaring surge again!

[*She goes into the interior of the palace, followed by*
DIEGO.

The Scene changes to the Garden.

Both Choruses, afterwards BEATRICE.

The Chorus of DON MANUEL *enters in solemn procession,*
adorned with garlands, and bearing the bridal ornaments
above mentioned. The Chorus of DON CÆSAR *opposes*
their entrance.

First Chorus (CAJETAN).
        Begone!
Second Chorus (BOHEMUND).
                    Not at thy bidding!
CAJETAN.   Seest thou not
        Thy presence irks?
BOHEMUND.   Thou hast it, then, the longer!
CAJET. My place is here! What arm repels me?
BOHEMUND.   Mine!
CAJET. Don Manuel sent me hither.
BOHEMUND.   I obey
        My Lord Don Cæsar.
CAJETAN.   To the eldest born
        Thy master reverence owes.
BOHEMUND.   The world belongs
        To him that wins!
CAJETAN.   Unmannered knave, give place!

BOHEM. Our swords be measured first!
CAJETAN.   I find thee ever
     A serpent in my path.
BOHEMUND.   Where'er I list
     Thus will I meet thee!
CAJETAN.   Say, why cam'st thou hither,
     To spy? ——
BOHEMUND.   And thou to question and command?
CAJET. To parley I disdain!
BOHEMUND.   Too much I grace thee
     By words!
CAJETAN.   Thy hot, impetuous youth should bow
     To reverend age.
BOHEMUND.   Older thou art — not braver.
BEATRICE (*rushing from her place of concealment*).
     Alas! What mean these warlike men?
CAJETAN (*to* BOHEMUND).   I heed not
     Thy threats and lofty mien.
BOHEMUND.   I serve a master
     Better than thine.
BEATRICE.   Alas! Should he appear!
CAJET. Thou liest! Don Manuel thousandfold excels.
BOHEM. In every strife the wreath of victory decks
     Don Cæsar's brows!
BEATRICE.   Now he will come! Already
     The hour is past!
CAJETAN.   'Tis peace, or thou shouldst know
     My vengeance!
BOHEMUND.   Fear, not peace, thy arm refrains.
BEAT. Oh! Were he thousand miles remote!
CAJETAN.   Thy looks
     But move my scorn; the compact I obey.
BOHEM. The coward's ready shield!
CAJETAN.   Come on! I follow.
BOHEM. To arms!
BEATRICE (*in the greatest agitation*).
      Their falchions gleam — the strife begins!
   Ye heavenly powers, his steps refrain! Some
      snare
   Throw round his feet, that in this hour of dread
   He come not: all ye angels, late implored

To give him to my arms, reverse my prayers;
Far, far from hence convey the loved one!
[*She runs into the alcove. At the moment when the two
Choruses are about to engage,* DON MANUEL *ap-
pears.*

DON MANUEL, *the Chorus.*

DON MANUEL.   Hold!
What do I see!

First Chorus to the Second (CAJETAN, BERENGAR, MAN-
FRED).

Come on! Come on!

Second Chorus (BOHEMUND, ROGER, HIPPOLYTE).

Down with them!

DON MANUEL (*stepping between them with drawn sword*).
Hold!

CAJETAN.   'Tis the prince!

BOHEMUND.   Be still!

DON MANUEL.   I stretch him dead
Upon this verdant turf that with one glance
Of scorn prolongs the strife, or threats his foe!
Why rage ye thus? What maddening fiend impels
To blow the flames of ancient hate anew,
Forever reconciled? Say, who began
The conflict? Speak ——

First Chorus (CAJETAN, BERENGAR).

My prince, we stood ——

Second Chorus (ROGER, BOHEMUND) *interrupting them.*

They came ——

DON MANUEL (*to the First Chorus*).
Speak thou!

First Chorus (CAJETAN).

With wreaths adorned, in festal train,
We bore the bridal gifts; no thought of ill
Disturbed our peaceful way; composed forever
With holy pledge of love we deemed your strife,
And trusting came; when here in rude array
Of arms encamped they stood, and loud defied us!

DON M.   Slave! Is no refuge safe? Shall discord thus
Profane the bower of virgin innocence,
The home of sanctity and peace?

[*To the Second Chorus.*

Retire ——
Your warlike presence ill beseems; away!
I would be private. [*They hesitate.*
In your master's name
I give command; our souls are one, our lips
Declare each other's thoughts; begone!
[*To the First Chorus.*
Remain ——
And guard the entrance.

BOHEMUND. So! What next? Our masters
Are reconciled; that's plain; and less he wins
Of thanks than peril, that with busy zeal
In princely quarrel stirs; for when of strife
His mightiness aweary feels, of guilt
He throws the red-dyed mantle unconcerned
On his poor follower's luckless head, and stands
Arrayed in virtue's robes! So let them end
E'en as they will their brawls, I hold it best
That we obey.

[*Exit Second Chorus. The first withdraws to the
back of the stage; at the same moment* BEATRICE
rushes forward, and throws herself into DON
MANUEL'S *arms.*

BEATRICE. 'Tis thou! Ah! cruel one,
Again I see thee — clasp thee — long appalled,
To thousand ills a prey, trembling I languish
For thy return: no more — in thy loved arms
I am at peace, nor think of dangers past,
Thy breast my shield from every threatening
harm.
Quick! Let us fly! they see us not! — away!
Nor lose the moment.
Ha! Thy looks affright me!
Thy sullen, cold reserve! Thou tear'st thyself
Impatient from my circling arms, I know thee
No more! Is this Don Manuel? My beloved?
My husband?

DON MANUEL. Beatrice!
BEATRICE. No words! The moment
Is precious! Haste.
DON MANUEL. Yet tell me ——

BEATRICE.   Quick! Away
  Ere those fierce men return.
DON MANUEL.   Be calm, for naught
  Shall trouble thee of ill.
BEATRICE.   Oh, fly! alas,
  Thou know'st them not!
DON MANUEL.   Protected by this arm
  Canst thou fear aught?
BEATRICE.   Oh, trust me; mighty men
  Are here!
DON MANUEL.   Beloved! mightier none than I!
BEAT.   And wouldst thou brave this warlike host alone?
DON M.   Alone! the men thou fear'st ——
BEATRICE.   Thou know'st them not,
  Nor whom they serve.
DON MANUEL.   Myself! I am their lord!
BEAT.   Thou art — a shudder creeps through all my
      frame!
DON M.   Far other than I seemed; learn at last
  To know me, Beatrice.   Not the poor knight
  Am I, the stranger and unknown, that loving
  Taught thee to love; but what I am — my race —
  My power ——
BEATRICE.   And art thou not Don Manuel? Speak —
  Who art thou?
DON MANUEL.   Chief of all that bear the name,
  I am Don Manuel, Prince of Messina!
BEAT.   Art thou Don Manuel, Don Cæsar's brother?
DON M.   Don Cæsar is my brother.
BEATRICE.   Is thy brother!
DON M.   What means this terror?   Know'st thou, then,
      Don Cæsar?
  None other of my race?
BEATRICE.   Art thou Don Manuel,
  That with thy brother liv'st in bitter strife
  Of long inveterate hate?
DON MANUEL.   This very sun
  Smiled on our glad accord!   Yes, we are brothers!
  Brothers in heart!
BEATRICE.   And reconciled?   This day?
DON M.   What stirs this wild disorder? Hast thou known

Aught but our name? Say, hast thou told me all?
Is there no secret? Hast thou naught concealed?
Nothing disguised?

BEATRICE.   Thy words are dark; explain,
What shall I tell thee?

DON MANUEL.   Of thy mother naught
Hast thou e'er told; who is she? If in words
I paint her, bring her to thy sight——

BEATRICE.   Thou know'st her!
And thou wert silent!

DON MANUEL.   If I know thy mother,
Horrors betide us both!

BEATRICE.   Oh, she is gracious
As the sun's orient beam! Yes! I behold her;
Fond memory wakes; — and from my bosom's depths
Her godlike presence rises to my view!
I see around her snowy neck descend
The tresses of her raven hair, that shade
The form of sculptured loveliness; I see
The pale, high-thoughted brow; the darkening
    glance
Of her large lustrous orbs; I hear the tones
Of soul-fraught sweetness!

DON MANUEL.   'Tis herself!

BEATRICE.   This day,
Perchance had give me to her arms, and knit
Our souls in everlasting love; — such bliss
I have renounced, yes! I have lost a mother
For thee!

DON MANUEL.   Console thyself, Messina's princess
Henceforth shall call thee daughter; to her feet
I lead thee; come — she waits.

BEATRICE.   What hast thou said?
Thy mother and Don Cæsar's? Never! never!

DON M. Thou shudderest! Whence this horror? Hast
    thou known
My mother? Speak ——

BEATRICE.   O grief! O dire misfortune!
Alas! that e'er I live to see this day!

DON M. What troubles thee? Thou know'st me, thou
    hast found,
In the poor stranger knight, Messina's prince

BEAT. Give me the dear unknown again! With him
On earth's remotest wilds I could be blest!
DON CÆSAR (*behind the scene*).
Away! What rabble throng is here?
BEATRICE.   That voice!
Oh heavens! Where shall I fly!
DON MANUEL.   Know'st thou that voice?
No! thou hast never heard it; to thine ear
'Tis strange ——
BEATRICE.   Oh, come — delay not ——
DON MANUEL.   Wherefore I fly?
It is my brother's voice! He seeks me — how
He tracked my steps ——
BEATRICE.   By all the holy saints!
Brave not his wrath! oh quit this place — avoid
     him ——
Meet not thy brother here!
DON MANUEL.   My soul! thy fears
Confound; thou hear'st me not; our strife is o'er.
Yes! we are reconciled.
BEATRICE.   Protect me, heaven,
In this dread hour!
DON MANUEL.   A sudden dire presage
Starts in my breast — I shudder at the thought:
If it be true! Oh, horror! Could she know
That voice! Wert thou — my tongue denies to utter
The words of fearful import — Beatrice!
Say, wert thou present at the funeral rites
Of my dead sire?
BEATRICE.   Alas!
DON MANUEL.   Thou wert !
BEATRICE.   Forgive me!
DON M. Unhappy woman! —
BEATRICE.   I was present!
DON MANUEL.   Horror!
BEAT. Some mighty impulse urged me to the scene —
Oh, be not angry — to thyself I owned
The ardent fond desire; with darkening brow
Thou listened'st to my prayer, and I was silent,
But what misguiding inauspicious star
Allured, I know not; from my inmost soul

The wish, the dear emotion spoke; and vain
Aught else :—Diego gave consent — oh, pardon me!
I disobeyed thee.
[*She advances towards him imploringly ; at the same
moment* Don Cæsar *enters, accompanied by the
whole Chorus.*

Both Brothers, both Choruses, Beatrice.

Second Chorus (Bohemund) *to* Don Cæsar.
Thou believ'st us not —
Believe thine eyes!
Don Cæsar (*rushes forward furiously, and at the sight
of his brother starts back with horror.*
Some hell-born magic cheats
My senses; in her arms! Envenomed snake!
Is this thy love ? For this thy treacherous heart
Could lure with guise of friendship! Oh, from heav
Breathed my immortal hate! Down, down to hell,
Thou soul of falsehood!
[*He stabs him,* Don Manuel *falls.*
Don Manuel. Beatrice!— my brother!
I die! [*Dies.* Beatrice *sinks lifeless at his side.*
First Chorus (Cajetan).
Help! Help! To arms! Avenge with blood
The bloody deed!
Second Chorus (Bohemund). The fortune of the day
Is ours! The strife forever stilled :— Messina
Obeys one lord.
First Chorus (Cajetan, Berengar, Manfred).
Revenge! The murderer
Shall die! Quick, offer to your master's shade
Appeasing sacrifice!
Second Chorus (Bohemund, Roger, Hippolyte).
My prince! fear nothing,
Thy friends are true.
Don Cæsar (*steps between them, looking around*).
Be still! The foe is slain
That practised on my trusting, honest heart
With snares of brother's love. Oh, direful shows
The deed of death! But righteous heaven hath
judged.

First Chorus (CAJETAN).
    Alas to thee, Messina! Woe forever!
    Sad city! From thy blood-stained walls this deed
    Of nameless horror taints the skies; ill fare
    Thy mothers and thy children, youth and age,
    And offspring yet unborn!
DON CÆSAR.   Too late your grief —
    Here give your help.   [*Pointing to* BEATRICE.
                Call her to life, and quick
    Depart this scene of terror and of death.
    I must away and seek my sister: — Hence!
    Conduct her to my mother —
    And tell her that her son, Don Cæsar, sends her!
                     [*Exit.*

  [*The senseless* BEATRICE *is placed on a litter and*
  carried away by the Second Chorus. The First
  Chorus remains with the body, round which the
  boys who bear the bridal presents range themselves
  in a semicircle.

Chorus (CAJETAN).
    List, how with dreaded mystery
      Was signed to my prophetic soul,
    Of kindred blood the dire decree: —
    Hither with noiseless, giant stride
    I saw the hideous fiend of terror glide!
      'Tis past! I strive not to control
    My shuddering awe — so swift of ill
    The Fates the warning sign fulfil.
      Lo! to my sense dismayed,
    Sudden the deed of death has shown
    Whate'er my boding fears portrayed
      The visioned thought was pain;
      The present horror curdles every vein!

One of the Chorus (MANFRED).
    Sound, sound the plaint of woe!
      Beautiful youth!
    Outstretched and pale he lies,
    Untimely cropped in early bloom;
    The heavy night of death has sealed his eyes; —

In this glad hour of nuptial joy,
  Snatched by relentless doom,
He sleeps — while echoing to the sky,
Of sorrow bursts the loud, despairing cry!

A second (CAJETAN).

We come, we come, in festal pride,
To greet the beauteous bride;
Behold! the nuptial gifts, the rich attire:
  The banquet waits, the guests are there;
They bid thee to the solemn rite
  Of hymen quick repair.
Thou hear'st them not — the sportive lyre,
  The frolic dance, shall ne'er invite;
Nor wake thee from thy lowly bed,
For deep the slumber of the dead!

The whole Chorus.

No more the echoing horn shall cheer
Nor bride with tones of sweetness charm his ear.
On the cold earth he lies,
In death's eternal slumber closed his eyes.

A third (CAJETAN).

What are the hopes, and fond desires
  Of mortals' transitory race?
This day, with harmony of voice and soul,
  Ye woke the long-extinguished fires
  Of brothers' love — yon flaming orb
Lit with his earliest beams your dear embrace
  At eve, upon the gory sand
Thou liest — a reeking corpse!
  Stretched by a brother's murderous hand.
  Vain projects, treacherous hopes,
Child of the fleeting hour are thine;
Fond man! thou rear'st on dust each bold design,

Chorus (BERENGAR).

To thy mother I will bear
The burden of unutterable woe!
Quick shall yon cypress, blooming fair,
  Bend to the axe's murderous blow

Then twine the mournful bier!
For ne'er with verdant life the tree shall smile
That grew on death's devoted soil;
Ne'er in the breeze the branches play,
Nor shade the wanderer in the noontide ray;
'Twas marked to bear the fruits of doom,
Cursed to the service of the tomb.

First (CAJETAN).

Woe to the murderer! Woe!
That sped exulting in his pride,
Behold! the parched earth drinks the crimson tide.
Down, down it flows, unceasingly,
    To the dim caverned halls below,
Where throned in kindred gloom the sister train,
    Of Themis progeny severe,
Brood in their songless, silent reign!
Stern minister of wrath's decree,
They catch in swarthy cups thy streaming gore,
And pledge with horrid rites for vengeance evermore

Second (BERENGAR).

Though swift of deed the traces fade
    From earth, before the enlivening ray;
As o'er the brow the transient shade
    Of thought, the hues of fancy flit away: —
Yet in the mystic womb unseen,
    Of the dark ruling hours that sway
Our mortal lot, whate'er has been,
    With new creative germ defies decay.
The blooming field is time
For nature's ever-teeming shoot,
    And all is seed, and all is fruit.
[*The Chorus goes away, bearing the corpse of* DON
    MANUEL *on a bier.*

SCENE — *The hall of pillars. It is night.*
The stage is lighted from above by a single large lamp.
DONNA ISABELLA *and* DIEGO *advance to the front.*
ISAB.   As yet no joyful tidings, not a trace
    Found of the lost one!

DIEGO.   Nothing have we heard,
My mistress; yet o'er every track, unwearied,
Thy sons pursue. Ere long the rescued maid
Shall smile at dangers past.
ISABELLA.   Alas! Diego,
My heart is sad; 'twas I that caused this woe!
DIEGO. Vex not thy anxious bosom; naught escaped
Thy thoughtful care.
ISABELLA.   Oh! had I earlier shown
The hidden treasure!
DIEGO.   Prudent were thy counsels,
Wisely thou left'st her in retirement's shade;
So, trust in heaven.
ISABELLA.   Alas! no joy is perfect —
Without this chance of ill my bliss were pure.
DIEGO. Thy happiness is but delayed; enjoy
The concord of thy sons.
ISABELLA.   The sight was rapture
Supreme, when, locked in one another's arms,
They glowed with brothers' love.
DIEGO.   And in the heart
It burns; for ne'er their princely souls have stooped
To mean disguise.
ISABELLA.   Now, too, their bosoms wake
To gentler thoughts, and own their softening sway
Of love. No more their hot, impetuous youth
Revels in liberty untamed, and spurns
Restraint of law, attempered passion's self,
With modest, chaste reserve.
                               To thee, Diego,
I will unfold my secret heart; this hour
Of feeling's opening bloom, expected long,
Wakes boding fears: thou know'st to sudden rage
Love stirs tumultuous breasts; and if this flame
With jealousy should rouse the slumbering fires
Of ancient hate — I shudder at the thought!
If these discordant souls perchance have thrilled
In fatal unison! Enough; the clouds
That black with thundering menace o'er me hung
Are past; some angel sped them tranquil by,
And my enfranchised spirit breathes again.

DIEGO. Rejoice, my mistress; for thy gentle sense
And soft, prevailing art more weal have wrought
Than all thy husband's power.   Be praise to thee
And thy auspicious star !

ISABELLA.   Yes, fortune smiled;
Nor light the task, so long with apt disguise
To veil the cherished secret of my heart,
And cheat my ever-jealous lord : more hard
To stifle mighty nature's pleading voice,
That, like a prisoned fire, forever strove
To rend its confines.

DIEGO.   All shall yet be well;
Fortune, propitious to our hopes, gave pledge
Of bliss that time will show.

ISABELLA.   I praise not yet
My natal star, while darkening o'er my fate
This mystery hangs : too well the dire mischance
Tells of the fiend whose never-slumbering rage
Pursues our house.   Now list what I have done,
And praise or blame me as thou wilt ; from thee
My bosom guards no secret : ill I brook
This dull repose, while swift o'er land and sea
My sons unwearied, track their sister's flight,
Yes, I have sought ; heaven counsels oft, when vain
All mortal aid.

DIEGO.   What I may know, my mistress,
Declare.

ISABELLA.   On Etna's solitary height
A reverend hermit dwells, — benamed of old
The mountain seer, — who to the realms of light
More near abiding than the toilsome race
Of mortals here below, with purer air
Has cleansed each earthly, grosser sense away ;
And from the lofty peak of gathered years,
As from his mountain home, with downward glance
Surveys the crooked paths of worldly strife.
To him are known the fortunes of our house ;
Oft has the holy sage besought response
From heaven, and many a curse with earnest prayer
Averted : thither at my bidding flew,
On wings of youthful haste, a messenger,

To ask some tidings of my child : each hour
I wait his homeward footsteps.

DIEGO.   If mine eyes
Deceive me not, he comes ; and well his speed
Has earned thy praise.

MESSENGER, ISABELLA, DIEGO.

ISABELLA (*to* MESSENGER).

Now speak, and nothing hide
Of weal or woe ; be truth upon thy lips !
What tidings bear'st thou from the mountain seer ?

MESS.   His answer : " Quick ! retrace thy steps ; the
lost one
Is found."

ISABELLA.   Auspicious tongue ! Celestial sounds
Of peace and joy ! thus ever to my vows.
Thrice honored sage, thy kindly message spoke !
But say, which heaven-directed brother traced
My daughter ?

MESSENGER.   'Twas thy eldest born that found
The deep-secluded maid.

ISABELLA.   Is it Don Manuel
That gives her to my arms ? Oh, he was ever
The child of blessing ! Tell me, hast thou borne
My offering to the aged man ? the tapers
To burn before his saint ? for gifts, the prize
Of wordly hearts, the man of God disdains.

MESS.   He took the torches from my hands in silence
And stepping to the altar — where the lamp
Burned to his saint — illumed them at his fire,
And instant set in flames the hermit cell,
Where he has honored God these ninety years !

ISAB.   What hast thou said ? What horrors fright my
soul ?

MESS.   And three times shrieking " Woe ! " with down-
ward course,
He fled ; but silent with uplifted arm
Beckoned me not to follow, nor regard him
So hither I have hastened, terror-sped.

ISAB.   Oh, I am tossed amid the surge again

Of doubt and anxious fears; thy tale appals
With ominous sounds of ill. My daughter found —
Thou sayest; and by my eldest born, Don Manuel?
The tidings ne'er shall bless, that heralded
This deed of woe!

MESSENGER.   My mistress! look around
Behold the hermit's message to thine eyes
Fulfilled. Some charm deludes my sense, or hither
Thy daughter comes, girt by the warlike train
Of thy two sons!

[BEATRICE *is carried in by the Second Chorus on a
litter, and placed in the front of the stage. She is
still without perception, and motionless.*

ISABELLA, DIEGO, MESSENGER, BEATRICE.

Chorus (BOHEMUND, ROGER, HIPPOLYTE, *and the other
nine followers of* DON CÆSAR.)

Chorus (BOHEMUND).   Here at thy feet we lay
The maid, obedient to our lord's command:
'Twas thus he spoke — " Conduct her to my mother;
And tell her that her son, Don Cæsar, sends her!

ISABELLA (*is advancing towards her with outstretched
arms, and starts back in horror*).
Heavens! she is motionless and pale!

Chorus (BOHEMUND).   She lives,
She will awake, but give her time to rouse
From the dread shock that holds each sense enthralled

ISAB. My daughter! Child of all my cares and pains!
And is it thus I see thee once again?
Thus thou returnest to thy father's halls!
Oh, let my breath relume thy vital spark;
Yes! I will strain thee to a mother's arms
And hold thee fast — till from the frost of death
Released thy life-warm current throbs again.

[*To the Chorus.*
Where hast thou found her? Speak! What dire
    mischance
Has caused this sight of woe?

Chorus (BOHEMUND).   My lips are dumb!
Ask not of me: thy son will tell thee all —
Don Cæsar — for 'tis he that sends her.

ISABELLA 'Tell me
Would'st thou not say Don Manuel?
Chorus (BOHEMUND). 'Tis Don Cæsar
That sends her to thee.
ISABELLA (*to the* MESSENGER). How declared the Seer?
Speak! Was it not Don Manuel?
MESSENGER. 'Twas he!
Thy elder born.
ISABELLA. Be blessings on his head
Which e'er it be; to him I owe a daughter,
Alas! that in this blissful hour, so long
Expected, long implored, some envious fiend
Should mar my joy! Oh, I must stem the tide
Of nature's transport! In her childhood's home
I see my daughter; me she knows not — heeds
not —
Nor answers to a mother's voice of love!
Ope, ye dear eyelids — hands be warm — and hea
Thou lifeless bosom with responsive throbs
To mine! 'Tis she! Diego, look! 'tis Beatrice!
The long-concealed — the lost — the rescued one!
Before the world I claim her for my own!
Chorus (BOHEMUND).
New signs of terror to my boding soul
Are pictured; — in amazement lost I stand!
What light shall pierce this gloom of mystery?
ISABELLA (*to the Chorus, who exhibit marks of confusion
and embarrassment*).
Oh, ye hard hearts! Ye rude unpitying men!
A mother's transport from your breast of steel
Rebounds, as from the rocks the heaving surge!
I look around your train, nor mark one glance
Of soft regard. Where are my sons? Oh, tell me
Why come they not, and from their beaming eyes
Speak comfort to my soul? For here environed
I stand amid the desert's raging brood,
Or monsters of the deep!
DIEGO. She opes her eyes!
She moves! She lives!
ISABELLA. She lives! On me be thrown
Her earliest glance!

DIEGO.   See! They are closed again —
  She shudders!
ISABELLA (*to the Chorus*).
              Quick! Retire — your aspect frights her.
                            [*Chorus steps back.*
BOHEM. Well pleased I shun her sight.
DIEGO.   With outstretched eyes,
  And wonderstruck, she seems to measure thee.
BEAT. Not strange those lineaments — where am I?
ISABELLA.   Slowly
  Her sense returns.
DIEGO.   Behold! upon her knees
  She sinks.
BEATRICE.   Oh, angel visage of my mother!
ISAB. Child of my heart!
BEATRICE.   See! kneeling at thy feet
  The guilty one!
ISABELLA.   I hold thee in my arms!
  Enough — forgotten all!
DIEGO.   Look in my face,
  Canst thou remember me?
BEATRICE.   The reverend brows
  Of honest old Diego!
ISABELLA.   Faithful guardian
  Of thy young years.
BEATRICE.   And am I once again
  With kindred?
ISABELLA.   Naught but death shall part us more!
BEAT. Will thou ne'er send me to the stranger?
ISABELLA.   Never!
  Fate is appeased.
BEATRICE.   And am I next thy heart?
  And was it all a dream — a hideous dream?
  My mother! at my feet he fell! I know not
  What brought me hither — yet 'tis well. Oh, bliss!
  That I am safe in thy protecting arms;
  They would have ta'en me to the princess, mother —
  Sooner to death!
ISABELLA.   My daughter, calm thy fears;
  Messina's princess ——
BEATRICE.   Name her not again!

At that ill-omened sound the chill of death
Creeps through my trembling frame.

ISABELLA.   My child! but hear me ——

BEAT. She has two sons by mortal hate dissevered,
Don Manuel and Don Cæsar ——

ISABELLA.   'Tis myself!
Behold thy mother!

BEATRICE.   Have I heard thee? Speak!

ISAB. I am thy mother, and Messina's princess!

BEAT. Art thou Don Manuel's and Don Cæsar's mother?

ISAB. And thine! They are thy brethren whom thou
          namest.

BEAT. Oh, gleam of horrid light!

ISABELLA.   What troubles thee?
Say, whence this strange emotion?

BEATRICE.   Yes! 'twas they!
Now I remember all; no dream deceived me,
They met — 'tis fearful truth! Unhappy men!
Where have ye hid him?

*[She rushes towards the Chorus; they turn away from
   her. A funeral march is heard in the distance.*

CHORUS.   Horror! Horror!

ISABELLA.   Hid!
Speak — who is hid? and what is true? Ye
          stand
In silent dull amaze — as though ye fathomed
Her words of mystery! In your faltering tones —
Your brows — I read of horrors yet unknown,
That would refrain my tongue! What is it? Tell
          me!
I will know all! Why fix ye on the door
That awe-struck gaze? What mournful music
          sounds?

                    [The march is heard nearer.

Chorus (BOHEMUND).
It comes! it comes! and all shall be declared
With terrible voice. My mistress! steel thy heart,
Be firm, and bear with courage what awaits thee —
For more than women's soul thy destined griefs
Demand.

ISABELLA. What comes? and what awaits me? Hark!

With fearful tones the death-wail smites mine ear —
It echoes through the house ! Where are my sons ?
[*The first Semi-chorus brings in the body of* DON
MANUEL *on a bier, which is placed at the side of
the stage. A black pall is spread over it.*

ISABELLA, BEATRICE, DIEGO.

Both Choruses.

First Chorus (CAJETAN).

With sorrow in his train,
From street to street the King of Terror glides ;
   With stealthy foot, and slow,
He creeps where'er the fleeting race
   Of man abides !
In turn at every gate
Is heard the dreaded knock of fate,
The message of unutterable woe !

BERENGAR.

When, in the sere
And autumn leaves decayed,
The mournful forest tells how quickly fade
The glories of the year !
When in the silent tomb oppressed,
   Frail man, with weight of days,
Sinks to his tranquil rest ;
   Contented nature but obeys
Her everlasting law, —
The general doom awakes no shuddering awe !
   But, mortals, oh ! prepare
For mightier ills ; with ruthless hand
Fell murder cuts the holy band —
   The kindred tie : insatiate death,
With unrelenting rage,
Bears to his bark the flower of blooming age !

CAJETAN.

When clouds athwart the lowering sky
   Are driven — when bursts with hollow moan
   The thunder's peal — our trembling bosoms own

The might of awful destiny!
Yet oft the lightning's glare
Darts sudden through the cloudless air: —
  Then in thy short delusive day
Of bliss, oh! dread the treacherous snare;
Nor prize the fleeting goods in vain,
  The flowers that bloom but to decay!
Nor wealth, nor joy, nor aught but pain,
  Was e'er to mortal's lot secure: —
  Our first best lesson — to endure!

ISAB. What shall I hear? What horrors lurk beneath
This funeral pall?

[*She steps towards the bier, but suddenly pauses, and stands irresolute.*

                     Some strange, mysterious dread
Enthrals my sense. I would approach, and sudden
The ice-cold grasp of terror holds me back!

[*To* BEATRICE, *who has thrown herself between her and the bier.*

Whate'er it be, I will unveil ——

[*On raising the pall she discovers the body of* DON MANUEL.

                      Eternal Powers! it is my son!

[*She stands in mute horror.* BEATRICE *sinks to the ground with a shriek of anguish near the bier.*

CHORUS. Unhappy mother! 'tis thy son. Thy lips
Have uttered what my faltering tongue denied.

ISAB. My soul! My Manuel! Oh, eternal grief!
And is it thus I see thee? Thus thy life
Has bought thy sister from the spoiler's rage?
Where was thy brother? Could no arm be found
To shield thee? Oh, be cursed the hand that dug
These gory wounds! A curse on her that bore
The murderer of my son! Ten thousand curses
On all their race!

CHORUS.   Woe! Woe!

ISABELLA.   And is it thus
Ye keep your word, ye gods? Is this your truth?
Alas for him that trusts with honest heart
Your soothing wiles! Why have I hoped and
  trembled?

And this the issue of my prayers! Attend,
Ye terror-stricken witnesses, that feed
Your gaze upon my anguish; learn to know
How warning visions cheat, and boding seers
But mock our credulous hopes; let none believe
The voice of heaven!
           When in my teeming **womb**
This daughter lay, her father, in a dream,
Saw from his nuptial couch two laurels grow,
And in the midst a lily all in flames,
That, catching swift the boughs and knotted stems,
Burst forth with crackling rage, and o'er the house
Spread in one mighty sea of fire. Perplexed
By this terrific dream my husband sought
The counsels of the mystic art, and thus
Pronounced the sage: "If I a daughter bore,
The murderess of his sons, the destined spring
Of ruin to our house, the baleful child
Should see the light."
      Chorus (CAJETAN *and* BOHEMUND).
           What hast thou said, my mistress?
Woe! Woe!
ISABELLA.   For this her ruthless father spoke
The dire behest of death. I rescued her,
The innocent, the doomed one; from my arms
The babe was torn; to stay the curse of heaven,
And save my sons, the mother gave her child;
And now by robber hands her brother falls;
My child is guiltless; Oh, she slew him not!
CHORUS. Woe! Woe!
ISAB. No trust the fabling readers of the stars
Have e'er deserved. Hear how another spoke
With comfort to my soul, and him I deemed
Inspired to voice the secrets of the skies!
"My daughter should unite in love the hearts
Of my dissevered sons;" and thus their tales
Of curse and blessing on her head proclaim
Each other's falsehood. No, she ne'er has brought
A curse, the innocent; nor time was given
The blessed promise to fulfil; their tongues
Were false alike; their boasted art is vain:

With trick of words they cheat our credulous ears,
Or are themselves deceived! Naught ye may know
Of dark futurity, the sable streams
Of hell the fountain of your hidden lore,
Or yon bright spring of everlasting light!

First Chorus (CAJETAN).

Woe! Woe! thy tongue refrain!
Oh, pause, nor thus with impious rage
The might of heaven profane;
The holy oracles are wise ——
Expect with awe thy coming destinies!

ISAB. My tongue shall speak as prompts my swelling heart;
My griefs shall cry to heaven. Why do we lift
Our suppliant hands, and at the sacred shrines
Kneel to adore? Good, easy dupes! What win we
From faith and pious awe? to touch with prayers
The tenants of yon azure realms on high,
Were hard as with an arrow's point to pierce
The silvery moon. Hid is the womb of time,
Impregnable to mortal glance, and deaf
The adamantine walls of heaven rebound
The voice of anguish : — Oh, 'tis one, whate'er
The flight of birds — the aspect of the stars!
The book of nature is a maze — a dream
The sage's art — and every sign a falsehood!

Second Chorus (BOHEMUND).

Woe! Woe! Ill-fated woman, stay
Thy maddening blasphemies;
Thou but disown'st, with purblind eyes,
The flaming orb of day!
Confess the gods, — they dwell on high —
They circle thee with awful majesty!

All the Knights.

Confess the gods — they dwell on high —
They circle thee with awful majesty!

BEATRICE.

Why hast thou saved thy daughter, and defied
The curse of heaven, that marked me in thy womb
The child of woe? Short-sighted mother! — vain
Thy little arts to cheat the doom declared
By the all-wise interpreters, that knit
The far and near; and, with prophetic ken,
See the late harvest spring in times unborn.
Oh, thou hast brought destruction on thy race,
Withholding from the avenging gods their prey;
Threefold, with new embittered rage, they ask
The direful penalty; no thanks thy boon
Of life deserves — the fatal gift was sorrow!

Second Chorus (BERENGAR) *looking towards the door
with signs of agitation.*

Hark to the sound of dread!
The rattling, brazen din I hear!
Of hell-born snakes the hissing tones are near!
Yes — 'tis the furies' tread!

CAJETAN.

In crumbling ruin wide,
Fall, fall, thou roof, and sink, thou trembling floor
That bear'st the dread, unearthly stride!
Ye sable damps arise!
Mount from the abyss in smoky spray,
And pall the brightness of the day!
Vanish, ye guardian powers!
They come! The avenging deities!

DON CÆSAR, ISABELLA, BEATRICE.   *The Chorus.*

[*On the entrance of* DON CÆSAR *the Chorus station
themselves before him imploringly. He remains
standing alone in the centre of the stage.*

BEAT.   Alas! 'tis he —
ISABELLA (*stepping to meet him*).
                    My Cæsar! Oh, my son!
And is it thus I meet the? Look! Behold!
The crime of hand accursed!
                    [*She leads him to the corpse.*

First Chorus (CAJETAN, BERENGAR).

Break forth once more
Ye wounds! Flow, flow, in swarthy flood,
Thou streaming gore!

ISAB. Shuddering with earnest gaze, and motionless,
Thou stand'st : — yes! there my hopes repose, and all
That earth has of thy brother; in the bud
Nipped is your concord's tender flower, nor ever
With beauteous fruit shall glad a mother's eyes,

DON C. Be comforted; thy sons, with honest heart,
To peace aspired, but heaven's decree was blood!

ISAB. I know thou lovedst him well; I saw between ye,
With joy, the bands old Nature sweetly twined;
Thou wouldst have borne him in thy heart of hearts
With rich atonement of long wasted years!
But see — fell murder thwarts thy dear design,
And naught remains but vengeance!

DON CÆSAR.   Come, my mother,
This is no place for thee. Oh, haste and leave
This sight of woe. [*He endeavors to drag her away.*

ISABELLA (*throwing herself into his arms*).
                    Thou livest! I have a son!

BEAT. Alas! my mother!

DON CÆSAR.   On this faithful bosom
Weep out thy pains; nor lost thy son, — his love
Shall dwell immortal in thy Cæsar's breast.

First Chorus (CAJETAN, BERENGAR, MANFRED).

Break forth, ye wounds!
Dumb witness! the truth proclaim;
Flow fast, thou gory stream!

ISABELLA (*clasping the hands of* DON CÆSAR *and*
BEATRICE).
My children!

DON CÆSAR.   Oh, 'tis ecstasy! my mother,
To see her in thy arms! henceforth in love
A daughter — sister ——

ISABELLA (*interrupting him*).
                    Thou hast kept thy word.
My son; to thee I owe the rescued one;
Yes, thou hast sent her ——

DON CÆSAR (*in astonishment*).

      Whom, my mother, sayst thou,
 That I have sent?

ISABELLA.   She stands before thine eyes —
 Thy sister.

DON CÆSAR. She! My sister?

ISABELLA.   Ay, what other?

DON C. My sister!

ISABELLA,   Thou hast sent her to me!

DON CÆSAR.   Horror!
 His sister, too!

CHORUS.   Woe! woe!

BEATRICE.   Alas! my mother!

ISAB. Speak! I am all amaze!

DON CÆSAR.   Be cursed the day
 When I was born!

ISABELLA.   Eternal powers!

DON CÆSAR.   Accursed
 The womb that bore me; cursed the secret arts,
 The spring of all this woe; instant to crush thee,
 Though the dread thunder swept — ne'er should this
  arm
 Refrain the bolts of death: I slew my brother!
 Hear it and tremble! in her arms I found him;
 She was my love, my chosen bride; and he —
 My brother—in her arms! Thou hast heard all!
 If it be true — oh, if she be my sister —
 And his! then I have done a deed that mocks
 The power of sacrifice and prayers to ope
 The gates of mercy to my soul!

Chorus (BOHEMUND).

 The tidings on thy heart dismayed
  Have burst, and naught remains; behold!
 'Tis come, nor long delayed,
  Whate'er the warning seers foretold:
 They spoke the message from on high,
 Their lips proclaimed resistless destiny!
 The mortal shall the curse fulfil
 Who seeks to turn predestined ill.

ISAB. The gods have done their worst; if they be true
Or false, 'tis one — for nothing they can add
To this — the measure of their rage is full.
Why should I tremble that have naught to fear?
My darling son lies murdered, and the living
I call my son no more. Oh! I have borne
And nourished at my breast a basilisk
That stung my best-beloved child. My daughter, haste,
And leave this house of horrors — I devote it
To the avenging fiends! In an evil hour
'Twas crime that brought me hither, and of crime
The victim I depart. Unwillingly
I came — in sorrow I have lived — despairing
I quit these halls; on me, the innocent,
Descends this weight of woe! Enough — 'tis shown
That Heaven is just, and oracles are true!

[Exit, followed by DIEGO.

BEATRICE, DON CÆSAR, *the Chorus.*

DON CÆSAR (*detaining* BEATRICE).
My sister, wouldst thou leave me? On this head
A mother's curse may fall — a brother's blood
Cry with accusing voice to heaven — all nature
Invoke eternal vengeance on my soul —
But thou — oh! curse me not — I cannot bear it!

*[*BEATRICE *points with averted eyes to the body.*
I have not slain thy lover! 'twas thy brother,
And mine that fell beneath my sword; and near
As the departed one, the living owns
The ties of blood: remember, too, 'tis I
That most a sister's pity need — for pure
His spirit winged its flight, and I am guilty!

*[*BEATRICE *bursts into an agony of tears.*
Weep! I will blend my tears with thine — nay, more,
I will avenge thy brother; but the lover —
Weep not for him — thy passionate, yearning tears
My inmost heart. Oh! from the boundless depths
Of our affliction, let me gather this,
The last and only comfort — but to know

That we are dear alike.   One lot fulfilled
Has made our rights and wretchedness the same ;
Entangled in one snare we fall together,
Three hapless victims of unpitying fate,
And share the mournful privilege of tears.
But when I think that for the lover more
Than for the brother bursts thy sorrow's tide,
Then rage and envy mingle with my pain,
And hope's last balm forsakes my withering soul !
Nor joyful, as beseems, can I requite
This injured shade : — yet after him content
To mercy's throne my contrite spirit shall fly,
Sped by this hand — if dying I may know
That in one urn our ashes shall repose,
With pious office of a sister's care.
[*He throws his arms around her with passionate ten-*
derness.
I loved thee, as I ne'er had loved before,
When thou wert strange ; and that I bear the curse
Of brother's blood, 'tis but because I loved thee
With measureless transport : love was all my guilt,
But now thou art my sister, and I claim
Soft pity's tribute.
[*He regards her with inquiring glances, and an air of*
painful suspense — then turns away with vehemence.
                              No ! in this dread presence
I cannot bear these tears — my courage flies
And doubt distracts my soul.   Go, weep in secret —
Leave me in error's maze — but never, never,
Behold me more : I will not look again
On thee, nor on thy mother.   Oh ! how passion
Laid bare her secret heart !   She never loved me !
She mourned her best-loved son — that was her cry
Of grief — and naught was mine but show of fond-
                              ness !
And thou art false as she ! make no disguise —
Recoil with horror from my sight — this form
Shall never shock thee more — begone forever !
                                        [*Exit.*
[*She stands irresolute in a tumult of conflicting pas-*
sions — then tears herself from the spot.

Chorus (CAJETAN).

Happy the man — his lot I prize —
    That far from pomps and turmoil vain,
Childlike on nature's bosom lies
    Amid the stillness of the plain.
My heart is sad in the princely hall,
    When from the towering pride of state,
I see with headlong ruin fall,
    How swift! the good and great!
And he — from fortune's storm at rest —
    Smiles, in the quiet haven laid
Who, timely warned, has owned how blest
    The refuge of the cloistered shade;
To honor's race has bade farewell,
    Its idle joys and empty shows;
Insatiate wishes learned to quell,
    And lulled in wisdom's calm repose : —
No more shall passion's maddening brood
    Impel the busy scenes to try,
Nor on his peaceful cell intrude
    The form of sad humanity!
'Mid crowds and strife each mortal ill
    Abides — the grisly train of woe
Shuns like the pest the breezy hill,
    To haunt the smoky marts below.

BERENGAR, BOHEMUND, *and* MANFRED.

On the mountains is freedom! the breath of decay
    Never sullies the fresh flowing air;
Oh, Nature is perfect wherever we stray;
    'Tis man that deforms it with care.

The whole Chorus repeats.

On the mountains is freedom, etc., etc.

DON CÆSAR, *the Chorus.*

DON CÆSAR (*more collected*).
    I use the princely rights — 'tis the last time —
    To give this body to the ground, and pay
    Fit honors to the dead.   So mark, my friends,

My bosom's firm resolve, and quick fulfil
Your lord's behest. Fresh in your memory lives
The mournful pomp, when to the tomb ye bore
So late my royal sire; scarce in these halls
Are stilled the echoes of the funeral wail; —
Another corpse succeeds, and in the grave
Weighs down its fellow-dust — almost our torch
With borrowed lustre from the last, may pierce
The monumental gloom ; and on the stair,
Blends in one throng confused two mourning trains.
Then in the sacred royal dome that guards
The ashes of my sire, prepare with speed
The funeral rites; unseen of mortal eye,
And noiseless be your task — let all be graced,
As then, with circumstances of kingly state.

BOHEM.   My prince, it shall be quickly done; for still
Upreared, the gorgeous catafalque recalls
The dread solemnity; no hand disturbed
The edifice of death.

DON CÆSAR.   The yawning grave
Amid the haunts of life ?   No goodly sign
Was this : the rites fulfilled, why lingered yet
The trappings of the funeral show ?

BOHEMUND.   Your strife
With fresh embittered hate o'er all Messina
Woke discord's maddening flames, and from the
    deed
Our cares withdrew — so resolute remained,
And closed the sanctuary.

DON CÆSAR.   Make no delay ;
This very night fulfil your task, for well
Beseems the midnight gloom !   To-morrow's sun
Shall find this palace cleansed of every stain,
And light a happier race.

[*Exit the Second Chorus, with the body of* DON
    MANUEL.

CAJETAN.   Shall I invite
The brotherhood of monks, with rights ordained
By holy church of old, to celebrate
The office of departed souls, and hymn
The buried one to everlasting rest ?

Don C. Their strains above my tomb shall sound for-
        ever
    Amid the torches' blaze — no solemn rites
    Beseem the day when gory murder scares
    Heaven's pardoning grace.
CAJETAN.   Oh, let not wild despair
    Tempt thee to impious, rash resolve. My prince
    No mortal arm shall e'er avenge this deed;
    And penance calms, with soft, atoning power,
    The wrath on high.
DON CÆSAR.   If for eternal justice
    Earth has no minister, myself shall wield
    The avenging sword; though heaven, with gracious
        ear,
    Inclines to sinners' prayers, with blood alone
    Atoned is murder's guilt.
CAJETAN.   To stem the tide
    Of dire misfortune, that with maddening rage
    Bursts o'er your house, were nobler than to pile
    Accumulated woe.
DON CÆSAR.   The curse of old
    Shall die with me! Death self-imposed alone
    Can break the chain of fate.
CAJETAN.   Thou owest thyself
    A sovereign to this orphaned land, by thee
    Robbed of its other lord!
DON CÆSAR.   The avenging gods
    Demand their prey — some other deity
    May guard the living!
CAJETAN.   Wide as e'er the sun
    In glory beams, the realm of hope extends;
    But — oh remember! nothing may we gain
    From Death!
DON CÆSAR   Remember thou thy vassal's duty;
    Remember and be silent! Leave to me
    To follow, as I list, the spirit of power
    That leads me to the goal. No happy one
    May look into my breast: but if thy prince
    Owns not a subject's homage, dread at least
    The murderer! — the accursed! — and to the head
    Of the unhappy — sacred to the gods —

Give honors due.   The pangs that rend my soul —
What I have suffered — what I feel — have left
No place for earthly thoughts!

DONNA ISABELLA, DON CÆSAR, *The Chorus.*

ISABELLA (*enters with hesitating steps, and looks irreso-
lutely towards* DON CÆSAR; *at last she approaches,
and addresses him with collected tones*).
I thought mine eyes should ne'er behold thee more;
Thus I had vowed despairing!   Oh, my son!
How quickly all a mothers's strong resolves
Melt into air!   'Twas but the cry of rage
That stifled nature's pleading voice; but now
What tidings of mysterious import call me
From the desolate chambers of my sorrow?
Shall I believe it?   Is it true? one day
Robs me of both my sons?

Chorus.

Behold! with willing steps and free,
    Thy son prepares to tread
The paths of dark eternity —
    The silent mansions of the dead.
My prayers are vain; but thou, with power confessed,
Of nature's holiest passion, storm his breast!

ISAB.   I call the curses back — that in the frenzy
Of blind despair on thy beloved head
I poured.   A mother may not curse the child
That from her nourishing breast drew life, and gave
Sweet recompense for all her travail past;
Heaven would not hear the impious vows; they fell
With quick rebound, and heavy with my tears
Down from the flaming vault!
                                        Live! live! my son!
For I may rather bear to look on thee —
The murderer of one child — than weep for both!
DON C.   Heedless and vain, my mother, are thy prayers
For me and for thyself; I have no place
Among the living: if thine eyes may brook
The murderer's sight abhorred — I could not bear
The mute reproach of thy eternal sorrow.

ISAB. Silent or loud, my son, reproach shall never
Disturb thy breast — ne'er in these halls shall sound
The voice of wailing, gently on my tears
My griefs shall flow away : the sport alike
Of pitiless fate together we will mourn,
And veil the deed of blood.

DON CÆSAR (*with a faltering voice, and taking her hand*).
Thus it shall be,
My mother — thus with silent, gentle woe
Thy grief shall fade : but when one common tomb
The murderer and his victim closes round —
When o'er our dust one monumental stone
Is rolled — the curse shall cease — thy love no more
Unequal bless thy sons : the precious tears
Thine eyes of beauty weep shall sanctify
Alike our memories. Yes! In death are quenched
The fires of rage; and hatred owns subdued,
The mighty reconciler. Pity bends
An angel form above the funeral urn,
With weeping, dear embrace. Then to the tomb
Stay not my passage : — Oh, forbid me not,
Thus with atoning sacrifice to quell
The curse of heaven.

ISABELLA. All Christendom is rich
In shrines of mercy, where the troubled heart
May find repose. Oh! many a heavy burden
Have sinners in Loretto's mansion laid ;
And Heaven's peculiar blessing breathes around
The grave that has redeemed the world! The prayers
Of the devout are precious — fraught with store
Of grace, they win forgiveness from the skies ; —
And on the soil by gory murder stained
Shall rise the purifying fane.

DON CÆSAR. We pluck
The arrow from the wound — but the torn heart
Shall ne'er be healed. Let him who can, drag on
A weary life of penance and of pain,
To cleanse the spot of everlasting guilt ; —
I would not live the victim of despair ;
No! I must meet with beaming eye the smile
Of happy ones, and breathe erect the air

Of liberty and joy. While yet alike
We shared thy love, then o'er my days of youth
Pale envy cast his withering shade ; and now,
Think'st thou my heart could brook the dearer ties
That bind thee in thy sorrow to the dead ?
Death, in his undecaying palace throned,
To the pure diamond of perfect virtue
Sublimes the mortal, and with chastening fire
Each gathered stain of frail humanity
Purges and burns away : high as the stars
Tower o'er this earthly sphere, he soars above me ;
And as by ancient hate dissevered long,
Brethren and equal denizens we lived,
So now my restless soul with envy pines,
That he has won from me the glorious prize
Of immortality, and like a god
In memory marches on to times unborn !

ISAB. My sons! Why have I called you to Messina
To find for each a grave ? I brought ye hither
To calm your strife to peace. Lo! Fate has
        turned
My hopes to blank despair.

DON CÆSAR.   Whate'er was spoke,
My mother, is fulfilled ! Blame not the end
By Heaven ordained. We trode our father's halls
With hopes of peace ; and reconciled forever,
Together we shall sleep in death.

ISABELLA.   My son,
Live for thy mother ! In the stranger's land,
Say, wouldst thou leave me friendless and alone,
To cruel scorn a prey — no filial arm
To shield my helpless age ?

DON CÆSAR.   When all the world
With heartless taunts pursues thee, to our grave
For refuge fly, my mother, and invoke
Thy sons' divinity — we shall be gods !
And we will hear thy prayers : — and as the twins
Of heaven, a beaming star of comfort shine
To the tossed shipman — we will hover near thee
With present help, and soothe thy troubled soul !

ISAB. Live — for thy mother, live, my son —
Must I lose all?

[*She throws her arms about him with passionate emo-*
tion. He gently disengages himself, and turning
his face away extends to her his hand.

DON CÆSAR. Farewell!

ISABELLA. I can no more;
Too well my tortured bosom owns how weak
A mother's prayers: 'a mightier voice shall sound
Resistless on thy heart.

[*She goes towards the entrance of the scene.*
My daughter, come.
A brother calls him to the realms of night;
Perchance with golden hues of earthly joy
The sister, the beloved, may gently lure
The wanderer to life again.

[BEATRICE *appears at the entrance of the scene.*

DONNA ISABELLA, DON CÆSAR, *and the Chorus.*

DON CÆSAR (*on seeing her, covers his face with his hands*).
My mother!
What hast thou done?

ISABELLA (*leading* BEATRICE *forwards*).
A mother's prayers are vain!
Kneel at his feet — conjure him — melt his heart!
Oh, bid him live!

DON CÆSAR. Deceitful mother, thus
Thou triest thy son! And wouldst thou stir my soul
Again to passion's strife, and make the sun
Beloved once more, now when I tread the paths
Of everlasting night? See where he stands —
Angel of life! — and wondrous beautiful,
Shakes from his plenteous horn the fragrant store
Of golden fruits and flowers, that breathe around
Divinest airs of joy; — my heart awakes
In the warm sunbeam — hope returns, and life
Thrills in my breast anew.

ISABELLA (*to* BEATRICE). Thou wilt prevail!
Or none! Implore him that he live, nor rob
The staff and comfort of our days.

BEATRICE. The loved one
    A sacrifice demands. Oh, let me die
    To soothe a brother's shade! Yes, I will be
    The victim! Ere I saw the light forewarned
    To death, I live a wrong to heaven! The curse
    Pursues me still : —'twas I that slew thy son —
    I waked the slumbering furies of their strife —
    Be mine the atoning blood!
CAJETAN. Ill-fated mother!
    Impatient all thy children haste to doom,
    And leave thee on the desolate waste alone
    Of joyous life.
BEATRICE. Oh, spare thy precious days
    For nature's band. Thy mother needs a son ;
    My brother, live for her! Light were the pang
    To lose a daughter — but a moment shown,
    Then snatched away!
DON CÆSAR (*with deep emotion*). 'Tis one to live or die,
    Blest with a sister's love!
BEATRICE. Say — dost thou envy
    Thy brother's ashes ?
DON CÆSAR. In thy grief he lives
    A hallowed life! — my doom is death forever!
BEAT. My brother!
DON CÆSAR. Sister! are thy tears for me ?
BEAT. Live for our mother!
DON CÆSAR (*dropping her hand, and stepping back*).
                            For our mother?
BEATRICE (*hiding her head in his breast*). Live
    For her and for thy sister!
Chorus (BOHEMUND). She has won!
    Resistless are her prayers. Despairing mother,
    Awake to hope again — his choice is made!
    Thy son shall live!
    [*At this moment an anthem is heard. The folding-
    doors are thrown open, and in the church is seen the
    catafalque erected, and the coffin surrounded with
    candlesticks.*
DON CÆSAR (*turning to the coffin*). I will not rob thee,
    brother!
    The sacrifice is thine : — Hark! from the tomb,

Mightier than mother's tears, or sister's love,
Thy voice resistless cries: — my arms enfold
A treasure, potent with celestial joys,
To deck this earthly sphere, and make a lot
Worthy the gods! but shall I live in bliss,
While in the tomb thy sainted innocence
Sleeps unavenged? Thou, Ruler of our days,
All just — all wise — let not the world behold
Thy partial care! I saw her tears! — enough —
They flowed for me! I am content: my brother!
I come!
[*He stabs himself with a dagger, and falls dead at his
sister's feet. She throws herself into her mother's
arms.*

Chorus, CAJETAN (*after a deep silence*).
       In dread amaze I stand, nor know
If I should mourn his fate. One truth revealed
Speaks in my breast; — no good supreme is life;
But all of earthly ills the chief is — Guilt!

Lightning Source UK Ltd.
Milton Keynes UK
15 March 2010
151412UK00001B/9/A